Ohio Academic Content Standards

History

H1   Define and measure time by years, decades and centuries.

H2   Place local historical events in sequential order on a time line.

H3   Describe changes in the community over time including changes in: Businesses; Architecture; Physical features; Employment; Education; Transportation; Technology; Religion; Recreation.

People in Societies

PS1   Compare some of the cultural practices and products of various groups of people who have lived in the local community including: Artistic expression; Religion; Language; Food.

PS2   Compare the cultural practices and products of the local community with those of other communities in Ohio, the United States and countries of the world.

PS3   Describe settlement patterns of various cultural groups within the local community.

Geography

GEO1   Use political maps, physical maps and aerial photographs to ask and answer questions about the local community.

GEO2   Use a compass rose and cardinal directions to describe the relative location of places.

GEO3   Read and interpret maps by using the map title, map key, direction indicator and symbols to answer questions about the local community.

GEO4   Use a number/letter grid system to locate physical and human features on a map.

GEO5   Identify the location of the equator, Arctic Circle, Antarctic Circle, North Pole, South Pole, Prime Meridian, the tropics and the hemispheres on maps and globes.

GEO6   Identify and describe the landforms and climate, vegetation, population and economic characteristics of the local community.

GEO7   Identify ways that physical characteristics of the environment (i.e., landforms, bodies of water, climate and vegetation) affect and have been modified by the local community.

GEO8   Identify systems of transportation used to move people and products and systems of communication used to move ideas from place to place.

Economics

E1   Define opportunity cost and give an example of the opportunity cost of a personal decision.

E2   Identify people who purchase goods and services as consumers and people who make goods or provide services as producers.

E3   Categorize economic activities as examples of production or consumption.

E4   Explain the advantages and disadvantages of specialization and the division of labor to produce items.

E5   Identify different forms of money used over time, and recognize that money facilitates the purchase of goods, services and resources and enables savings.

E6   Explain how the local community is an example of a market where buyers and sellers exchange goods and services.

E7   Identify examples of economic competition in the local community.

D1283613

Government

GOV1   Explain the major functions of local government including: Promoting order and security; Making laws; Settling disputes; Providing public services; Protecting the rights of individuals.

GOV2   Explain the structure of local governments and identify local leaders (e.g., township trustees, county commissioners, city council members or mayor).

GOV3   Identify the location of local government buildings and explain the functions of government that are carried out there.

GOV4   Identify goods and services provided by local government, why people need them and the source of funding (taxation).

GOV5   Define power and authority.

GOV6   Explain why the use of power without legitimate authority is unjust (e.g., bullying, stealing).

Citizenship Rights and Responsibilities

CRR1   Describe how people help to make the community a better place in which to live including: Working to preserve the environment; Helping the homeless; Restoring houses in low-income areas; Supporting education; Planning community events; Starting a business.

CRR2   Demonstrate effective citizenship traits including: Civility; Respect for the rights and dignity of each person; Volunteerism; Compromise; Compassion; Persistence in achieving goals; Civic-mindedness.

CRR3   Describe the responsibilities of citizenship with emphasis on: Voting; Obeying laws; Respecting the rights of others; Being informed about current issues; Paying taxes.

Social Studies Skills and Methods

SSS1   Obtain information about local issues from a variety of sources including: Maps; Photos; Oral histories; Newspapers; Letters; Artifacts; Documents.

SSS2   Locate information using various parts of a source including: The table of contents; Title page; Illustrations; Keyword searches.

SSS3   Identify possible cause and effect relationships.

SSS4   Read and interpret pictographs, bar graphs and charts.

SSS5   Communicate information using pictographs and bar graphs.

SSS6   Use a problem-solving/decision-making process which includes: Identifying a problem; Gathering information; Listing and considering options; Considering advantages and disadvantages of options; Choosing and implementing a solution.

OHIO
Macmillan/McGraw-Hill TIMELINKS

Communities

PROGRAM AUTHORS

James A. Banks
Kevin P. Colleary
Linda Greenow
Walter C. Parker
Emily M. Schell
Dinah Zike

CONTRIBUTORS

Raymond C. Jones
Irma M. Olmedo

 Macmillan/McGraw-Hill

PROGRAM AUTHORS

James A. Banks, Ph.D.
Kerry and Linda Killinger Professor
  of Diversity Studies
  and Director, Center for
  Multicultural Education
University of Washington
Seattle, Washington

Kevin P. Colleary, Ed.D.
Curriculum and Teaching Department
Graduate School of Education
Fordham University
New York, New York

Linda Greenow, Ph.D.
Associate Professor and Chair
Department of Geography
State University of New York at New Paltz
New Paltz, New York

Walter C. Parker, Ph.D.
Professor of Social Studies Education,
  Adjunct Professor of Political Science
University of Washington
Seattle, Washington

Emily M. Schell, Ed.D.
Visiting Professor, Teacher Education
San Diego State University
San Diego, California

Dinah Zike
Educational Consultant
Dinah-Mite Activities, Inc.
San Antonio, Texas

CONTRIBUTORS

Raymond C. Jones, Ph.D.
Director of Secondary Social Studies
  Education
Wake Forest University
Winston-Salem, North Carolina

Irma M. Olmedo
Associate Professor
University of Illinois-Chicago
College of Education
Chicago, Illinois

HISTORIANS/SCHOLARS

Thomas Bender, Ph.D.
Professor of History
New York University
New York, New York

Ned Blackhawk
Associate Professor of History
  and American Indian Studies
University of Wisconsin
Madison, Wisconsin

Manuel Chavez, Ph.D.
Associate Director, Center for
  Latin American & Caribbean Studies
Assistant Professor, School of Journalism
Michigan State University
East Lansing, Michigan

Sheilah F. Clarke-Ekong, Ph.D.
Professor of Anthropology
University of Missouri-St. Louis
St. Louis, Missouri

Larry Dale, Ph.D.
Director, Center for Economic Education
Arkansas State University
Jonesboro, Arkansas

Brooks Green, Ph.D.
Associate Professor of Geography
University of Central Arkansas
Conway, Arkansas

Thomas C. Holt, Ph.D.
Professor of History
University of Chicago
Chicago, Illinois

Paula Kluth, Ph.D.
Independent Scholar
  and Special Education Consultant
Oak Park, Illinois

Andrei V. Korobkov, Ph.D.
Associate Professor
Department of Political Science
Middle Tennessee State University
Murfreesboro, Tennessee

Nayanjot Lahiri
Professor, Department of History
University of Delhi
Delhi, India

Mac Dixon-Fyle, Ph.D.
Professor of History
DePauw University
Greencastle, Indiana

Oscar J. Martinez, Ph.D.
Regents Professor of History
University of Arizona
Tucson, Arizona

Nathan Rosenstein, Ph.D.
Professor of History
The Ohio State University
Columbus, Ohio

Douglas R. Skopp, Ph.D.
Distinguished University Teaching Professor
State University of New York at Plattsburgh
Plattsburgh, New York

Peter N. Stearns
Provost and Professor of History
George Mason University
Fairfax, Virginia

Rebecca L. Torstrick, Ph.D.
Associate Professor of Anthropology
  and Director, Women's Studies Program
Indiana University
South Bend, Indiana

The *McGraw·Hill* Companies

Macmillan
McGraw-Hill

MHID 0-02-151719-3

ISBN 978-0-02-151719-0

Printed in the United States of America

1 2 3 4 5 6 7 8 9 10   079/043   13 12 11 10 09 08

Communities
CONTENTS

Unit 1 Communities and Geography — 1

EXPLORE The Big Idea How does where you live affect how you live?

PEOPLE, PLACES, AND EVENTS — 2

Lesson 1: What Is a Community? — 4

Map and Globe Skills Use Intermediate Directions — 10

Lesson 2: Communities Big and Small — 12

Lesson 3: Our Country's Geography — 18

Map and Globe Skills Use a Map Scale — 26

Lesson 4: Our Natural Resources — 28

Lesson 5: People and the Environment — 36

Global Connections Saving Animals — 41

Ohio Connections Land and Resources — 44

Review and Assess/Test Preparation — 46

The Big Idea Activities — 48

Unit 2 Communities Change   49

How do communities change over time?

PEOPLE, PLACES, AND EVENTS	50
Lesson 1: First Communities	52
Global Connections Buildings Made Long Ago	54
Lesson 2: A New Country	60
Chart and Graph Skills Use Time Lines	68
Lesson 3: Moving West	70
Map and Globe Skills Understand Hemispheres	76
Lesson 4: Communities Become Cities	78
Chart and Graph Skills Use Bar Graphs	84
Lesson 5: Daily Life Changes	86
Ohio Connections Your Community's History	92
Review and Assess/Test Preparation	94
The Big Idea Activities	96

Unit 3 Many Cultures, One Country 97

The Big Idea How do people change communities?

PEOPLE, PLACES, AND EVENTS 98

Lesson 1: A Land of Immigrants 100

Lesson 2: All About Culture 108

Lesson 3: Sharing Culture Through Stories 116

Lesson 4: Local Celebrations 124

   Global Connections Independence in India 129

Lesson 5: Cultures Around the World 132

   Map and Globe Skills Understand Latitude and Longitude 138

   Ohio Connections Food in Your Community 140

Review and Assess/Test Preparation 142

The Big Idea Activities 144

Unit 4 Communities at Work 145

The Big Idea How do people in a community meet their needs?

PEOPLE, PLACES, AND EVENTS 146

Lesson 1: Businesses in the Community 148

   Global Connections A Dollar in Canada 153

Lesson 2: Making Money Choices 156

Lesson 3: Farm Communities 164

   Chart and Graph Skills Use Line Graphs 170

Lesson 4: Making Goods 172

Lesson 5: Working Together 180

   Ohio Connections Businesses in Your Community 188

Review and Assess/Test Preparation 190

The Big Idea Activities 192

Why do communities need governments?

PEOPLE, PLACES, AND EVENTS 194

Lesson 1: National Government 196

 Chart and Graph Skills Use Flow Charts 204

Lesson 2: State Government 206

 Map and Globe Skills Use Road Maps 212

Lesson 3: Local Government 214

 Global Connections Adelaide, Australia 218

Lesson 4: Rules and Laws 220

Lesson 5: Taking Action 228

 Ohio Connections Symbols and Landmarks 236

Review and Assess/Test Preparation 238

The Big Idea Activities 240

Reference Section

Reading Skills	R2	Glossary	REF1
Geography Handbook	GH1	Index	REF6
Atlas	GH14	Credits	REF16

Maps

The Great Lakes	11	Chicago's Sister Cities	186
Regions of the United States	20	Indiana Highways	213
Part of Toledo	27	Adelaide, Australia	218
New Jersey	46	The Hopi Reservation	225
East Coast of America	61	Connecticut Highways	238
Lewis and Clark's Journey	72	A Map of the World	GH7
The Hemispheres	76	Historical Map	GH13
The Transcontinental Railroad	87	United States: Political	GH14
Central America	101	United States: Physical	GH16
The Global Grid	139	World: Political	GH18
Illinois: Latitude and Longitude	142	North American Political	GH20
United States Farm Products	166	North American: Physical	GH21
Global Trade Map	176	Ohio: Political	GH22
U.S. Car Exports, 2005	183	Ohio: Physical	GH23
U.S. Domestic Trade	184	The 50 United States	GH24

Skills and Features

Reading Skills

Main Idea and Details	R2	Understand Hemispheres	76
Sequence	R4	Understand Latitude and Longitude	138
Summarize	R6	Use Road Maps	212
Cause and Effect	R8		
Compare and Contrast	R10		

Map and Globe Skills

Use Intermediate Directions	10		
Use a Map Scale	26		

Chart and Graph Skills

Use Time Lines	68
Use Bar Graphs	84
Use Line Graphs	170
Use Flow Charts	204

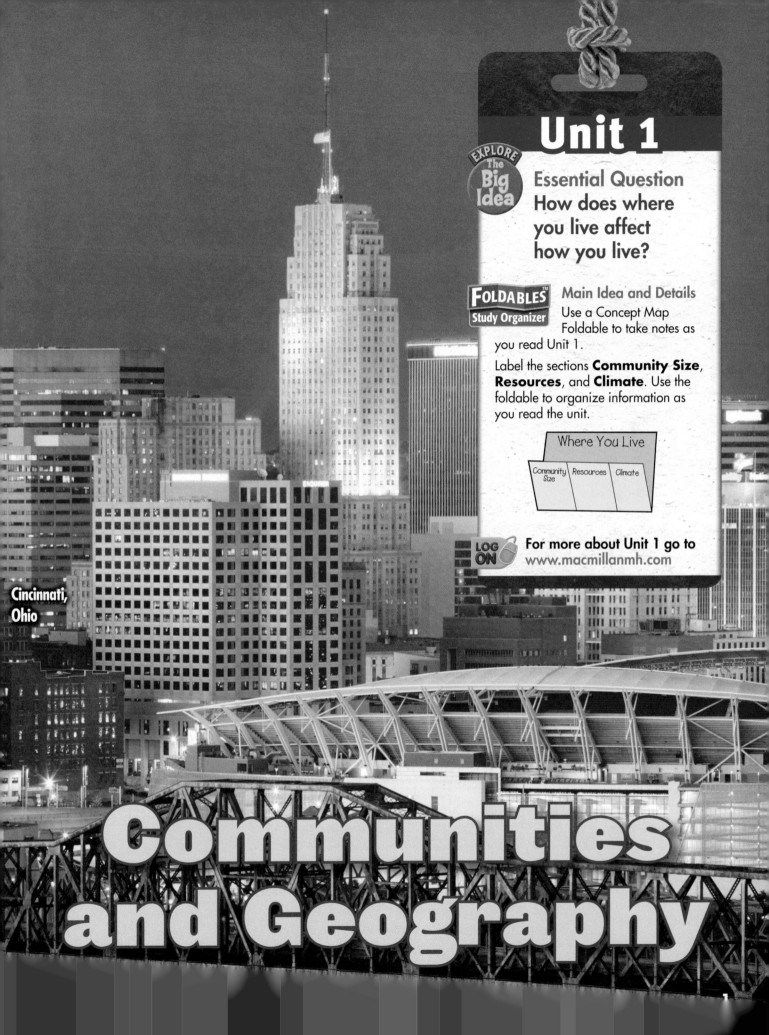

Cincinnati, Ohio

Unit 1

EXPLORE
The Big Idea

Essential Question
How does where you live affect how you live?

FOLDABLES ™
Study Organizer

Main Idea and Details
Use a Concept Map Foldable to take notes as you read Unit 1.

Label the sections **Community Size**, **Resources**, and **Climate**. Use the foldable to organize information as you read the unit.

Where You Live

| Community Size | Resources | Climate |

LOG ON

For more about Unit 1 go to
www.macmillanmh.com

Communities and Geography

1

PEOPLE, PLACES, AND EVENTS

People visit Ohio Caverns

Ohio Caverns

Ohio Caverns open for tours

1928 | The Ohio Caverns were discovered in 1897 and opened for tours in 1928.

The **Ohio Caverns** are limestone caverns with many rock formations that look like white crystals. These formations are called stalactites and stalagmites.

Today students visit the Ohio Caverns in West Liberty, Ohio.

Garrett Morgan

Cleveland, Ohio

Patent for traffic light

1923

Morgan created a T-shaped traffic light to help prevent accidents on busy roads.

Garrett Morgan is famous for being one of the first inventors to hold a patent on the **traffic light.** He invented the light in **Cleveland, Ohio**.

Today traffic lights are used all around the world.

What Is a Community?

Lesson 1

VOCABULARY

community p. 5

geography p. 5

capital p. 6

festival p. 7

READING SKILL

Main Idea and Details
Copy the chart below.
As you read, fill it in with
ideas and details about
people who live, work,
and play in Columbus.

Main Idea	Details

OHIO ACADEMIC CONTENT STANDARDS

PS2, GEO1, GEO2, GEO7, GEO8, CRR1, CRR2, SSS6

Jazz and Rib Fest
Columbus, Ohio

Visual Preview

What makes a community?

A Communities are where people live, work, and play.

B People in a community work at many kinds of jobs.

C People in many communities help one another.

THINK ABOUT COMMUNITIES

Columbus is a city in Ohio. The people of Columbus think their city is a great place to live and work and have fun together.

Where do you live? No matter where you live, you live in a **community**. A community is a place where people live, work, play, and help each other. All communities have homes. They have places for people to work and places to have fun, too.

Is your community near a river? Is the land hilly, or is it flat? Are there grasslands or forests nearby? Thinking about **geography** helps us understand communities. Geography is the study of Earth and the way people and animals live on it.

A community's geography can affect its size. Large communities like Columbus, Ohio are often built near major roads. People traveling these roads bring business to the community. Being close to a major road helped Columbus grow into a big city.

QUICK CHECK

Main Idea and Details **What is a community?**

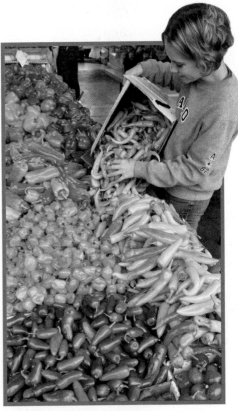

▲ Some people in Columbus work at this farmers' market.

5

B WORK AND PLAY

What do people in your community do for work and fun? The people of Columbus work at many kinds of jobs. They have many ways to have fun, too.

Work in Columbus

Columbus is the **capital** of the state of Ohio. A capital is a city where a country or state has its government. Some people in Columbus work for the state government.

Other people in Columbus work as doctors, teachers, or construction workers. A community like Raleigh needs people with many different skills. People in Columbus use these different skills to help each other.

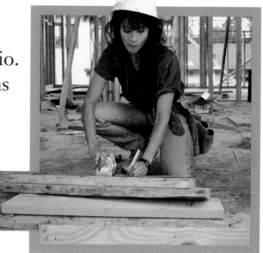

▲ Some people in Columbus construct houses.

Fun in Columbus

In Columbus there are many ways to have fun outdoors. You can fish at Hoover Reservoir, hike in Blendon Woods State Park, or canoe along the Big Darby Creek. There is an arts festival every summer, too. A festival is a celebration. You can listen to music and see artists show their paintings.

The Columbus Jazz and Rib Fest is held once a year. At this festival, you can enjoy a concert, great food, and fun. Many people work together to make these festivals successful.

▼ People in Columbus can canoe on the Big Darby Creek.

QUICK CHECK

Summarize **What are some kinds of work people do in Columbus?**

▼ The Ohio State Fair is held in Columbus.

7

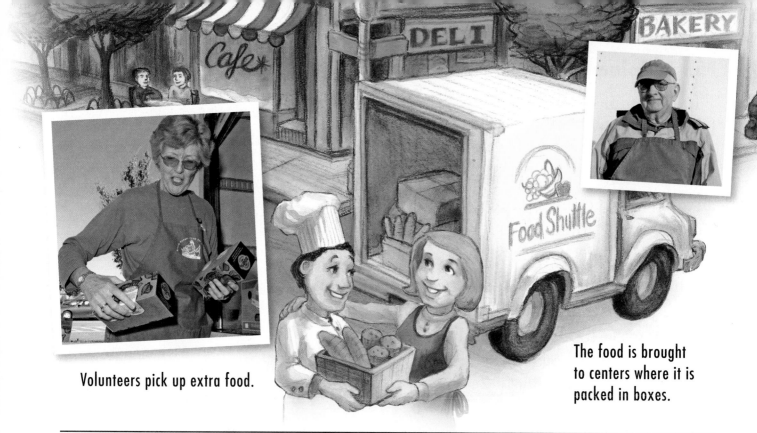

Volunteers pick up extra food.

The food is brought to centers where it is packed in boxes.

C HELPING HANDS

Communities are places where people help each other. The Mid-Ohio FoodBank is a program that donates food and other grocery products to those who don't have enough to eat in the central Ohio area.

Program Helpers at Work

The Mid-Ohio FoodBank collects unused food from grocery stores, restaurants, and farmers. Workers use the food to provide meals for people who are hungry.

Helpers at the FoodBank do many things. Some sort through donated food. Others pack the food for delivery. About 40,000 meals are provided every day through the FoodBank. That is over 2 million pounds of food donated each month!

PLACES

The **Mid-Ohio FoodBank** in central Ohio is dedicated to building a community that makes food available to all people. Each year, more than 5,000 volunteers sort and repack food at the Mid-Ohio FoodBank.

Mid-Ohio FoodBank Workers

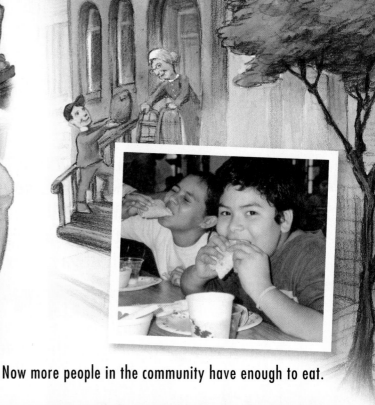

Other volunteers prepare meals for people who need food.

Now more people in the community have enough to eat.

Because of programs like the Mid-Ohio FoodBank, people have food to eat and the food is not wasted. The workers feel good about helping others, too. When people work to help others, it makes the community a better place to live!

QUICK CHECK

Summarize How do people at the FoodBank help the community?

Check Understanding

1. **VOCABULARY** Write one sentence for each vocabulary word below.
   community   geography   festival

2. **READING SKILL Main Idea and Details** Use your chart from page 4 to write a paragraph about ways people live, work, and play in Columbus.

Main Idea	Details

3. **Write About It** Make a list of some ways to have fun in your community.

Map and Globe Skills

Use Intermediate Directions

VOCABULARY

cardinal direction

intermediate direction

You know that the compass rose on a map shows north, east, south, and west. These are the **cardinal directions**. A compass rose can also show **intermediate directions**. An intermediate direction is halfway between two cardinal directions.

Learn It

Follow these steps for using a compass rose to find the cardinal and intermediate directions.

- The long points of the compass rose show the cardinal directions. The letters **N**, **E**, **S**, and **W** stand for north, east, south, and west.

- The short points of the compass rose show the intermediate directions. For example, northeast is halfway between north and east. The abbreviations **NE**, **SE**, **SW**, and **NW** stand for northeast, southeast, southwest, and northwest. Intermediate directions are not always labeled on a compass rose.

Try It

Study the compass rose. Use it to answer the questions.

- Which intermediate direction is halfway between north and east?

- What two cardinal directions is southwest between?

Apply It

The map below shows the states near the Great Lakes. Use the map to answer the questions.

- If you go from Cleveland to Buffalo, in what direction are you going?

- What direction would you go to travel from Duluth to Cincinnati?

The Great Lakes

International boundary
State boundary
• City

0   100   200 miles
0   100   200 kilometers

Lake Superior

Duluth
MN
Hayward
Minneapolis
WI
Milwaukee
IA
Cedar Rapids
Chicago
Des Moines
IL
MO

Lake Michigan
Lake Huron
MI
Bay City
Detroit

Lake Ontario
Buffalo
NY

Lake Erie
Cleveland
PA
Pittsburgh
MD
Toledo
OH
Columbus
Ft. Wayne
Indianapolis
IN
Cincinnati
WV
VA
KY

Lesson 2

VOCABULARY

urban p. 13

suburb p. 14

rural p. 15

commute p. 16

transportation p. 16

READING SKILL

Main Idea and Details
Copy the chart below. As you read fill it with a main idea and details that describe a suburb.

Main Idea	Details

OHIO ACADEMIC CONTENT STANDARDS

H3, PS1, PS2, PS3, GEO8, SSS6

Communities Big and Small

E. 9 St

Cleveland, Ohio

Visual Preview

How are communities different?

A City communities are filled with many people and tall buildings.

B Areas that are just outside of cities have more space and fewer people.

C In other communities people may live far from one another.

A LOOK AT CITIES

New York City has about 8 million people. That's a big city! Only 48 people live in Rendville, Ohio. That's a very small community.

Cleveland, Ohio, is a big city, with almost half a million people. It is an **urban** area—a city and the communities that surround it. Urban areas like Cleveland have many tall buildings close together.

There's lots to see and do in urban areas. In Cleveland you can visit the Rock and Roll Hall of Fame and Museum, or go to a ball game. On hot summer days you can go to the beach on Lake Erie, one of the five Great Lakes.

Like other cities, Cleveland is made up of neighborhoods. People from Eastern Europe moved to one neighborhood known as Slavic Village. You can still hear Slavic languages, such as Polish and Czech, there. You can taste Slavic foods and listen to Slavic music, too.

▲ People enjoy watching baseball games at Jacobs Field in Cleveland.

QUICK CHECK

Main Idea and Details **What makes Cleveland an urban area?**

B   NEAR AND FAR

Many cities in the United States have **suburbs** near them. A suburb is a community near a city that has its own homes and stores, and its own schools. Houses and stores in a suburban area are farther apart than in a city. Sidewalks and streets are less crowded, too. Most people drive cars to get around. They might drive to a mall to shop.

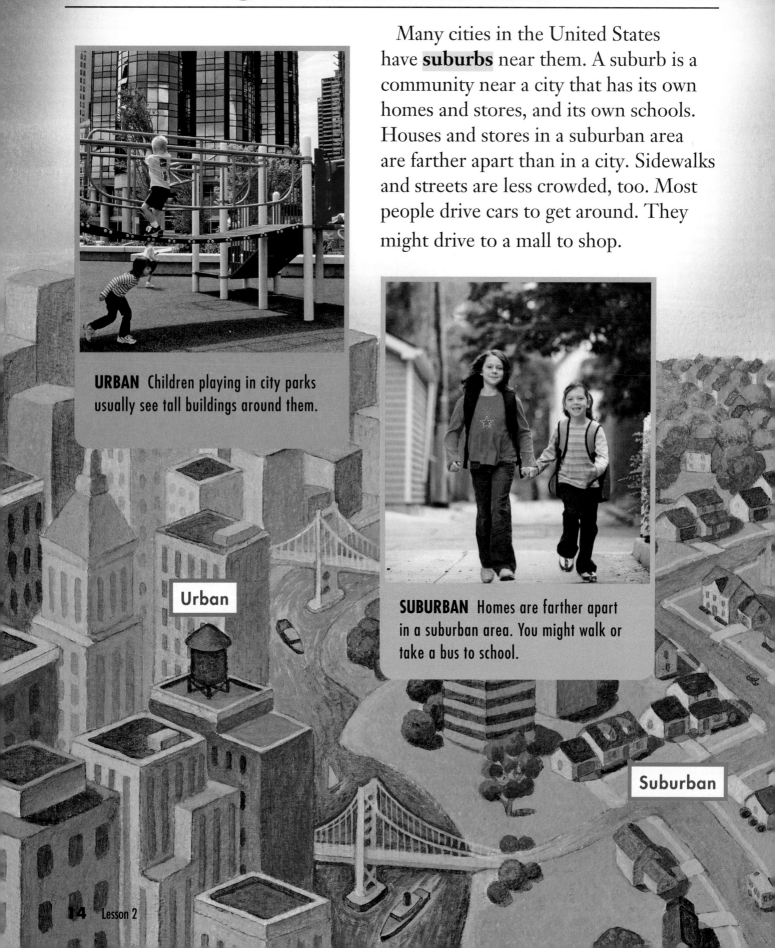

URBAN Children playing in city parks usually see tall buildings around them.

Urban

SUBURBAN Homes are farther apart in a suburban area. You might walk or take a bus to school.

Suburban

Farms and Open Land

If you live on a farm or a ranch, or in a small town or village near farms and ranches, you live in a **rural** community. A rural community is one that has farms and open land around it. Rural communities have fewer people than suburbs.

About 225 people live in the rural community of Rossburg, Ohio. Rossburg has many farms—some are bigger than the town itself! If you lived there, your best friend might live on a farm 10 miles away!

QUICK CHECK

Summarize **How are suburbs and rural communities different?**

RURAL In a rural area there's enough room to keep a pet like this mule.

Rural

15

Chicago, Illinois, is a big city. There are a lot of jobs there, but many of the people who work in Chicago do not live there. Instead they live in suburbs like Oak Park and **commute** to their jobs in Chicago. To commute means to travel a distance to and from work.

Some commuters drive their cars to work in Chicago, but the roads get pretty crowded. So many commuters use other kinds of **transportation**. Transportation means a way to get from one place to another. Some use public transportation, such as a bus or train. The fastest way to commute from Oak Park to Chicago is by train— it only takes about twenty minutes.

How many kinds of transportation can you find in this photo of Chicago? ▼

Homes in rural communities are far apart.

Traveling Takes Time

People who live in rural areas often have to drive to another community to get what they need. If you lived in Rossburg, Ohio you might go to school in Ansonia, about five miles away. Rossburg does not have its own school. To buy some things that you need, you might have to go to Greenville, about 15 minutes away. To visit Columbus, the capital of Ohio, you would have to travel more than two hours!

QUICK CHECK

Main Idea and Details **How do people in Oak Park commute to and from Chicago?**

Check Understanding

1. **VOCABULARY** Use the words below to write a description of an urban community.

   urban   **suburb**   **commute**

2. **READING SKILL** **Main Idea and Details** Use your chart from page 12 to write a paragraph about suburbs.

Main Idea	Details

 3. **Write About It** Write a letter to a friend explaining where you would choose to live and why.

17

Lesson 3

VOCABULARY

landform p. 19

adapt p. 19

region p. 20

plain p. 20

plateau p. 21

natural resource p. 23

READING SKILL

Main Idea and Details
Copy the chart below. As you read list how landforms and weather affect daily life.

Main Idea	Details

OHIO ACADEMIC CONTENT STANDARDS

H3, GEO1, GEO3, GEO6, GEO7, SSS6

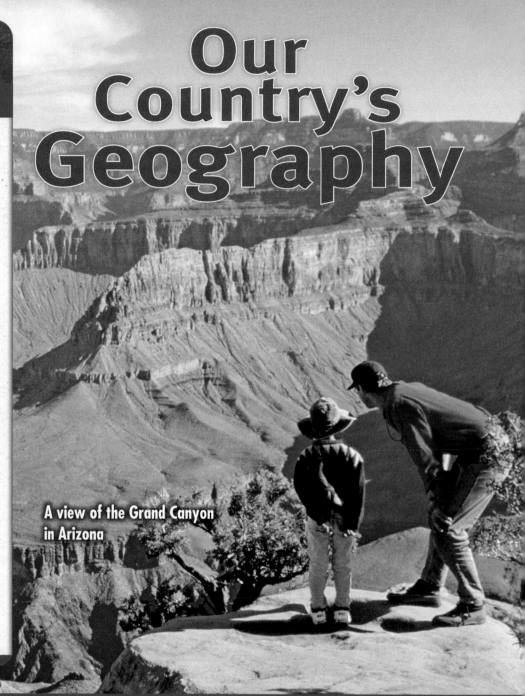

Our Country's Geography

A view of the Grand Canyon in Arizona

Visual Preview

How does geography affect people in a community?

A Geography affects the homes people build.

B Different types of land affect how people live, travel, and work.

C Water covers much of Earth and people use it in many ways.

D People adapt to weather and climate wherever they live.

Ⓐ LAND AND PEOPLE

If you could fly like a bird across the United States, you'd see snow-covered mountains, sandy deserts, dark forests, and rushing waters. So many kinds of land and water!

Our country has mountains, hills, valleys, and flat land. These are **landforms**, or shapes of Earth's surface. Landforms are part of geography, and they affect how people live. Water is part of geography, too. People **adapt** to the landforms and water in their communities. To adapt means to change the way you live.

The photo below shows Creek Street in Ketchikan, Alaska. The creek is near the sea, so the water level in the creek rises with the tide in the sea. People who live on Creek Street built their houses on stilts, or posts, to keep the homes above the water. This is how they adapt to the geography of their area.

People affect geography, too. They change the land when they build roads, tunnels, bridges, and buildings.

QUICK CHECK

Main Idea and Details How did people in Ketchikan adapt to the geography?

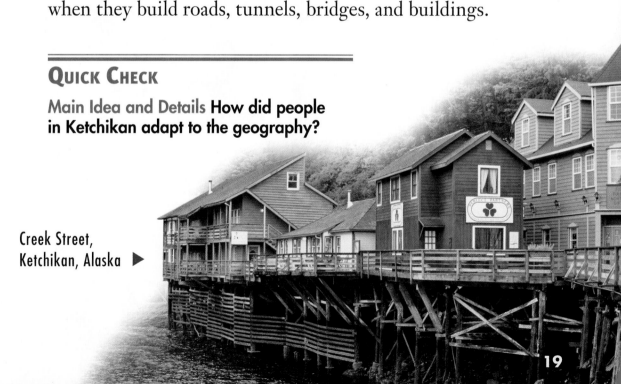

Creek Street,
Ketchikan, Alaska ▶

TYPES OF LAND

The United States is a really big country with many kinds of land. To make learning about it easier, we can think of the country as having five **regions**—the Northeast, Southeast, Midwest, Southwest, and West. A region is an area with things in common—like geography. The landforms in each region make the region different from other areas. Look at the map to see the different landforms in each region.

Landforms Affect Daily Life

Pete lives on a mountain in the West. In the winter when it snows, traveling up and down the mountain is hard. Pete's dad needs special tires on his car to make it easier to drive in ice and snow. So the mountain affects how Pete's family lives. Landforms in other regions affect how people live, too.

QUICK CHECK

Summarize Which region has land that is flat with no mountains?

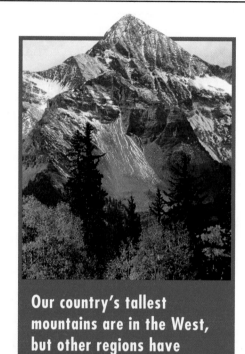

Our country's tallest mountains are in the West, but other regions have mountains, too.

West

Much of the Midwest is flat land as far as the eye can see. This flat land, called a **plain**, is good for farming.

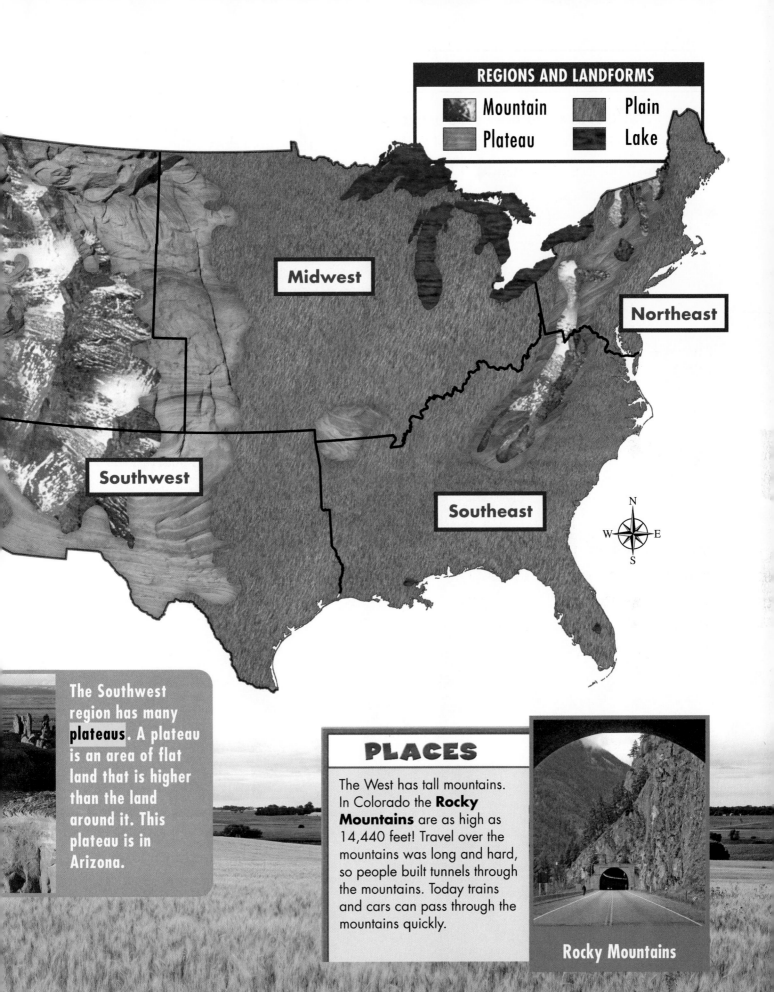

Mountain

Plateau

Plain

Lake

Midwest

Northeast

Southwest

Southeast

N
W   E
S

The Southwest region has many **plateaus**. A plateau is an area of flat land that is higher than the land around it. This plateau is in Arizona.

PLACES

The West has tall mountains. In Colorado the **Rocky Mountains** are as high as 14,440 feet! Travel over the mountains was long and hard, so people built tunnels through the mountains. Today trains and cars can pass through the mountains quickly.

Rocky Mountains

C WATER ALL AROUND US

Did you know that oceans cover most of Earth's surface? Besides lots of ocean, Earth also has lakes, rivers, and ponds. The photo below was taken from outer space and you can see lots of that blue water! Read below to find out more about what Earth looks like from outer space.

Primary Sources

" . . . there emerges [appears] a sparkling blue and white jewel, a . . . sky-blue sphere [round ball] with slowly swirling veils of white, rising gradually like a small pearl in the thick sea of black . . . "

Edgar Mitchell, United States astronaut, January 1971

Write About It What does astronaut Edgar Mitchell compare Earth to?

Using Water

Water is one of our most important **natural resources**. A natural resource is something found in nature that people use. People use water from lakes, rivers, and ponds, for drinking and to grow crops. Most Americans use about 153 gallons every day. How much do you use?

People also use rivers and lakes for transportation. Large boats pull or push barges up and down rivers to move things from place to place. Rivers and lakes are useful for transportation, so many cities are located near rivers.

▲ Water helps these corn stalks grow.

QUICK CHECK

Summarize What are some things water is used for?

▼ Tow boat pushing barge down the Ohio River

It rained all morning and now there are puddles on the ground. Before you go outside, you put on a rain slicker and rubber rain boots. Then you grab your umbrella. Why? To stay dry! Weather is a part of geography that changes every day.

Climate is the weather in a place or region over a long period of time. Climate tells what the weather is usually like in an area. How does climate affect you? If you live in a cold climate you need warm clothes. You may live in a different kind of house than people who live where it is always warm.

Blizzards are heavy snowstorms with very strong winds. ▼

▲ Tornadoes have strong winds that form a funnel-shaped cloud.

▲ Hurricanes are storms with very strong winds and heavy rain.

Dangerous Weather

Some weather—like tornadoes, hurricanes, and blizzards—can be dangerous. People who live in communities that may have dangerous weather adapt to keep safe. For example, many people in Florida now build strong homes that hurricane winds cannot easily destroy or damage.

QUICK CHECK

Main Idea and Details **How do people adapt to the climate where they live?**

Check Understanding

1. **VOCABULARY** Write one sentence for each vocabulary term below.
   landform   region   natural resource

2. **READING SKILL Main Idea and Details** Use your chart from page 18 to write how weather and landforms affect daily life.

Main Idea	Details

3. **Write About It** Write a paragraph telling one way people have changed water or a landform in your area.

Map and Globe Skills

Use a Map Scale

VOCABULARY
map scale

A map is always much smaller than the place it shows. So a map uses a **map scale** to show the real distances between two places on a map.

Learn It

- Read the title of the map on page 27. This map shows part of Toledo, Ohio.

- Look at the map scale. The line is about 1 inch long. The map scale shows that about 1 inch on the map equals 1 mile on Earth.

- Place the edge of a piece of paper under The Docks and COSI. Make two marks on the paper—one at the dot for The Docks and the other at the dot for COSI. Now put your paper on the map scale and place your first mark under the zero. Where is your second mark? The distance from The Docks to COSI is almost 1 mile.

Try It

Using your map scale, measure distances on the map.

- Is the distance from Raceway Park to the Firefighters Museum more or less than 1 mile?

- Is it more or less than 1 mile from The Docks to Raceway Park?

Apply It

- About how far is it from COSI to the Firefighters Museum?

- About how far is it from The Docks to the Toledo Museum of Art?

- How would you use the scale to measure 4 miles on the map?

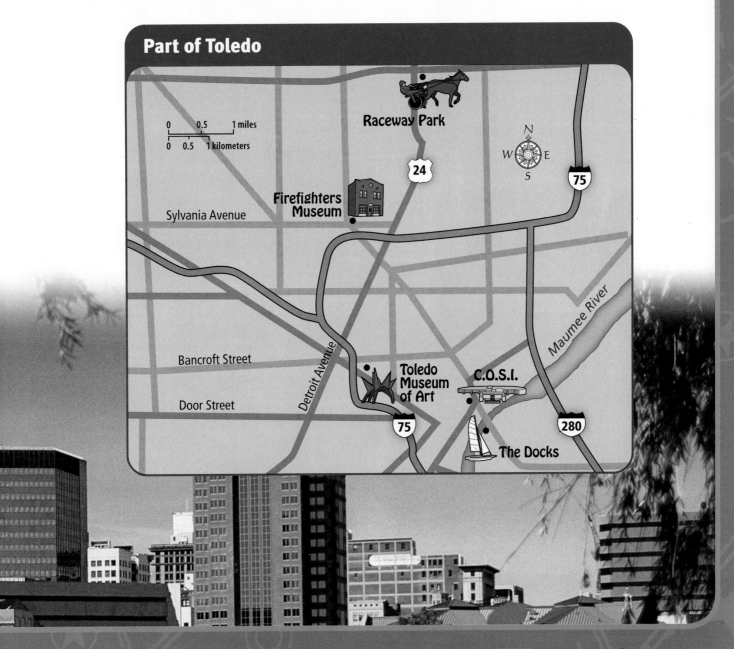

Part of Toledo

Lesson 4

VOCABULARY

mineral p. 29

nonrenewable resource p. 30

environment p. 32

recycle p. 34

READING SKILL

Main Idea and Details
Copy the chart below. As you read, list how you can protect natural resources.

Main Idea	Details

OHIO ACADEMIC CONTENT STANDARDS

H3, GEO6, GEO7, CRR1, SSS6

OUR NATURAL RESOURCES

Trees are an important natural resource.

Visual Preview

How do we get and use our natural resources?

A Minerals like copper and salt are found in the ground.

B Oil is a very important resource that cannot be replaced.

C We must protect our resources and use them wisely.

D People can work together to save natural resources.

28

USING NATURAL RESOURCES

Every day you use pencils and paper in school. You get water from the faucet to drink. You add salt to your food at dinner. Where do these things come from?

What do air, water, soil, plants, and animals have in common? They are all natural resources. We use natural resources every day. We breathe air and drink water. We grow crops using soil, and make paper and other things from the wood of trees.

Can you name something that comes from the ground that you sprinkle on your food? It's salt, of course! Salt is a **mineral**. Minerals are natural resources—they are found in nature, but they are not plants or animals. Salt, coal, and copper are minerals. Coal is burned as fuel, and copper is used in many things, including wire and coins.

QUICK CHECK

Main Idea and Details **What are some ways people use natural resources?**

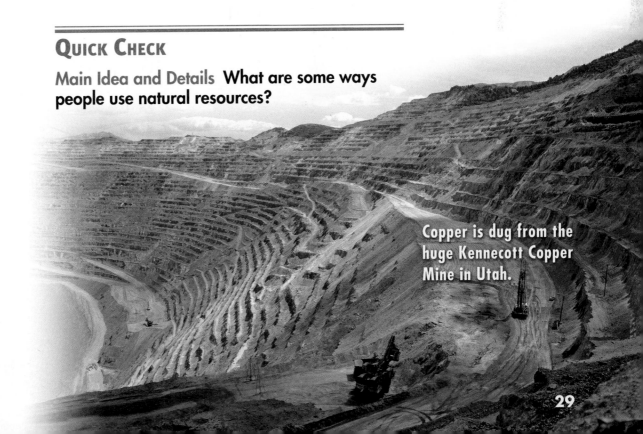

Copper is dug from the huge Kennecott Copper Mine in Utah.

Nature has many things we need to live. Depending on where they are located, communities have different resources they can use. Communities must also find ways to get resources that may not be found in their area, such as oil or water.

Types of Resources

When you are out of fruit at home, you can buy or pick more fruit. This is an example of replacing something. Water is a renewable resource, a natural resource that can be replaced, or renewed. When it rains or snows, water is replaced in nature. Sunlight, wind, and trees are renewable resources, too.

Other natural resources cannot be replaced. These are **nonrenewable resources**. Oil, copper, coal, iron, and gold are all nonrenewable resources. Oil is a very valuable resource that is used to make gasoline and to heat homes. The United States does not produce all the oil it needs, so we must buy oil from other countries.

Oil rigs in the Gulf of Mexico drill below the ocean floor for oil. ▶

As you can see on the datagraphic, our country's natural resources are found in different regions.

QUICK CHECK

Summarize How are renewable resources and nonrenewable resources different?

Copper and zinc are used to make pennies. ▼

DataGraphic

Natural Resources of the United States

Study the map and chart. Then answer the questions.

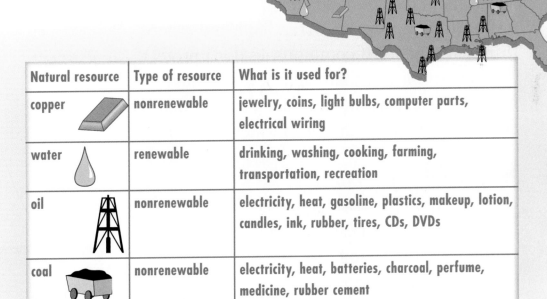

Natural resource	Type of resource	What is it used for?
copper	nonrenewable	jewelry, coins, light bulbs, computer parts, electrical wiring
water	renewable	drinking, washing, cooking, farming, transportation, recreation
oil	nonrenewable	electricity, heat, gasoline, plastics, makeup, lotion, candles, ink, rubber, tires, CDs, DVDs
coal	nonrenewable	electricity, heat, batteries, charcoal, perfume, medicine, rubber cement

Think About Natural Resources

1. Which natural resource on the map is renewable?

2. Which resource is used in plastics, candles, and ink?

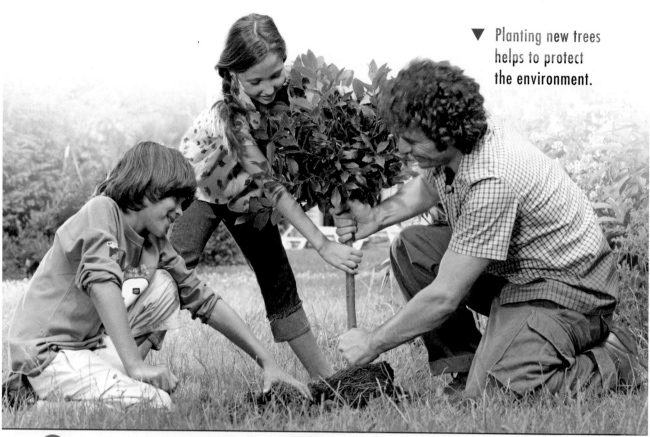

▼ Planting new trees helps to protect the environment.

Ⓒ PROTECTING OUR RESOURCES

Our natural resources come from the **environment**—the air, water, land, and other things around us. If communities don't protect their environment, there may not be enough natural resources. People, plants, and animals need clean air to breathe and clean water to drink.

Saving Oil

Oil is a nonrenewable resource that is made into gasoline to run cars. To save oil some companies are making cars that use less gasoline. Other companies make cars that run on fuels that aren't made from oil.

Cars called hybrids run on both gasoline and electricity, so they use less oil. ▶

How Can People Help?

People need to protect the environment. One way is by building "green buildings." A green building has features that make it environmentally friendly. The Hearst Tower in New York City is a green building. It has special windows that allow sunshine in, but keep the sun from heating the building too much in the summer. This means it uses less electricity for lights and air conditioners. Rain water is collected on the roof and stored in a tank. Some of the water is used to water plants inside and outside the building. The water is also used for a giant waterfall inside the building.

PEOPLE

John Muir loved the outdoors and wanted to protect natural places. Muir began to write about Yosemite Valley, an area in California that later became a national park. John Muir's work led to the creation of many national parks.

John Muir

QUICK CHECK

Summarize **Why do communities need to protect the environment?**

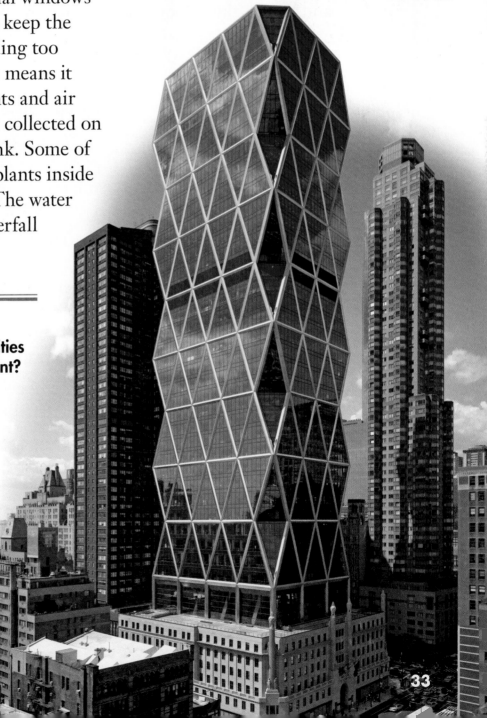

Hearst Tower in New York City ▶

33

Ⓓ OTHER WAYS TO HELP

You can help the environment by **recycling**, too. To recycle means to reuse something. Glass jars, cans, newspapers, and some plastics can be recycled. They can be made into something that can be used again. Recyling also means that there is less waste to get rid of.

People can work together to help the environment. Earth Force is an environmental group. Students in this group start recycling programs, clean up parks, and teach others about helping our environment.

QUICK CHECK

Main Idea and Details **What can people do to take care of natural resources?**

Caring for Earth is everyone's job. ▼

Check Understanding

1. **VOCABULARY** Use the words below to write a paragraph on natural resources.
   environment   **recycle**

2. **READING SKILL** Main Idea and Details Use your chart from page 28 to write a paragraph about protecting natural resources.

Main Idea	Details

3. **Write About It** Write a paragraph telling one way natural resources affect communities.

Citizenship

Points of View

Toledo

Wooster

Urbana

Should Trees Be Protected?

Most communities have some trees. As communities grow, trees are sometimes cut down to make room for roads or new buildings. Read three points of view on whether special rules are needed to protect trees.

"Before people cut down trees, they should make sure there are lots of other trees nearby. I would like to see people save more trees than they cut down."

Ama
Toledo, Ohio

"Trees sometimes get in the way of buildings like houses, hospitals, and schools, so we have to cut them down to make room. I think trees should be planted to replace those that are cut down."

Nate
Wooster, Ohio

"I think people can decide what to do with their trees on their own land. Maybe there should be some rules when they decide to cut down a lot of trees, like they can only cut down one-third or one-half of the trees."

Julia
Urbana, Ohio

Write About It Explain why the trees in your community should or should not be protected.

Lesson 5

People and the Environment

Hoover Dam holds back
the Colorado River and
makes electricity for
many communities.

Visual Preview

How do people interact with the environment?

A Building dams is
one change
people may make
to the environment.

B People find new
ways to get
energy that don't
harm the environment.

C People work to
protect animals
and plants and the
places they live.

D Some people
work to protect
special environments.

CHANGING THE ENVIRONMENT

You are sitting on the shore of Lake Mead, the largest man-made lake in the country. It's hard to believe this huge lake wasn't always here.

You've already learned that people adapt to the environment. But they also change the environment to meet their needs. In the 1920s communities and farms in Arizona and Nevada needed mor e water. The government built Hoover Dam across the Colorado River. A **dam** is a wall across a river or stream that holds back and controls the water.

After the Hoover Dam was built, the water backed up and formed Lake Mead. People use Lake Mead as a **reservoir**, a place to store water. Farmers use this water for crops. The water is also carried through pipes to cities miles away. The dam has another use, too. Water that passes through the dam turns huge machines to make electricity. The electricity is used by communities many miles away.

QUICK CHECK

Main Idea and Details Why are dams sometimes built?

Besides using Lake Mead as a reservoir, people can use it for fun! ▶

◀ Many Earth Day celebrations include parades like this one in Los Angeles, California.

B HELPING THE ENVIRONMENT

Unfortunately some things people do can hurt the environment. So in some communities people are working to teach people how to protect the environment.

Gaylord Nelson was a United States Senator from Wisconsin. He always cared about protecting the environment. In 1970 Nelson organized the first Earth Day celebration. Nelson wanted a day that would teach people how important it is to take care of our Earth.

Since then many people celebrate Earth Day every year on April 22. People take part in many ways. The Earth Day Groceries Project began in Seattle, Washington, in 1994. Students decorated brown paper grocery bags with messages about the environment. On Earth Day supermarket customers learned about protecting the environment by reading their grocery bags!

Gaylord Nelson

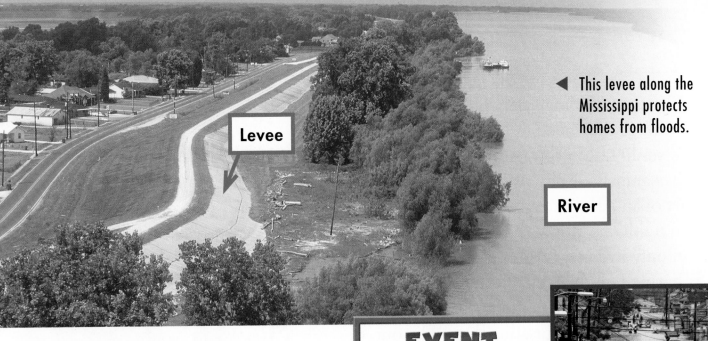

Levee

River

◄ This levee along the Mississippi protects homes from floods.

Using Land

St. Louis, Missouri, is built next to the Mississippi River. A **levee** along the river protects St. Louis. A levee is a long wall made of dirt or concrete built next to a river to prevent flooding. Levees protect the cities and farms near the water.

Hurricane Katrina, August 2005

Some people live in windy areas. The wind can be used to turn windmills that make electricity. Wind is a renewable resource. It is also clean and free! Some people build wind farms and use their land to create energy.

QUICK CHECK

Main Idea and Details Why is Earth Day celebrated?

A wind farm makes electricity. ▶

C PLANTS AND ANIMALS

Plants and animals depend on the environment for things they need to live. Plants use air, water, and sunlight to grow. Animals eat plants or other animals. Animals and plants together are part of an **ecosystem**—a community of living and nonliving things. Many plants and animals can only live in a certain place. If an ecosystem is harmed or changed, all the plants and animals in the ecosystem are affected. If the ecosystem is destroyed, a plant or animal may die out.

In Missouri a group of scientists is studying the prairie ecosystem. A prairie is flat land covered with grasses and flowers. The group works to protect plants like the Missouri bladderpod and animals like the jackrabbit. They want to keep these endangered plants and animals from dying out forever.

Animals and plants need help in other places, too. On the next page, read how people on islands near Africa work to protect animals there.

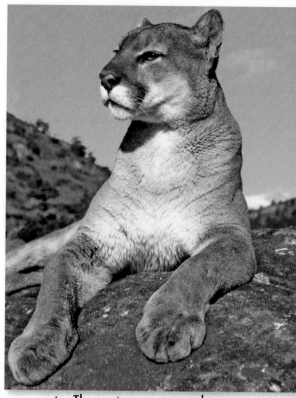

▲ The eastern puma used to be seen all across the United States. Now it is seen only in the West.

QUICK CHECK

Summarize Why is it important to protect ecosystems?

Yellow bladderpods ▼

PLACES

In some places people have drained wetlands to build on the land. But at **Eagle Bluffs**, near Columbia, Missouri, people restored a wetland. The wetland provides homes for special plants and animals.

Eagle Bluffs

Global Connections

Saving Animals

Mauritius, a group of islands near Africa, once had many animals found nowhere else. Two of these were the pink pigeon and the giant tortoise. Then things changed.

▲ The Aldabran Giant Tortoise is similar to the one once found on Mauritius.

Long ago ships brought both rats and cats to Mauritius. Both escaped and began to live on the islands. They ate the birds and the tortoise eggs. People changed the ecosystem, too. They cut the trees where the pigeons nested, and they ate the tortoises. Soon all the tortoises were gone, and there were very few pink pigeons left.

▼ Pink pigeon

Today the people of Mauritius are working to save the pink pigeons. They have made a park to protect places where pigeons nest. They also are raising another kind of tortoise on a nearby island. Someday they may bring these tortoises to live on Mauritius.

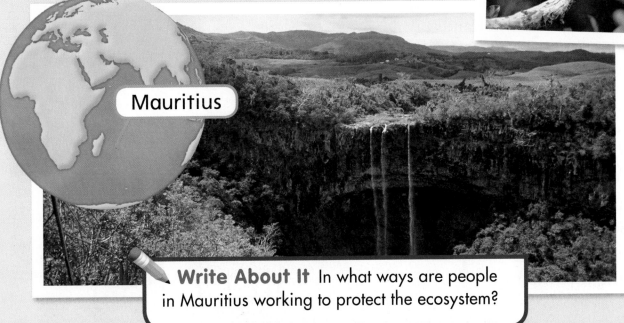

Mauritius

Write About It In what ways are people in Mauritius working to protect the ecosystem?

THE GREAT LAKES ECOSYSTEM

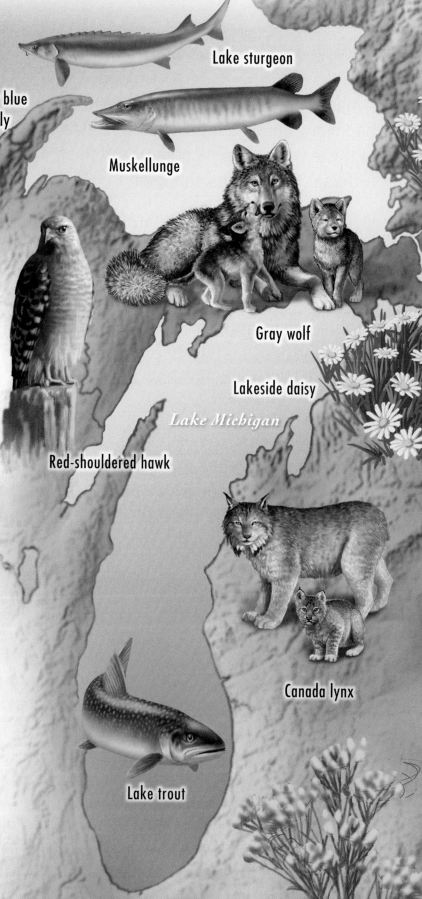

Dwarf lake iris

Black tern

Karner blue butterfly

Lake Superior

Lake sturgeon

Muskellunge

Gray wolf

Lakeside daisy

Lake Michigan

Red-shouldered hawk

Canada lynx

Lake trout

The Great Lakes hold more freshwater than any other place on Earth. The shores of the Great Lakes have prairies, sand dunes, and forests. Hundreds of kinds of fish, turtles, insects, birds, and plants live in and around the lakes.

Around the shores of the lake, though, are cities and factories. People have drained wetlands and cut forests to build homes and businesses. Because of this, almost 30 types of plants and animals now struggle to survive in the Great Lakes. The Hine's emerald dragonfly, for example, lives in wetland and grassy areas. Because people have drained many wetlands, these dragonflies are losing their homes.

A Safe and Healthy Ecosystem

Some people work in groups to keep plants and animals in the Great Lakes safe and healthy. The Great Lakes Basin Ecosystem Team is one such group. They work to protect the ecosystem and to teach visitors how to enjoy the area without harming it.

QUICK CHECK

Main Idea and Details **Why are some animals in the Great Lakes ecosystem endangered?**

▲ Whooping cranes are on the list of birds that need protection.

Yellow perch

Grasshopper sparrow

Brook trout

Eastern prairie fringed orchid

Lake Huron

Lake Erie water snake

Golden-winged warbler

Houghton's goldenrod

Lake Erie

Check Understanding

1. **VOCABULARY** Write one sentence for each of the vocabulary words below.
   dam   reservoir   levee

2. **READING SKILL** **Main Idea and Details** Use your chart from page 36 to write a paragraph about how people interact with the environment.

Main Idea	Details

3. **Write About It** Write two or three sentences to explain how dams and levees affect the way people live.

43

Ohio Connections

Your Community's Land and Resources

Lee learned about the geography and natural resources near his community. Here's what you can do to learn about the geography of your community.

- At the library, find a map of your community that shows landforms. This is also called a topographic map. Look for the landforms and bodies of water near your community, such as mountains, lakes, rivers, oceans, or ponds.

- Use encyclopedias, newspapers, or the Internet to find pictures and information about your community's natural resources.

LOG ON For more help with your project visit www.macmillanmh.com

Geography Activity

Make a Clay Landform Model

1 Use a map to learn about the landforms and bodies of water in your area. Decide what to include on your model.

2 Copy the map onto the cardboard. If you decide to make your model larger than the map, you could use a copy machine to make the map larger.

3 Cover the map with clay. Build up each type of feature using different colors of clay.

4 Use your paper to make labels and a key for your model. Use glue, tape, and toothpicks to attach your labels and key to the model.

5 Share your model with your classmates.

Materials
- map of your community
- markers
- cardboard
- clay of different colors
- paper
- glue or tape
- toothpicks

Unit 1 Review and Assess

Vocabulary

Number a paper from 1 to 4. Beside each number write the word from below that matches the description.

community **natural resource**

suburb **environment**

1. something found in nature that people use

2. a community not far from a city

3. the air, water, land, and living things around us

4. a place where people live, work, play, and help each other

Comprehension and Critical Thinking

5. **Reading Skill** Describe three kinds of communities.

6. How can people protect the environment?

7. **Critical Thinking** Why should people in communities help each other?

8. **Critical Thinking** How could a change to the environment be both good and bad?

Skill

Use Intermediate Directions

Write a complete sentence to answer each question.

9. In which direction would you travel if you were going from Camden to Atlantic City?

10. If you were in Trenton, which direction would you travel to reach Elizabeth?

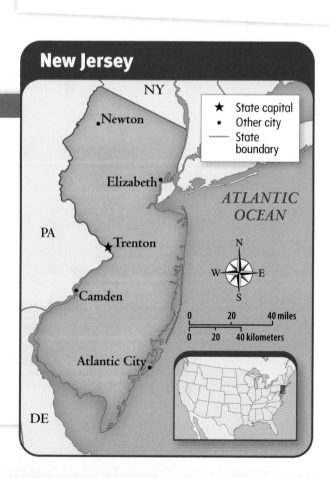

New Jersey

★ State capital
• Other city
— State boundary

NY

Newton

Elizabeth

PA

Trenton

Camden

Atlantic City

ATLANTIC OCEAN

N W E S

0 20 40 miles
0 20 40 kilometers

DE

Directions: Read the selection.

Ohio has a variety of natural resources. There are many trees and areas with rich soil. Lakes and streams provide water and have fish that people like to eat.

Some resources, such as trees, soil, and fish, are renewable. Renewable resources can be replaced, but people still need to use them wisely. If too many of one kind of fish are taken from the water, they may die out forever. It is important to use only as much of a renewable resource as we need. That way we will be sure that we always have enough.

Directions: Use the selection to answer questions 1-4.

1. What type of resources are trees, soil, and fish?

    ○ A. minerals

    ○ B. renewable resources

    ○ C. nonrenewable resources

2. What is the main idea here?

    ○ A. Renewable resources can be used again.

    ○ B. It is important to use renewable resources wisely.

    ○ C. Water is an important resource.

3. What are some ways we could protect renewable resources?

    Write your answer on a separate piece of paper.

4. Should we use renewable resources as much as we want? Explain why we should or should not.

    Write your answer on a separate piece of paper.

How does where you live affect how you live?

Write About the Big Idea

Expository Essay

Use the Unit 1 foldable to write an essay that answers the Big Idea question, "How does where you live affect how you live?" Begin with an introduction. Write one paragraph for each section of the foldable. Use the notes you wrote on your foldable to help you. End with a paragraph that answers the question.

FOLDABLES™ Study Organizer

Where You Live

| Community Size | Resources | Climate |

Projects About the Big Idea

Make a Drawing Think about your community. Draw a picture that shows everyday activities in your community.

Make a Poster Design a poster showing how people use one renewable or one nonrenewable resource. Work in a small group to make a poster that shows the steps needed to bring that resource from nature to your community.

EXPLORE
The Big Idea

Essential Question
How do communities change over time?

FOLDABLES
Study Organizer

Sequence
Make a Trifold Book Foldable to take notes as you read Unit 2. Label the sections **Newcomers, Seeking Freedom**, and **Inventions**.

Newcomers

Seeking Freedom

Inventions

LOG ON

For more about Unit 2 go to
www.macmillanmh.com

Communities Change

PEOPLE, PLACES, AND EVENTS

Rufus Putnam

Marietta, Ohio

Ohio Settlement

1788
Marietta became the first permanent settlement in the Northwest Territory.

Rufus Putnam was an explorer who founded **Marietta**, the first **settlement** in the Ohio Territory.

Today you can visit the **Sternwheel Festival** on the Ohio River in Marietta.

LOG ON For more about People, Places, and Events, visit www.macmillanmh.com

Blue Jacket

Fort Recovery, Ohio

Battle of St. Clair

1791

The Battle of St. Clair was between the United States and the Western Confederacy of American Indians.

Blue Jacket, a great Shawnee leader, fought under Little Turtle at the **Battle of St. Clair** in **Fort Recovery, Ohio**.

Today you can visit the site of the Battle of St. Clair in Fort Recovery, Ohio.

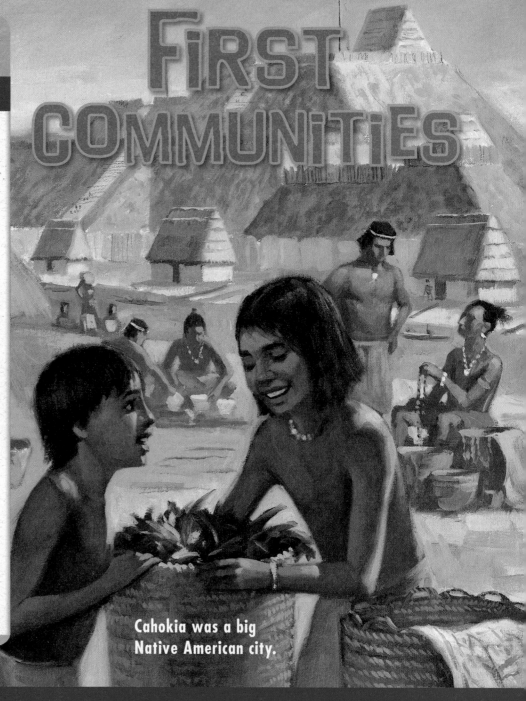

FIRST COMMUNITIES

Cahokia was a big
Native American city.

VOCABULARY

culture p. 53

barter p. 53

artifact p. 53

settler p. 56

slavery p. 59

READING SKILL

Sequence

Copy the chart below. As you read list what happened when new people arrived in America.

First
Next
Last

OHIO ACADEMIC CONTENT STANDARDS

H3, PS1, PS3, GEO7, SSS1

Visual Preview

How did the first communities grow?

A Cahokia was built by Native Americans in what is now Illinois.

B The Powhatan, a Native American group, lived in what is now Virginia.

C People from England built a community called Jamestown.

D Africans worked in Jamestown and helped it to grow.

Ⓐ CAHOKIA

It is the year 1200 in the Native American city of Cahokia, in what is now Illinois. From the fields you can see a huge mound of earth, as tall as a ten-story building.

Once the land in this area was nearly flat. Then the people began to build mounds. It took more than 300 years to build the largest mound. At the top the chief and other important people held ceremonies to honor the sun. Sun ceremonies and mound building were all part of the **culture**, or way of life, in Cahokia.

Life in Cahokia

Life in Cahokia was busy. Men fished in nearby rivers. Women and children picked corn and squash to eat. Others made tools and pots to trade in the market.

Artifacts, things made or used by people in the past, tell us how people lived long ago.

Cahokia was then one of the biggest cities in the world. It was built near several rivers. People traveled the rivers and **bartered**, or traded goods, with other villages near and far. Trading brought an exchange of things like language, ideas, and technology.

QUICK CHECK

Sequence **What did Cahokia look like before mound building began?**

53

Global Connections

Buildings Made Long Ago

About 2,000 years ago, Teotihuacan, Mexico, was at the center of a Native American civilization. A civilization is a culture that has advanced systems of learning, arts, and government. Teotihuacan was even bigger than Cahokia.

People from both Cahokia and Teotihuacan made the mounds and pyramids that we study today. Cahokians built their dirt mounds up to 100 feet tall. Some mounds were used as temples where people worshipped.

The people of Teotihuacan built their huge pyramids of stone. The Pyramid of the Sun is twice the size of the biggest Cahokian mounds! This pyramid has a temple on top.

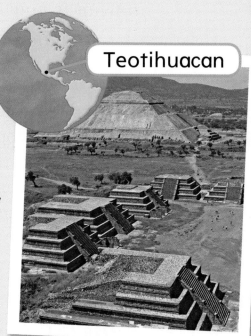

Teotihuacan

▲ Some pyramids in Teotihuacan were used to bury the dead.

Cahokia

Cahokian mounds had temples on top. Others had homes for important people. ▶

Write About It Write a paragraph about the ways people in Cahokia and Teotihuacan made and used their buildings.

yahikan

canoe

▲ A Powhatan home was called a yahikan. Each had a fire in the center for warmth.

ⓑ POWHATAN'S VILLAGES

It is a winter morning in the year 1606. A young girl, Pocahontas, follows her family to the river to bathe. Bathing in the river every day is part of her group's culture. Later she will help her mother make clothing.

Meeting Community Needs

Pocahontas lived in a Native American village in what is now Virginia. Her father, Powhatan, was a powerful chief. During the early 1600s he ruled over many villages. The people he led were also called the Powhatan.

The Powhatan used the natural resources around them to meet many needs. They carved canoes out of trees and used them on the rivers and the ocean to fish and trade. The Powhatan also hunted turkey and deer in the forests. They grew and stored corn and squash. Everyone worked together so there was enough to eat.

▼ The Powhatan used stone knives like these.

QUICK CHECK

Main Idea and Details **How did the Powhatan use resources?**

55

Do you know why the year 1492 is important? That's when Christopher Columbus discovered America. After that people from many countries in Europe started coming to the Americas. Some came looking for land, gold, or adventure. Others came to build new communities and to find freedom.

Making a New Home

People from England first came to Powhatan lands in 1607. These **settlers** began making this land their home. A settler is a person who moves from one area to another to find land. The settlers called their new home Jamestown. Many of them were unwilling to work. They only wanted to look for gold!

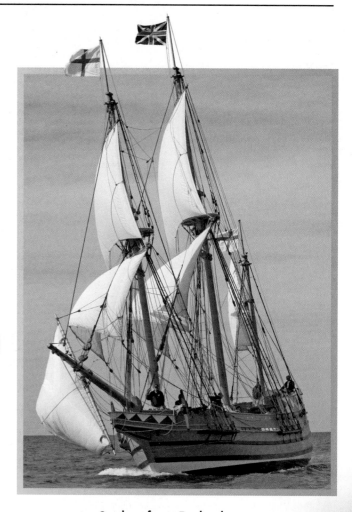

▲ Settlers from England came to America by ship.

Jamestown

Life in Jamestown was very hard in the winter of 1609. The settlers soon ran out of food. One settler wrote, "Now all of us at James Town, beginning to feel that sharp prick of hunger . . ." Even so, new settlers continued to arrive.

You can visit Jamestown Settlement to see how Jamestown looked long ago. ▶

Help From the Powhatan

The land was new and strange to the English. They had to learn how to hunt and grow food. To whom did the settlers go for help? Their neighbors, the Powhatan. Sometimes Pocahontas brought fish, corn, and squash to the hungry settlers. She became friends with Jamestown's leader, John Smith, and later married John Rolfe, another English settler.

As Jamestown grew, there was less land for the Powhatan. In just ten years the Powhatan had lost much of their land to the Jamestown settlers.

John Smith

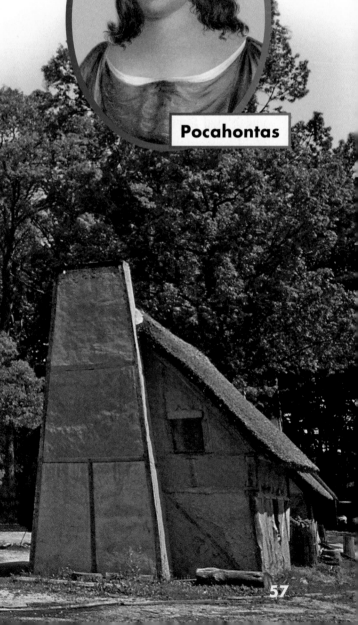

Pocahontas

QUICK CHECK

Sequence **What did the English have to do after settling in Jamestown?**

This photo shows how people in Jamestown made glass. ▶

▲ Artifacts help us understand Jamestown. What do you think these glass objects were used for?

Ⓓ HERE TO STAY

Settlers kept coming to Jamestown. As more people arrived, Jamestown grew stronger. Settlers chopped down trees for wood. They planted tobacco. They also made glass. Wood, tobacco, and glass could then be sent back to England for sale.

Growing tobacco was hard work! In 1619 a Dutch ship brought some people from Africa to Jamestown. The English settlers were happy to have the African workers.

Africans in Jamestown

The Africans who came to Jamestown helped it to grow even more. They cooked, made clothes, worked on farms, took care of children, and made buildings.

Though the first Africans in Jamestown did not choose to come and were not free, they were not all kept in **slavery**. Slavery is forcing people to work without pay and without freedom. The first Africans in Jamestown were servants who earned their freedom in time. Slavery would be far worse for the Africans who followed.

QUICK CHECK

Main Idea and Details **What types of work did people do in Jamestown?**

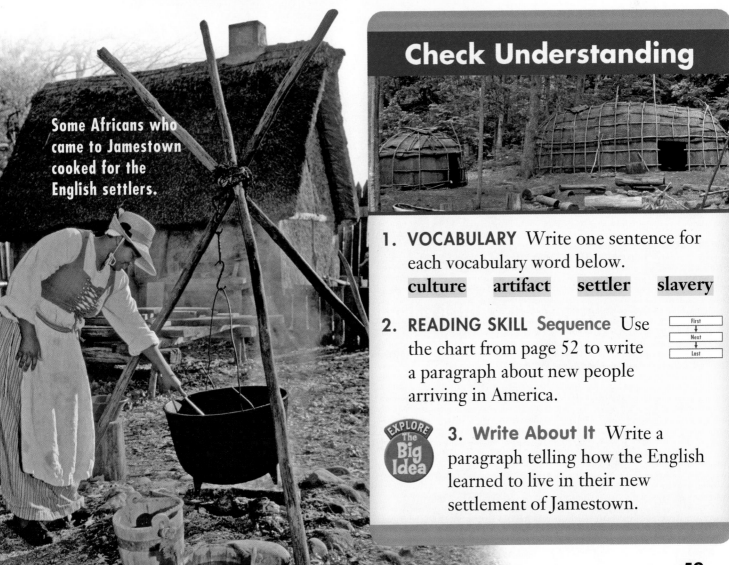

Some Africans who came to Jamestown cooked for the English settlers.

Check Understanding

1. **VOCABULARY** Write one sentence for each vocabulary word below.
   culture   artifact   settler   slavery

2. **READING SKILL Sequence** Use the chart from page 52 to write a paragraph about new people arriving in America.

   | First |
   | Next |
   | Last |

3. **Write About It** Write a paragraph telling how the English learned to live in their new settlement of Jamestown.

EXPLORE The Big Idea

Lesson 2

VOCABULARY

colony p. 61

tax p. 62

revolution p. 65

Patriot p. 65

constitution p. 66

READING SKILL

Sequence

Copy the chart. As you read fill it in with events that led up to the American Revolution.

First
↓
Next
↓
Last

OHIO ACADEMIC CONTENT STANDARDS

H1, H2, H3, PS1, GOV4, GOV5, GOV6, CRR2, CRR3

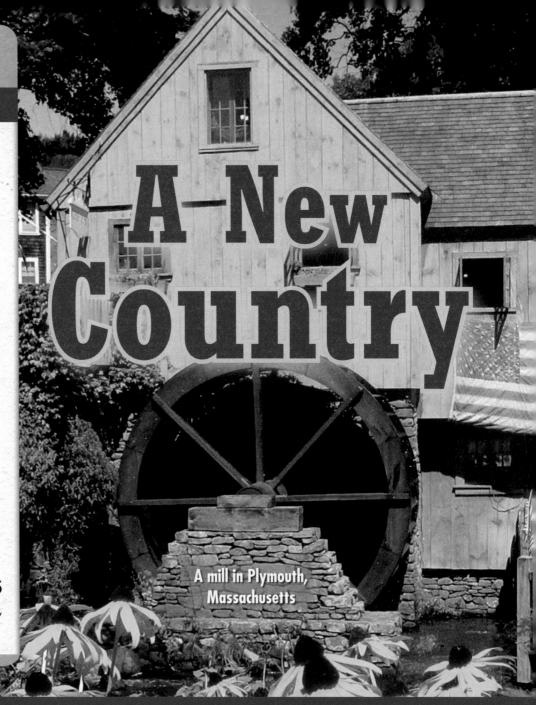

A New Country

A mill in Plymouth, Massachusetts

Visual Preview

How did the British colonies grow and become a new country?

A People from Europe built new communities in North America.

B Boston became one of the biggest colonial cities.

C Colonists won their freedom from British rule.

D Leaders wrote a plan for the new government.

Ⓐ COMMUNITIES GROW

A sailor calls, "Land ahead!" You rush to the front of the ship and stare into the mist. Then you see it. America!

After people back in Europe learned about the success of Jamestown, more and more people sailed across the huge Atlantic Ocean. They wanted a chance to start a better life in America, too.

A Better Life

Jamestown wasn't big enough for everyone! Many of the newcomers settled in different areas along the Atlantic coast. By the 1750s there were 13 British **colonies** stretching along the east coast of North America. A colony is a place that is ruled by another country. Most colonists, or people who live in a colony, were farmers who raised crops to sell and make money.

Many British people traveled to America to live in the colonies. Some came for religious freedom. Others came hoping to start a business or to own their own land.

This old map shows the east coast of America in 1770.

▲ Farmers in the colonies grew crops such as corn, rice, and tobacco.

QUICK CHECK

Sequence What happened after people heard about the success of Jamestown?

BOSTON, A COLONIAL CITY

Boston was one of the biggest colonial cities. What was life in Boston like in colonial times? People bought fish from the fishermen and vegetables from their neighbors. They could buy wooden chests, beds, and barrels made right in Boston. But items like silk and tea came from Great Britain.

▲ Colonists bought tea from Great Britain.

Paying Money to the British

Colonists had to pay **taxes** on things from Great Britain. A tax is money paid to a government. A new law called the Stamp Act said that colonists had to pay a tax on items such as sugar, newspapers, tea, paper, and glass. These were things colonists used every day.

People in Boston were unhappy about paying these taxes and started to complain. They were especially angry about the tax on tea. Why should they pay if they didn't have a say in how the tax money was used, they thought.

Unfair Rules

There were other rules the colonists thought were unfair. For example, the colonists were not allowed to meet in groups. They also said they did not get fair trials in courts with judges. Some rules said British soldiers could eat and sleep in colonists' homes whenever they wanted. The colonists knew it was time to make some important changes.

▼ Many things shipped to and from Great Britain passed through Boston's busy harbor.

QUICK CHECK

Main Idea and Details **Why were people in Boston unhappy with the British?**

In 1774 colonial leaders met in the Philadelphia State House, now called Independence Hall. ▶

© TAKING ACTION

Many colonists wanted to let the British government know that they were unhappy with these rules. First they took peaceful actions. Some, like Samuel Adams, wrote newspaper articles. Others met to talk and to make decisions. Many people stopped buying British items such as tea.

These actions weren't enough. Colonists soon took other actions that were not peaceful. In 1773 a group of men, dressed as Native Americans so the British would not recognize them, secretly went onto British ships. As a protest they dumped 342 chests of British tea into Boston Harbor. This event became known as the Boston Tea Party.

▼ As punishment after the Boston Tea Party, Great Britain closed Boston Harbor. No ships could enter or leave.

Fighting for Freedom

The British government would not change its unfair rules. Nothing the colonists did worked. It was time to declare independence in writing. The job of writing such a declaration was given to a Virginia lawyer named Thomas Jefferson.

The Declaration of Independence told King George III of Great Britain that Americans would be free. The colonists' leaders approved the declaration on July 4, 1776. The British king was not happy—and the American **Revolution** began. A revolution is a fight that often leads to the end of one government and the beginning of another. British soldiers came to fight the **Patriots**—the people who fought for independence. After seven years of war, the Patriots finally won independence from Great Britain. The 13 colonies were now a new country—the United States of America.

▲ African Americans were among those who fought during the American Revolution.

QUICK CHECK

Sequence What happened after colonial leaders approved the Declaration of Independence?

George Washington

PEOPLE

George Washington was a general who led Patriots during the American Revolution. In 1789 Washington was elected President of the United States of America. We honor President Washington by celebrating his birthday on President's Day, the third Monday in February.

D AFTER THE WAR

▲ Representatives signed the United States Constitution in 1788.

A new country needs a **constitution**, or a written plan of government. In 1787 representatives, or people who speak or act for others, met in Philadelphia to write a constitution. After talking and thinking about different ideas, they reached a compromise. In 1788 the United States Constitution was approved by the 13 states and was now the law.

QUICK CHECK

Sequence What did representatives need to do after the war was over?

Check Understanding

1. **VOCABULARY** Use the words below to write a paragraph about the Patriots' fight for freedom.

   tax   **revolution**   **constitution**

2. **READING SKILL Sequence** Use your chart from page 60 to write a paragraph about the events that led to the American Revolution.

First
Next
Last

3. **Write About It** Make a list of some ways to have fun in your community. Write a letter about what it might have been like to live during the American Revolution.

Citizenship

Democracy in Action

Cooperation and Compromise

Like people long ago, people today cooperate and compromise. A fifth-grade class in Lutz, Florida, wanted a dog park at Nye Park. At a town meeting the students found out that Nye Park was too small. So the students compromised and asked for a leash-only dog area. Finally the town agreed to create a dog park elsewhere. Read the steps below to learn how to compromise.

How to Work Together

1. **Identify the problem.** Find out what each group or person thinks is the problem.

2. **Express points of view.** Share the reasons why people disagree. Find out what each person wants.

3. **Look for common goals or interests.** Talk about the ideas or goals that all groups share.

4. **Find ways that everyone can gain from compromise.** Look for a way to give each group or person at least part of what they want, so that everyone can agree.

Write About It Write a paragraph about a school activity that requires cooperation.

Chart and Graph Skills

Use Time Lines

VOCABULARY

time line

year

decade

century

You have read about events in America's history. It is not always easy to remember what happened first, next, and last. A **time line** shows the order of events. Learning to use time lines will help you learn about events in the past.

Learn It

Follow these steps and look at the time line below as you read.

- **Look at the dates.** Time lines are divided to show time periods, such as **years**, **decades**, or **centuries**. A year is any period of 12 months. A decade is 10 years, and a century is 100 years.

- **Look at the order of events.** Events are listed in time order from left to right. The earliest event on this time line is "Christopher Columbus lands in the Americas."

- **Use the dates to tell the number of years between events.** Subtract the date of the earlier event from the date of the later event.

First Communities

1560 - Spanish people come to Powhatan lands

1450   1500   1550   1600   1650

1492 - Christopher Columbus lands in the Americas

1607 - English settlers arrive in Jamestown

Fighting for Freedom

1783 - Patriots win the American Revolution

1770   1775   1780   1785   1790

1776 - Declaration of Independence approved

1789 - George Washington becomes the first President of the United States

Try It

Use the time line above to answer the questions.

- How many years does this time line cover?

- What is the last event on the time line?

- What happened in 1776?

- How many years after the end of the Revolution did George Washington become President?

Apply It

- Make a time line of your own life.

- Divide your time line into years.

- Make the first event the year you were born.

- Include five important events on your time line. Also include an event in the future—your 13th birthday. In what year will you be 13?

MOVING WEST

Daniel Boone led people west.

VOCABULARY

explorer p. 71

frontier p. 71

pioneer p. 71

territory p. 72

READING SKILL

Sequence

Copy the chart below. As you read list the events that helped change the United States after the Revolutionary War.

| First |
| Next |
| Last |

OHIO ACADEMIC CONTENT STANDARDS

H3, PS3, GEO5, GEO8

Visual Preview

How did the United States change after the American Revolution?

A As the country grew, people began to move west.

B Lewis and Clark led a team to find out about the land to the west.

C Many people traveled west in covered wagons.

LOOKING WEST

You are traveling west but you are not even on a road. You are following a Native American trail over the mountains.

The country was growing quickly! Soon people began thinking about moving west. Daniel Boone was an **explorer** who followed Native American trails west in the 1770s. An explorer is someone who goes to a new place to find out about it. Boone found forests filled with bear, deer, and fox. He also discovered Native American communities as he traveled through the **frontier**. A frontier is the far edge of a country where new people are just beginning to settle.

Boone explored the area that is now Kentucky. Later he helped settlers cross the Appalachian Mountains to make new homes on the other side.

QUICK CHECK

Sequence **What did Daniel Boone do after he explored Kentucky?**

PLACES

Daniel Boone helped build a new settlement in Kentucky called **Fort Boonesborough**. Today people can visit Fort Boonesborough State Park to see what life was like for **pioneers**. A pioneer is the first of a group of people to settle in an area.

Fort Boonesborough

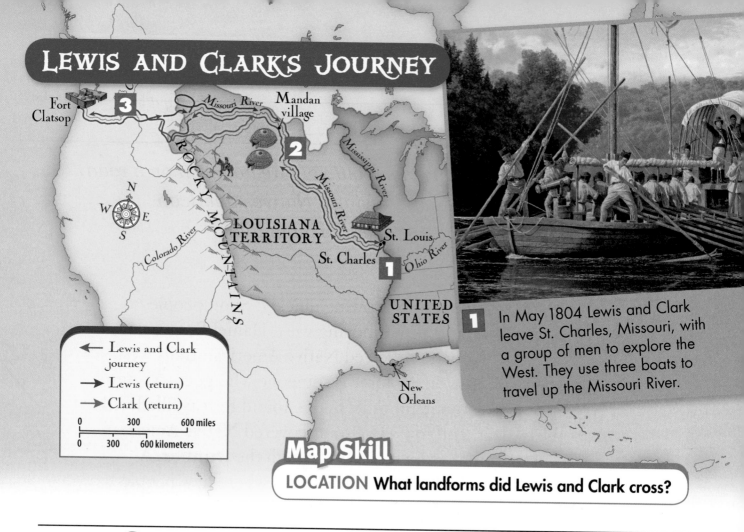

LEWIS AND CLARK'S JOURNEY

3 Fort Clatsop

Missouri River — Mandan village

2

LOUISIANA TERRITORY

Mississippi River

Missouri River

St. Louis

St. Charles

1

Ohio River

UNITED STATES

New Orleans

Colorado River

ROCKY MOUNTAINS

← Lewis and Clark journey
→ Lewis (return)
→ Clark (return)

0   300   600 miles
0 300   600 kilometers

1 In May 1804 Lewis and Clark leave St. Charles, Missouri, with a group of men to explore the West. They use three boats to travel up the Missouri River.

Map Skill

LOCATION What landforms did Lewis and Clark cross?

B   ACROSS THE CONTINENT

The Mississippi River was important for trade and travel. President Thomas Jefferson wanted to get control of the Mississippi River from France. He tried to buy New Orleans, the city where the Mississippi River flows into the sea. Instead, in 1803 France sold all of the Louisiana **Territory**. A territory is land owned by a country. This deal, called the Louisiana Purchase, doubled the size of the United States, all for $15 million!

Learning About the New Land

The United States knew very little about this huge territory. So Jefferson hired Meriwether Lewis and William Clark to go and explore the new land. During their journey Lewis and Clark made maps that would help settlers who moved west later.

2 Lewis and Clark meet a Native American woman named Sacagawea. She travels with them as their guide. She tells them which plants are safe to eat and helps them get horses to finish their journey.

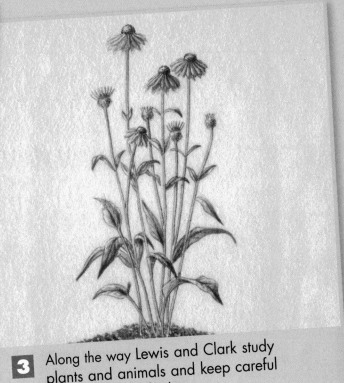

3 Along the way Lewis and Clark study plants and animals and keep careful records of their findings.

People, Plants, and Animals

During their two-year journey, Lewis and Clark met some of the Native Americans who lived in the West. Sacagawea, their Native American guide, helped them talk with the people they met because she knew many of their languages. Lewis and Clark wrote about all these different people and their ways of life.

Lewis and Clark also studied plants and animals. They wrote about at least 170 plants. They also described animals such as the white-tailed deer and the plains gray wolf.

EVENT

The **Louisiana Purchase** included all or part of 15 states and even parts of Canada. In New Orleans the event was celebrated by raising the American flag!

Louisiana Purchase

QUICK CHECK

Summarize **What did Lewis and Clark do during their journey?**

C TRAILS TO THE WEST

Pioneers and settlers followed Native American and explorers' trails to the West. Many trails, like the Oregon Trail, began in Independence, Missouri. Settlers often traveled in wagon trains, a group of covered wagons traveling together across country.

The Oregon Trail

The Oregon Trail was difficult to travel. Rivers were good for drinking water, but they were hard to cross. Families always looked for food and fuel for cooking fires. Have you ever written a letter or journal entry about a trip you have taken? Below, read how a 17-year-old girl described her journey on the trail.

Primary Sources

"We traveled but nine miles. . . . The roads were very hilly and the sand six inches deep. We traded with the Indians this evening for salmon; they are the best fish I ever saw."

Journal Entry
Abigail Jane Scott, August 5, 1852

Write About It Write a paragraph describing what Scott's journal entry tells you about traveling on the Oregon Trail.

Traveling by wagon train was slow and difficult.

Why Move West?

By 1870 thousands of pioneers had traveled across the Oregon Trail. Many had listened to the words of John Soule, an Indiana journalist who said,

" Go West, young man, and grow up with the country. **"**

Some settlers started farms in Oregon. Others hoped to find gold in California! Others went just for adventure. All who went west hoped for better lives.

QUICK CHECK

Main Idea and Details **Why did pioneers travel the Oregon Trail?**

Check Understanding

1. **VOCABULARY** Make a drawing that shows the meaning of each word below.
   explorer   **frontier**   **pioneer**

2. **READING SKILL** **Sequence** Use your chart from page 70 to write a paragraph telling how the United States changed after the American Revolution.

First
Next
Last

 EXPLORE The Big Idea

3. **Write About It** Write a diary entry that a pioneer traveling west might have written.

Map and Globe Skills

Understanding Hemispheres

VOCABULARY

sphere

hemisphere

prime meridian

equator

Today people come to the United States from all over the world. You can find these places on a globe, a model of Earth. A globe is a **sphere**. It is round, like a ball. You can see only half of a globe at a time. The part of the globe that you see is called a **hemisphere**, which means "half of a sphere."

Learn It

We can divide Earth two ways— around the middle or top to bottom.

- The **equator** is an imaginary line around Earth halfway between the North Pole and the South Pole. Any place north of this line is in the Northern Hemisphere. Any place south of this line is in the Southern Hemisphere.

- The **prime meridian** is an imaginary line that runs from the North Pole to the South Pole through Greenwich, England. Places east of this line are in the Eastern Hemisphere. Places west of this line are in the Western Hemisphere.

- A continent can lie in more than one hemisphere.

Western Hemisphere

Eastern Hemisphere

Northern Hemisphere

Southern Hemisphere

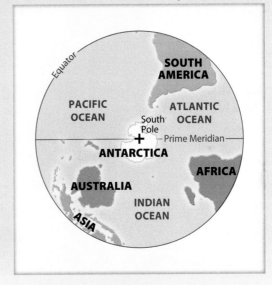

Try It

Look at the maps above.

● Name the four hemispheres.

● Which hemisphere is entirely south of the equator?

Apply It

● Which two hemispheres is North America in?

● Which two hemispheres is Australia in?

Lesson 4

VOCABULARY

industry p. 79

immigrant p. 80

migration p. 82

discrimination p. 83

READING SKILL

Sequence

Copy the chart below. As you read list ways small towns and cities grew.

First

↓

Next

↓

Last

OHIO ACADEMIC CONTENT STANDARDS

H1, H3, PS3, SSS4, SSS5

COMMUNITIES BECOME CITIES

The Statue of Liberty greeted newcomers.

Visual Preview

How did small communities grow into large cities?

A As more people moved to find jobs, small towns grew into cities.

B People arriving from other countries helped cities grow.

C Many African Americans moved to cities in the North and Midwest.

A FROM TOWN TO CITY

New York City was once a small town with just a few streets and buildings. Today it is our country's largest city, with more than 8 million people!

When the population of a place grows, communities grow, too. Population means the number of people who live in an area. More people means more houses, schools, and roads. Soon towns become small cities. Small cities may grow into large urban areas.

What makes a population grow? One answer is jobs! People often move to new places to find work. For example, many people moved to northern Pennsylvania to get jobs in the coal **industry**. An industry makes one kind of product or provides one kind of service. Coal mining is an industry. So is banking.

Geography also affects population. People often move to a new place because of its geography. Some people like a warm climate. They move to an area where it is warm.

QUICK CHECK

Sequence What happens after new people move to an area?

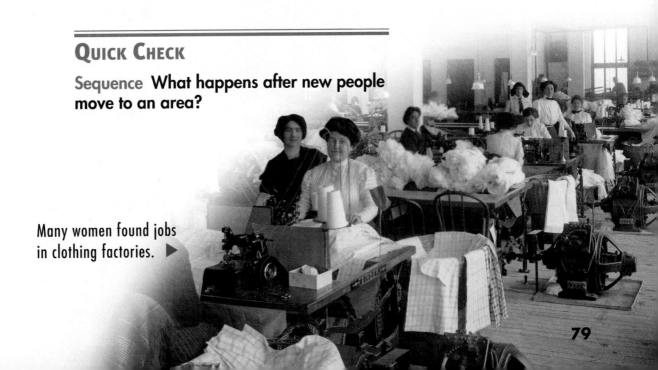

Many women found jobs in clothing factories. ▶

79

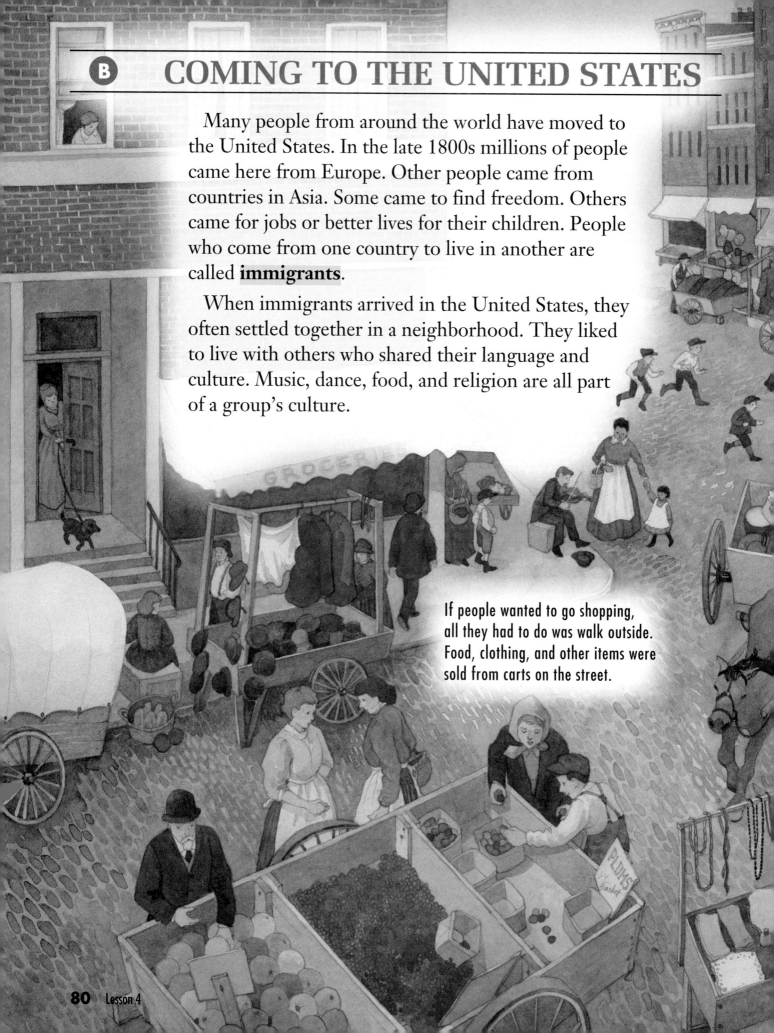

COMING TO THE UNITED STATES

B

Many people from around the world have moved to the United States. In the late 1800s millions of people came here from Europe. Other people came from countries in Asia. Some came to find freedom. Others came for jobs or better lives for their children. People who come from one country to live in another are called **immigrants**.

When immigrants arrived in the United States, they often settled together in a neighborhood. They liked to live with others who shared their language and culture. Music, dance, food, and religion are all part of a group's culture.

If people wanted to go shopping, all they had to do was walk outside. Food, clothing, and other items were sold from carts on the street.

With large numbers of immigrants, the populations of cities grew. The streets were often filled with traffic. In New York City most immigrants lived in tenements—apartment buildings with many people.

Sometimes musicians, dancers, and other performers provided entertainment for people living in and visiting a neighborhood.

Sometimes immigrants moved into communities that were already settled. Over time, their culture helped shape the neighborhood. For example, some neighborhood restaurants serve food from a particular culture, and museums show paintings made by immigrant artists.

QUICK CHECK

Main Idea and Details **How do immigrants change communities?**

PEOPLE

Many **immigrant** parents came to this country so their children could have a better education. When they weren't in school, many immigrant children worked to help earn money.

Immigrants

About the same time that immigrants were arriving from other countries, people were also on the move in the United States. Many African Americans in the South decided to move to the North and the Midwest. This **migration**, or movement from one part of a country to another, changed our country. Thousands of African Americans left farms in the South and moved to big cities like New York, Chicago, Detroit, and Pittsburgh to find work in factories.

Those that moved had to adapt to life in an urban community. They now lived in crowded cities full of people, tall buildings, and traffic. Life was very different from life on farms in the rural South.

▼ The movement of African Americans from the South to the North became known as the Great Migration.

▲ African Americans at work in New York around 1917

Life in the North

Like the immigrants, African Americans were looking for a better life. In the South they faced **discrimination**. Discrimination happens when people are treated unfairly because of how they look or what they believe. They faced discrimination in the North, too, but life was better for them there. People found jobs and some started their own businesses.

___

QUICK CHECK

Compare and Contrast **How is migration different from immigration?**

Check Understanding

1. **VOCABULARY** Write one sentence for each vocabulary word below. **immigrant migration discrimination**

2. **READING SKILL** Sequence Use your chart from page 78 to write a paragraph about how small towns grew into cities.

First
Next
Last

3. **Write About It** Write a paragraph that tells how immigrants added to America's way of life.

Chart and Graph Skills

Use Bar Graphs

VOCABULARY

graph

bar graph

You have read about changes in population and the growth of cities. You can learn information about population by reading a **graph**. A graph is a special kind of picture that shows information in a way that is easy to understand. A **bar graph** uses bars to show information. You can use bar graphs to compare amounts of different items.

Learn It

Look at the graph as you follow the steps.

- **Read the title.** The graph shows the population of New York City from 1900 to 1930.

- **Read the labels.** The labels along the bottom show the years the graph is about. The labels along the side show the number of people in millions.

- **Put the information together.** Put your finger at the top of the blue bar, the bar for 1920. Move your finger to the left. You can see the blue bar reaches just past the mark for 5 million. This means that in 1920 the population of New York City was just over 5 million people. In which year shown on the graph did New York City have the lowest population?

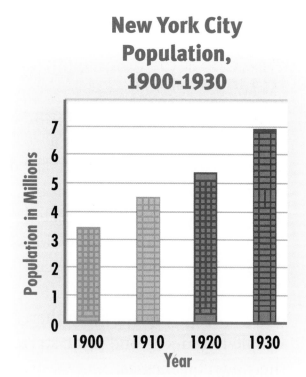

New York City Population, 1900-1930

Try It

Now look at the graph on this page to answer the questions.

- What does this graph show?

- What do the bars stand for?

- About how many people lived in Cincinnati in 1920?

Cincinnati Population, 1900–1930

Apply It

Find out the number of students in each class in your school. Show the information on a bar graph. Decide which information will go along the bottom and the side of the graph. Give your graph a title.

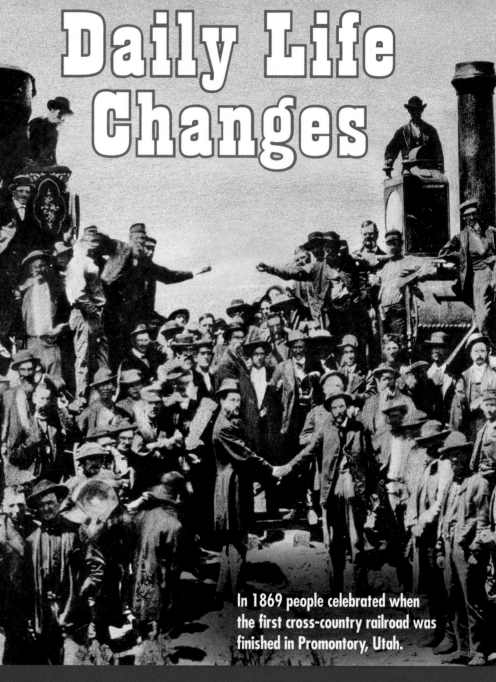

Daily Life Changes

Lesson 5

VOCABULARY

transcontinental p.87

skyscraper p. 89

elevator p. 89

manufacture p. 91

assembly line p. 91

READING SKILL

Sequence
Copy the chart below. As you read list the events that changed daily life in the United States.

First
↓
Next
↓
Last

OHIO ACADEMIC CONTENT STANDARDS

H1, H2, H3, GEO8, SSS1, SSS4, SSS5, SSS6

In 1869 people celebrated when the first cross-country railroad was finished in Promontory, Utah.

Visual Preview

How did inventions change lives in the mid 1800s?

A By 1869 railroad lines stretched across the country.

B New inventions improved lives in many ways.

C Automobiles and other inventions improved ways of traveling.

A TRAVELING MADE EASIER

As the eastern part of the United States got even more crowded, people began moving west. Traveling was hard. There were no trains, airplanes, cars, or even roads!

As more people moved west, a safer, faster way to travel was needed. Traveling west by wagon or ship took too long. In 1862 workers began building the first **transcontinental** railroad. This railroad ran across the continent. The Central Pacific Railroad was built eastward from Sacramento, California, mostly by Chinese immigrants. Irish immigrants worked on the Union Pacific Railroad, which was built westward from Omaha, Nebraska.

The two railroads met in Promontory, Utah, in 1869. Now travel that used to take months took only days. Railroads also made it easier to carry things, like food and mail, between the East and the West.

QUICK CHECK

Sequence How many years after work began on the transcontinental railroad was it completed?

▲ The Golden Spike was the last spike used to finish the transcontinental railroad.

NEW WAYS OF DOING THINGS

The railroad was an invention that helped people travel faster than they had before. An invention is something that has been made for the first time. As new communities and industries grew, people made more inventions that changed life everywhere.

Before

◄ **1830** Until the 1830s news traveled only as fast as a galloping horse. It could take days for news to travel across the country.

1853 Climbing many stairs wasn't easy, so most buildings were only a few stories tall.

◄ **1879** If you wanted to see at night you had to light a candle or an oil lamp. This was dangerous—fires could start easily.

1955 Germs spread in crowded cities. Schools and public places were sometimes closed so people couldn't pass on sicknesses.

PEOPLE

After **Granville T. Woods** invented a railway telegraph in 1887, train operators could send and receive messages between moving trains and the station. This helped people keep track of where trains were. It also helped prevent accidents.

Granville T. Woods

Inventions Change Communities

How did inventions change communities? Very tall building called **skyscrapers** made it possible for more people to work and live in big cities. Changes in medicine helped people avoid getting sick. Inventions made life easier and communities safer.

After

1830 ▶ Joseph Henry invented the telegraph in 1830, but it was not until 1843 that telegraph lines were put up. Then news could travel with lightning speed.

1853 In 1853 Elisha Otis made the first safe **elevator**, a machine for moving people up and down in a building. Now buildings could be taller.

1879 ▶ After 1879 when Thomas Edison improved the lightbulb, homes, workplaces, and schools got much brighter and a lot safer, too.

1955 In 1955 Jonas Salk made a vaccine that prevented a serious disease called polio. Vaccines made it safer for people to live in crowded cities.

QUICK CHECK

Sequence Why do you think skyscrapers weren't built until after the elevator was invented?

MORE WAYS TO GET AROUND

By the early 1900s people had invented even faster ways to travel—cars and airplanes. People could travel longer distances and make trips faster with these new forms of transportation. The Datagraphic below shows how these better forms of transportation changed the time it took to cross the country.

DataGraphic
Changes in Transportation

Study the map and pictograph below.
Then answer the questions that follow.

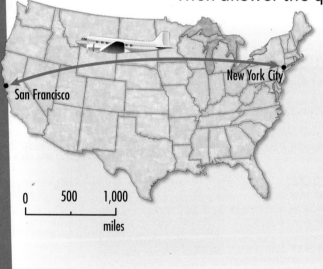

From New York City to San Francisco

1860 stagecoach		
1869 train		
1925 car		
1935 airplane		

☀ = 1 day of travel

Think About Changes in Transportation

1. About how many days did it take to travel by train from New York City to San Francisco in 1869?

2. About how many miles is it from New York to San Francisco?

▲ Each worker on the assembly line added one part to a car until it was finished.

▼ By 1923 almost half the cars sold in the United States were Model Ts.

Making Cars

In 1903 a man named Henry Ford started a company in Detroit, Michigan, to **manufacture** cars. Manufacture means to make something using machines. Ford used an **assembly line**. On an assembly line, each worker performs a certain task. All the tasks together make the product. Using an assembly line made it faster and cheaper to produce goods. Henry Ford sold his first Model T car in 1908. It was cheap enough so many more people could afford to own one.

QUICK CHECK

Cause and Effect **What happened because of the assembly line?**

Check Understanding

1. **VOCABULARY** Make a drawing showing what each vocabulary word means.
   elevator   skyscraper   assembly line

2. **READING SKILL Sequence** Use your chart from page 86 to write a paragraph on how inventions changed daily life in the United States.

First
Next
Last

3. **Write About It** Write a paragraph to explain how transportation changed from 1830 through the early 1900s.

Ohio Connections
Your Community's History

Janet wanted to learn about her town's history. She interviewed an older resident to find out how her community has changed. Then she created a poster about early leaders and historic areas in her community.

Here are some ways you can learn about your town's past:

- Interview an older relative or neighbor who has lived in your community for a long time.

- Look in your school or local library or on the Internet for information about your community's history. Look at old newspapers and photos to see what your community looked like long ago.

- Make a time line of three or four key events in your community's history.

- Take photographs or draw sketches of older buildings or businesses in your community.

LOG ON For help with your project visit www.macmillanmh.com

History Activity

Conduct an Interview

1. Before your interview, prepare a list of questions.

2. Take notes during the interview. If you decide to tape your interview, ask permission first.

3. Write a report of your interview and what you learned about your town's history.

Materials
- notebook
- pencil or pen
- lined paper

Make a Poster

Materials
- notebook
- crayons
- poster board
- photos and drawings
- markers

1. Gather the photos you found. Use these to draw pictures of older buildings. Arrange the drawings and your own photos on your poster board.

2. Use a marker to print labels for each building. Include the building's name, the year it was built, and what it is used for today.

3. Include a time line of important community events.

4. Share your poster with the class.

Historic Elkhart

1876 Musical Instrument Company G.G. Conn

1889 Electric Streetcars

1937 Travel Trailers

1831 Dr. Havilah Beardsly buys land and names the area Elkhart.

1852 The population increases because trains brought people to Elkhart.

1884 Miles Medical Co. is created by Dr. Franklin Miles.

Unit 2 Review and Assess

Vocabulary

Number a paper from 1 to 4. Beside each number write the word from the list below that matches the description.

settler   **explorer**

constitution   **migration**

1. a written plan of government

2. a person who makes a home in a new land

3. movement from one part of a country to another

4. a person who goes to a new place to find out about it

Comprehension and Critical Thinking

5. How did the Powhatan help settlers in Jamestown?

6. **Reading Skill** Why do immigrants often settle together in a community?

7. **Critical Thinking** How is travel today different from travel long ago?

8. **Critical Thinking** Why do people move to new places?

Skill

Use Bar Graphs

Look at the graph on the right. Write a complete sentence to answer each question.

9. What does this graph show?

10. Between 1890 and 1917, from which place did the most immigrants come?

Immigration to the United States, 1890-1917

Ohio Achievement Test Preparation

Directions: Read the selection.

In the late 1800s, the bicycle changed the way of life for many Ohio people. The new form of transportation allowed people to easily get away from the city. It also meant children could visit friends without their parents having to **escort** them.

Bicycles were cheaper than horses, and they were less difficult to repair. After bicycles came along, the government improved the roads to make them smoother and easier to ride on.

Early bicycles had iron or steel wheels. Later, rubber tires were made to make a more comfortable ride into town.

Directions: Use the selection to answer questions 1-3.

1. How did the invention of the bicycle change lives?

   ○ A. The bicycle was faster than the horse and buggy.

   ○ B. The bicycle cost more money compared to other transportation.

   ○ C. The bicycle allowed people to travel more easily.

2. What do you think the word **escort** means in the selection above?

   ○ A. to run away from someone

   ○ B. to hide from someone

   ○ C. to go with someone

3. Tell how bicycles were better than horses for traveling. Then tell some ways horses might have been better.

   Write your answer on a separate piece of paper.

The Big Idea Activities

How do communities change over time?

Write About the Big Idea

Descriptive Essay

In Unit 2 you read about how communities in the United States changed. Review the notes you made on your foldable. Begin your essay with a paragraph that states how communities changed over time.

Write one paragraph for each section of the foldable. Each paragraph should describe how communities were affected by the three topics.

Your final paragraph should summarize the main ideas of your essay.

Newcomers

Seeking Freedom

Inventions

Projects About the Big Idea

Make a Pictograph Find out the different ways of transportation that your classmates use to get to school. Make a pictograph that shows how many students use each type of transportation.

Write and Perform a Play You have read about traveling west on the Oregon Trail. Work in a small group to write a play about the pioneers' journey on the trail. Think of a problem a wagon train might have. Include the problem and the solution in your play. Perform your play for the class.

How We Get to School

car	
bus	
bicycle	
walking	

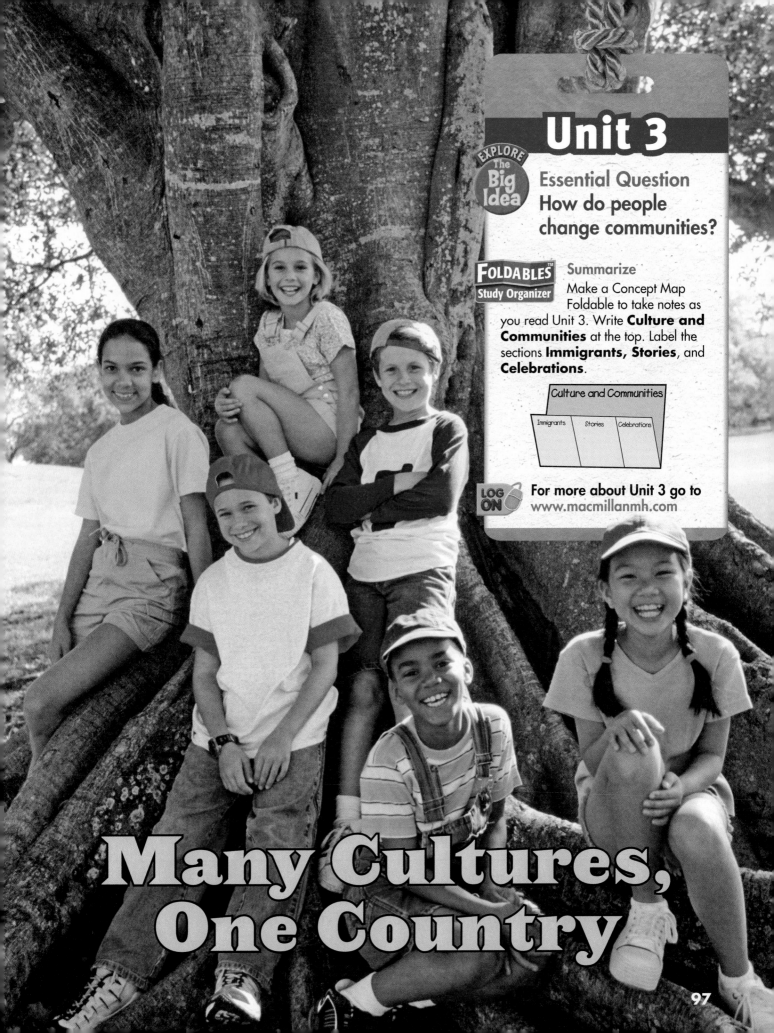

EXPLORE
The Big Idea

Essential Question
How do people change communities?

FOLDABLES™
Study Organizer

Summarize
Make a Concept Map Foldable to take notes as you read Unit 3. Write **Culture and Communities** at the top. Label the sections **Immigrants, Stories**, and **Celebrations**.

Culture and Communities

Immigrants	Stories	Celebrations

LOG ON

For more about Unit 3 go to
www.macmillanmh.com

Many Cultures, One Country

PEOPLE, PLACES, AND EVENTS

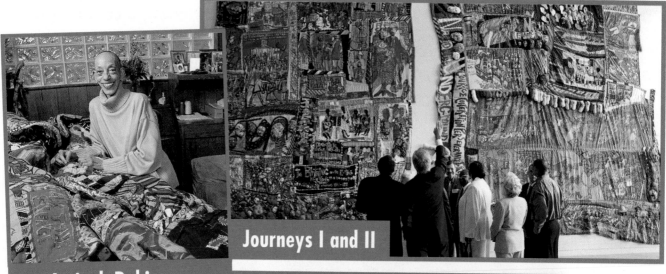

Aminah Robinson

Journeys I and II

National Underground Railroad Freedom Center

2004
The National Underground Railroad Freedom Center opened in 2004.

Aminah Robinson was born in 1940 in Columbus, Ohio. Her pieces titled **Journeys I and II** are on display at the **National Underground Railroad Freedom Center.**

Today you can see Aminah Robinson's work at the Freedom Center in Cincinnati, Ohio.

LOG ON For more about People, Places, and Events, visit
www.macmillanmh.com

Jim Tressel

Ohio Stadium

Fiesta Bowl

2003 The Ohio State University football team celebrates after winning the 2003 Fiesta Bowl in Tempe, Arizona.

The **Ohio Stadium** is home to The Ohio State University Buckeyes. Coach **Jim Tressel** led the Buckeyes to the **Fiesta Bowl** National Championship game in 2003.

Today you can visit the stadium to see exciting sporting events.

A Land of Immigrants

Lesson 1

VOCABULARY

custom p. 103

heritage p. 103

generation p. 103

READING SKILL

Summarize
Copy the chart. As you read, use it to summarize what happens when immigrants come to the United States.

| Summary |

OHIO ACADEMIC CONTENT STANDARDS

H1, PS1, PS2, PS3, SSS4, SSS5

Visual Preview

What happens when immigrants come to the United States?

A Immigrants come to the United States from many countries.

B Immigrants bring their culture and heritage with them.

C Immigrants face many new challenges in their new home.

D The immigrants' customs become part of their new community's culture.

COMING TO THE UNITED STATES

Maybe your family has stories about how they came to the United States. How was life here different from what they knew in their home country?

About 100 years ago, great numbers of immigrants came to the United States from Europe. Do you think that immigration was all in the past? Not at all! People still come here to make new homes every day. Today though, most immigrants come from Asia, Mexico, or Central America. Many also come from Africa and from islands in the Caribbean Sea.

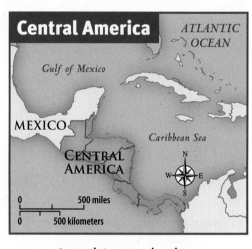

▲ Central America lies between North and South America.

Immigrants all have one thing in common. No matter where they come from or when they first arrive in the United States, they all move to this country to find a better life. Some come for jobs or so their children can go to good schools. Others come to find freedom. All of them help the United States grow.

QUICK CHECK

Summarize **Why do immigrants move to the United States?**

GROWTH AND CHANGE

As immigrants came to this country, the population of the United States grew. The Datagraphic below shows information about immigration and how it affected the population between 1950 and 2000.

DataGraphic
Immigration and Population

Study the pictograph and bar graph below. Answer the questions that follow.

Immigration to the United States, 1950–2000

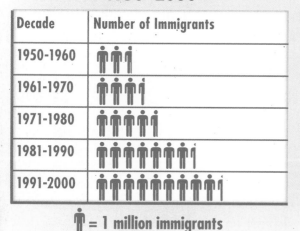

Decade	Number of Immigrants
1950-1960	
1961-1970	
1971-1980	
1981-1990	
1991-2000	

= 1 million immigrants

United States Population, 1950–2000

Think About Immigration and Population

1. In what year did the population of the United States first reach more than 200 million?

2. If the bar graph showed information for 2010, what do you think it would show?

Sharing Customs

Immigrants do more than add to the country's population—they bring new **customs**. A custom is a way of doing something that is shared by many people. Do you like to snack on chips and salsa? Not long ago most Americans did not eat these items. Immigrants from Mexico, like Maria's family, brought these things with them from Mexico.

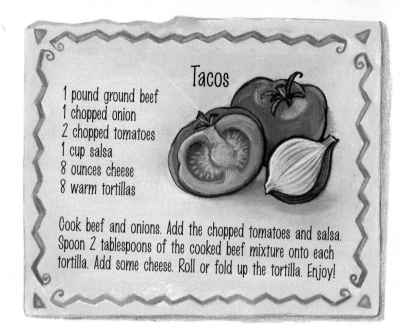

Tacos

1 pound ground beef
1 chopped onion
2 chopped tomatoes
1 cup salsa
8 ounces cheese
8 warm tortillas

Cook beef and onions. Add the chopped tomatoes and salsa. Spoon 2 tablespoons of the cooked beef mixture onto each tortilla. Add some cheese. Roll or fold up the tortilla. Enjoy!

Maria's mother taught her how to make tacos because they are part of her family's **heritage**—something handed down from the past. The heritage that people share is passed from one **generation** to the next. A generation is a group of people born and living around the same time. Someday Maria will teach her children how to make tacos. Teaching something to the next generation is one way to keep a group's heritage alive.

When immigrants like Maria's family come to the United States, they share their customs with their new American friends. People come here from all over the world. They bring their customs and share them with the rest of us. This is how we all get to enjoy things like tacos that might not be part of our own family's heritage.

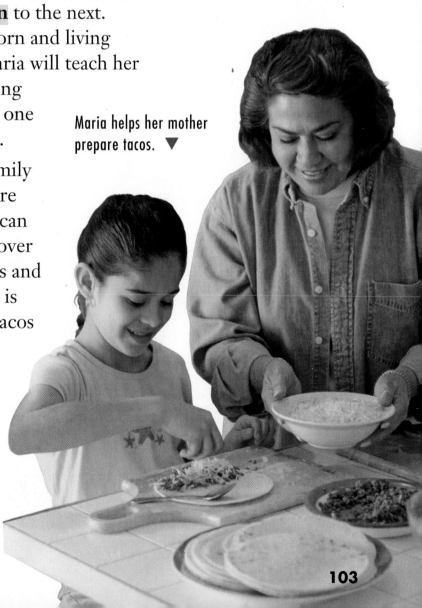

Maria helps her mother prepare tacos. ▼

QUICK CHECK

Main Idea and Details **How do Americans learn about the customs of other countries?**

C STARTING A NEW LIFE

Have you ever moved to a new place and had to start over to make friends? Was it difficult? Maybe you felt strange at first. Many immigrants feel that way when they first arrive in the United States. Living in a new place is a challenge! Many newcomers must learn to speak English. They must also learn their way around new neighborhoods, meet new people, and make new friends.

Think what it might be like if you couldn't read the street signs in your new neighborhood! ▶

◀ In Chau Lam's old school, all the students were Vietnamese.

Primary Sources

Write About It Write a paragraph describing how you felt on your first day of school. How is it similar to or different from how Chau Lam felt?

One Immigrant's Story

Chau Lam was 8 years old when she came from Vietnam, a country in Asia, to live in the United States. A war had just ended in her country—Chau Lam and her family were escaping to find a better life. They took a dangerous trip by boat. After many weeks they made their way safely to New York City. You can read above what Chau Lam remembers feeling about her first day of school in the United States.

Chau Lam's new classmates looked different from her classmates back in Vietnam. ▼

QUICK CHECK

Main Idea and Details
What are some challenges immigrants may face after coming to the United States?

105

Ada also came from another country to live in the United States. Ada was born in Nigeria, in West Africa. She had never seen a paved road, used an elevator, or eaten pizza! When she moved to Crownsville, Maryland, she experienced all of these strange new things.

When Ada came to Crownsville, she joined a community where other people from Nigeria were already living. This helped her feel at home as she got to know American culture. At the local market, she could buy Nigerian clothing and food. She also shared her customs with others in her community who were not familiar with Nigerian culture. People in Ada's community loved learning about her culture—and Ada enjoyed learning about other cultures, too.

◄ Kente is a colorful cloth from Africa.

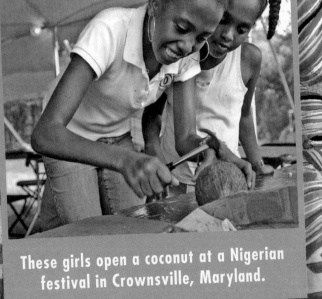

These girls open a coconut at a Nigerian festival in Crownsville, Maryland.

Playing drums at the Nigerian festival

▲ These young people are dressed in Nigerian clothing.

A Mixed Culture

In the United States, we learn from immigrants from other countries. That is how culture in the United States developed. American culture is like a stew of many ingredients! Over time the customs of many different immigrant groups have been added to the culture we all share today.

QUICK CHECK

Summarize **Why do immigrants sometimes live in communities with people from their home country?**

Check Understanding

1. **VOCABULARY** Use the vocabulary words below to write a letter to an older relative.
   custom **heritage** **generation**

2. **READING SKILL** Summarize
   Use your chart from page 100 to summarize what happens when immigrants come to the United States.

3. **Write About It** Write a paragraph that tells how a community shares customs.

EXPLORE The Big Idea

Lesson 2

VOCABULARY

ethnic group p. 109

diverse p. 109

architecture p. 110

READING SKILL

Summarize
Copy the chart below. As you read, list things that make up a culture.

Summary

OHIO ACADEMIC CONTENT STANDARDS

H3, PS1, PS2

All About Culture

Girls dancing the hula in Hawaii

Visual Preview

How have other cultures become part of American culture?

A New people bring their cultures when they immigrate.

B Artists may borrow some ideas from other cultures.

C Musicians make new types of music when cultures mix.

D Dances from many cultures are enjoyed in the United States.

A   LAND OF MANY CULTURES

You wake up and pull on your favorite jeans. You pour a bowl of cereal while you listen to your favorite music. Clothes, food, and music are all part of your culture.

By 2003 there were more than 33 million people living in the United States who were not born here. These people came here from other countries. They are from many different **ethnic groups**. An ethnic group is a group of people who share the same language and culture. People in every ethnic group bring their customs with them when they immigrate. The things different ethnic groups brought have helped make the United States a very **diverse**, or varied, land.

Some customs are brought to the United States by immigrants. Other customs are created right here. Together these customs from near and far mix and make one big, rich culture that we all share. In fact, the United States has one of the most diverse cultures on Earth!

QUICK CHECK

Summarize Why is United States culture so diverse?

These instruments come from countries in Asia and Africa. ▶

PAINTING AND ARCHITECTURE

Everywhere you look you can see how other cultures have added to American culture. This is especially true of things like painting and **architecture**. Architecture is the art of designing buildings. Artists often look to other cultures for ideas to use in their work. Here are two examples.

In the United States

African American artist Jacob Lawrence made a group of paintings about the Great Migration—the journey of African Americans who moved from the South to the North and Midwest in the early to mid-1900s. Where did Lawrence get his ideas?

The designers of the United States Supreme Court Building liked Greek ideas about freedom and government. They honored these Greek ideas by using Greek styles when they designed many of our government buildings.

The ideas that artists borrow become part of their art. If you go to a museum to look at Jacob Lawrence's paintings, or if you visit the United States Supreme Court Building, you will see different ideas that are now part of American culture.

QUICK CHECK

Main Idea and Details What kinds of ideas are borrowed from other places and cultures?

Around the World

African art often uses flat shapes and bright colors, as in this painting. Lawrence borrowed these ideas and made them part of his work. This is one way African ideas became part of American culture.

The Parthenon was built in Greece thousands of years ago. Huge columns carved from stone hold up the roof. What ideas do you think the designers of the Supreme Court building borrowed from the Parthenon? How are the buildings similar?

C MUSIC AND SPORTS

Every country and culture has its own special music. When people move from one place to another, they bring the music they love with them. Africans who came to the United States brought their songs and rhythms with them. Louis Armstrong and other musicians changed the African music and turned it into jazz—a new and exciting American music. Jazz, blues, and ragtime are all kinds of music that grew out of African music.

▲ Louis Armstrong became known as the "father of jazz."

The Harlem Renaissance was a time of great creativity that took place in the 1920s in Harlem in New York City. African American writers, artists, and musicians used their work to share African American culture.

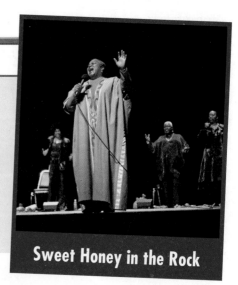

PEOPLE

Sweet Honey in the Rock is a Grammy Award-winning group of female African American singers. They were founded in 1973 by Dr. Bernice Johnson Reagon. Their songs are about freedom and equal rights.

Sweet Honey in the Rock

North America's First Sport

Sports are an important part of a group's culture. Lacrosse was probably North America's first sport. Native Americans created it hundreds of years ago. They used the game to help settle arguments. In 1636 French settlers in Canada saw the game. Soon they began playing lacrosse, too. In the 1800s new rules were added to the game, and lacrosse became more popular.

Lacrosse has changed a lot since the Native Americans played! It is now a combination of basketball, soccer, and hockey. Each player carries a crosse—a stick with a net on the end. The crosse is used to throw, catch, or scoop a ball off a grass field and into the goal.

▲ Native American lacrosse teams often had hundreds of players on a side.

QUICK CHECK

Summarize How did jazz and lacrosse become part of American culture?

Today more than 100,000 high school students play lacrosse.

113

Ⓓ DANCE

Dance is an important part of culture. Music and dance go together! In Mexico many villages have their own special dances. Mexicans brought these dances with them to the United States and passed them on to their children as part of their heritage.

Many dances are part of holiday celebrations. Chinese boys often learn the dragon dance or the fan dance to celebrate New Year.

▲ Chinese boys dance to celebrate the Chinese New Year.

QUICK CHECK

Main Idea **How are dances part of a culture?**

▲ Dancers celebrating Cinco de Mayo.

Check Understanding

1. **VOCABULARY** Write one sentence for each vocabulary term below.
   ethnic group   **diverse**   **architecture**

2. **READING SKILL**
   Summarize Use your chart from page 108 to write a paragraph that summarizes the things that are part of culture.

	Summary	

3. **Write About It** Write a paragraph that tells how people in a community learn about different cultures.

EXPLORE The Big Idea

Citizenship

Points of View

Should old buildings be torn down?

What should we do with old buildings? Do we need them? Read three points of view on whether old buildings should be saved.

Akron

Dayton

Portsmouth

"Old buildings should not be torn down. We have a building nearby that was President William Howard Taft's house. We wouldn't have been able to see what it was like to live back then if the house was torn down."

Hannah
Akron, Ohio

"It is OK to tear down some buildings. There is an old building near my house. I think it should be torn down and a park should go there. That would make the space useful."

Carlos
Portsmouth, Ohio

"Old historical buildings should be saved. If the entire building can't be saved, at least save part of it so that it can go somewhere like a museum. Then everyone could still see what buildings used to be like. Special American buildings, like the White House, should definitely be saved."

James
Dayton, Ohio

Write About It Write a paragraph about a building in your community that you think should be saved.

Sharing Culture Through Stories

VOCABULARY

hero p. 117

value p. 117

READING SKILL

Summarize
Copy the chart below. As you read, list information about stories from different cultures. Then write a summary statement.

OHIO ACADEMIC CONTENT STANDARDS

PS1

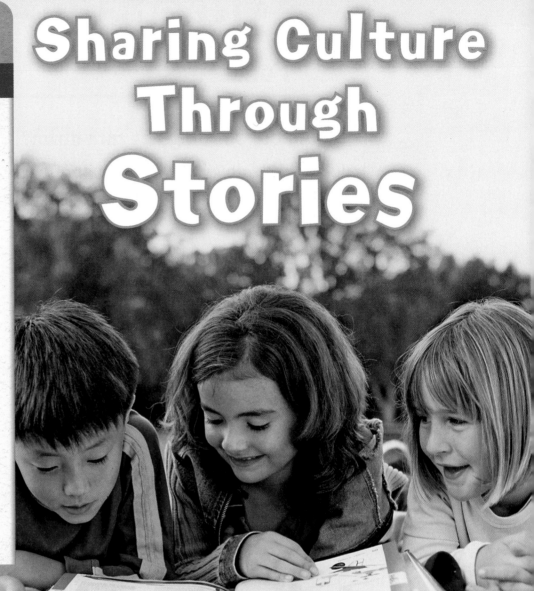

Visual Preview

Why are stories important to a culture?

A Stories are a way of sharing the important ideas of a culture.

B Myths and fables help explain important beliefs.

C Legends help tell us what is important to a culture.

D Some stories teach us about some qualities of our leaders.

Where did mountains come from? Why is the grass green? People in the past weren't sure how to answer these questions. So they told stories to explain the answers.

Some stories from the past are about **heroes**. A hero is someone you admire because of his or her achievements or personal qualities. These stories have been passed down over many generations. There are different kinds of stories, but they all teach us about the beliefs and **values** of a culture. A value is an idea—like honesty or courage—that people in a culture care about and think important. By listening to these stories we can learn about our own culture and other cultures as well.

We can tell stories, too. We can share stories we have heard from others, or we can tell stories of our own that have never been told before. No matter what kind of story is told, people can share their culture with others through stories. In this lesson you'll read about stories that are part of different cultures.

This Native American doll shows a storyteller surrounded by children. ▼

QUICK CHECK

Summarize What can we learn by listening to stories?

117

People from many cultures all over the world tell stories called myths. A myth can tell about or explain a belief shared by a group of people. Some myths are about heroes or gods and goddesses. Many myths explain how something came to be in nature or how a custom got started. A lot of myths use animals to explain things.

The Hopi—a Native American group that live in the southwestern United States—have a myth to explain where stars came from. In "How Coyote Placed the Stars," animals help make the world and put the rivers, mountains, and forests in their places. Read the story below to see what happened next.

"How Coyote Placed the Stars"

Long ago the animals helped make the world. The birds wanted to decorate the desert, so they gathered hundreds of small shiny rocks into a large pile. When they went home to sleep, Coyote crept from his hiding place to investigate. When he found the rocks were not good to eat, he took them one by one and threw them up into the sky. They still shine there today.

Stories With a Lesson

People everywhere have told stories for thousands of years. Over time, different stories from cultures around the world have become part of our American culture, too.

One type of story is called a fable. A fable is a short story that teaches a moral or lesson. In fables the characters are usually animals that talk and act just like people.

Aesop's Fables

A man named Aesop lived in Greece long ago. He was enslaved, but he was so good at telling stories that he earned his freedom by telling a story. Eventually he became famous for his fables.

One of Aesop's best known fables is "The Fox and the Grapes." Read this fable on the right of the page. Do you know anyone who acts like this fox? Like all fables, this one teaches us a lesson.

QUICK CHECK

Main Idea and Details **What do you think the story on this page is trying to teach?**

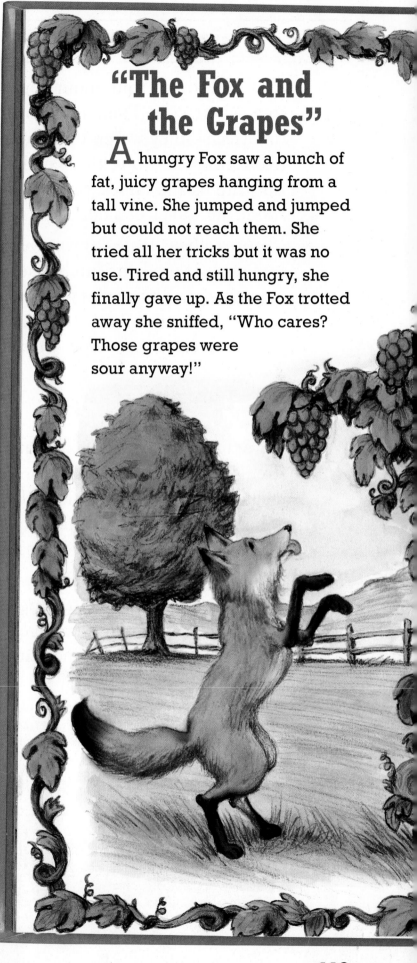

"The Fox and the Grapes"

A hungry Fox saw a bunch of fat, juicy grapes hanging from a tall vine. She jumped and jumped but could not reach them. She tried all her tricks but it was no use. Tired and still hungry, she finally gave up. As the Fox trotted away she sniffed, "Who cares? Those grapes were sour anyway!"

Not all stories told in our country come from somewhere else. The Paul Bunyan stories are American—they weren't borrowed or passed down from another culture the way Aesop's fables were. Like myths and fables, they can tell us something about the values of a culture.

Stories about Paul Bunyan were first told around campfires by real-life lumberjacks. They were told to entertain. The stories are actually a special kind of story called a tall tale. In a tall tale, many details are exaggerated, or "larger than life."

Paul's Adventures

Paul Bunyan was a make-believe person who was more than 50 feet tall! He became famous for his size, strength, and skill at clearing forests. Some stories include Bunyan's best friend, Babe, a blue ox that was as big as a mountain. The people who told these stories exaggerated the skills important to lumberjacks.

According to one story, Bunyan traveled across the country, clearing forests so pioneers could plant crops and build villages, houses, bridges, barns, and ships. One day he dragged his ax behind him and left a big ditch in his tracks. That was how the Grand Canyon was made!

PLACES

Johnny Appleseed was born John Chapman. He is known as a peaceful man who spread apple seeds across the United States. He is celebrated at the Johnny Appleseed Festival in **Brunswick, Ohio**.

Johnny Appleseed

Once Bunyan started a logging camp. He hired 1,000 men who were each more than 10 feet tall. Bunyan needed to make sure all these men had enough to eat and drink. Read below to find out what Paul did.

A selection from
"Paul Bunyan, the Mightiest Logger of Them All"
Then he built a gigantic logging camp with bunkhouses a mile long and bunks ten beds high. The camp's . . . table was so long that it took a week to pass the salt and pepper from one end to the other. Paul dug a few ponds to provide drinking water for everyone. Today we call those ponds the Great Lakes.

QUICK CHECK

Summarize **Why do you think the lumberjacks told the Paul Bunyan stories?**

Ⓓ LEARNING FROM A LEGEND

A legend is a story based on something that really happened, or on the life of a real person. The story has been added to over time, though, so it is not entirely true. Some legends are about heroes. Since heroes are people we admire, sharing stories about heroes is a way we teach others to be like our heroes.

An American Hero

Many Americans believe George Washington is a hero because he was such a great leader. On the next page you can read part of an American legend about George Washington.

From

"The Life of Washington" by Mason L. Weems

"George," said his father, "do you know who killed that beautiful little cherry-tree yonder in the garden?" . . . [George] bravely cried out, "I can't tell a lie, Pa; you know I can't tell a lie. I did cut it with my hatchet. . . ." "Run to my arms, you dearest boy," cried his father. . . . "Such an act of heroism [telling the truth] in my son, is [of] more worth than a thousand trees. . . ."

This story never really happened. Then why was it written? Because it helps us understand something about Washington—that he was an honest person. Honesty is an important quality for leaders to have. Stories like this are supposed to help us learn about heroes and leaders and want to be like them.

QUICK CHECK

Summarize What does the legend about George Washington teach us?

Check Understanding

1. **VOCABULARY** Use the words below to write a description of a hero.
   hero   **value**

2. **READING SKILL**
   Summarize Use your chart from page 116 to summarize what stories can teach us.

   Summary

3. **Write About It** Write a paragraph to explain why people tell stories about heroes.

Lesson 4

VOCABULARY

founder p. 125

holiday p. 130

READING SKILL

Summarize

Copy the chart below. Use it to summarize what communities celebrate.

Summary

OHIO ACADEMIC CONTENT STANDARDS

PS1, PS2

Local Celebrations

Children dress like Tom Sawyer and Becky Thatcher for National Tom Sawyer Days.

Visual Preview

What are some reasons communities celebrate?

A Communities celebrate both important and fun parts of their culture.

B Some places celebrate with county fairs to honor what people can do.

C Communities all over the world celebrate their nation's independence.

D Some Native Americans hold powwows to honor their heritage.

124

A CELEBRATING COMMUNITIES

Welcome to Hannibal, Missouri. Today is the day of the frog jumping contest at National Tom Sawyer Days. We set our frogs down at the starting line. They're off!

People in Hannibal, Missouri, celebrate National Tom Sawyer Days to honor the writer Mark Twain. Tom Sawyer was a character in one of Twain's books. People in Hannibal are proud of Mark Twain.

Barbourville, Kentucky, has a Daniel Boone Festival. Daniel Boone was the town's **founder**. A founder is a person who starts something, such as a business or a town. At the festival people enjoy events like a carnival, an art show, and a parade. Some even dress up like Daniel Boone!

Celebrating Food

Communities celebrate for many reasons. In some places food is the reason! People in Barnesville, Minnesota, celebrate a Potato Days festival every year. The potato is important to their community's culture. They have a parade, races, and even a "dress-the-potato" contest!

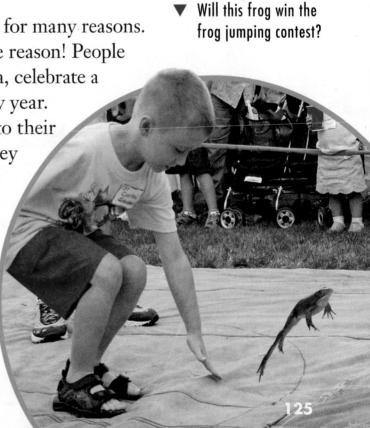

▼ Will this frog win the frog jumping contest?

QUICK CHECK

Summarize Why do communities celebrate certain people?

125

▲ At county fairs children often show off the animals they have raised. Some will win a blue ribbon!

Almost every community celebrates something. Across the country, people celebrate things we all have in common. For example, people in many towns plant and care for trees on Arbor Day. Many communities celebrate a Founder's Day, too.

Some communities celebrate by holding a county fair every year. In Goshen, Indiana, people enjoy the Elkhart County 4-H Fair. What is 4-H? It is an organization for young people between the ages of 5 and 19. Young people learn lots of skills in 4-H. They learn to raise animals and care for plants, and how to help their community. County fairs are often held by 4-H groups to celebrate young people and their accomplishments.

Some communities celebrate their pets with a parade.

Celebrating Children

More and more communities are celebrating El Día de los Niños, El Día de los Libros. That is Spanish for Children's Day, Book Day. The first celebrations took place at libraries in Arizona, New Mexico, and Texas. Now Children's Day is celebrated all over the country. If you like to read, this is the celebration for you. On this day children enjoy a parade, free books, gifts, music, and games.

▲ The power of books is celebrated on Children's Day, Book Day.

QUICK CHECK

Main Idea and Details What are some ways communities celebrate young people?

PEOPLE

Pat Mora writes children's books. In 1996 Mora learned that in Mexico, April 30 is Children's Day, or Día de Los Niños. Mora decided to start Children's Day, Book Day in the United States as a way to share books.

Pat Mora

C AMERICANS CELEBRATE FREEDOM

It's hard to believe there was ever a time when Americans weren't free. Americans celebrate the idea of freedom because it is so important to us. On Veteran's Day we celebrate all those who have served in the armed forces. Memorial Day is a time for us to remember those who died fighting for our country.

Some towns hold parades on the Fourth of July. ▼

Independence Day

Americans celebrate our independence from Great Britain on the Fourth of July, also known as Independence Day. We call it America's birthday. Many Americans celebrate with parades, fireworks, picnics, and concerts.

Communities celebrate the Fourth in different ways. Seward, Alaska, has a foot race. Lititz, Pennsylvania, has a Festival of Candles. How does your community celebrate Independence Day?

The United States is not the only country to celebrate independence. Read the next page to see how people in India celebrate their Independence Day.

QUICK CHECK

Main Idea and Details **How do Americans celebrate the idea of freedom?**

Global Connections

Independence in India

India is a large country in Asia. India celebrates its independence on August 15. Like people in the United States, people in India celebrate freedom from British rule. On Independence Day the Indian flag is raised in cities and towns all over India. The flag flies over government buildings in New Delhi, India's capital city. Students in schools raise the flag in special ceremonies.

Another popular activity on Independence Day in India is kite flying. Indian children fly kites of all shapes, colors, and sizes to celebrate their country's independence.

Young people love to wear the colors of India to celebrate Independence Day.

India

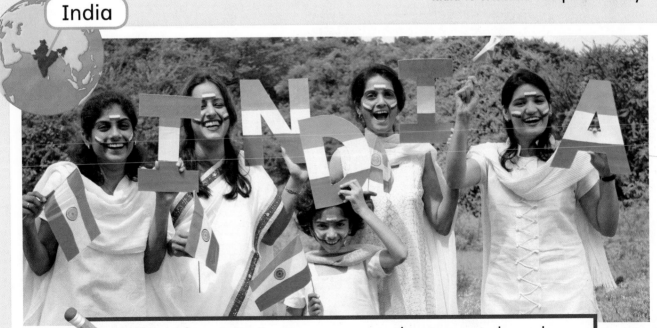

Write About It Suppose you were planning an Independence Day celebration. Write a paragraph describing the activities you would include in your celebration.

CELEBRATING HERITAGE

A **holiday** is a day on which we honor important heroes and special events by celebrating. These heroes and events are part of our heritage. Americans celebrate many different holidays.

Martin Luther King, Jr., Day is a holiday for all Americans. King was a hero who fought for equal rights. Other holidays celebrate events from our country's history. People in some states celebrate Juneteenth—June 19, 1865, the day slavery ended in Texas. Some African Americans think of Juneteenth as their independence day. Thanksgiving Day started with the Pilgrims in Plymouth, Massachusetts. We celebrate it today as a day to give thanks.

▲ Members of a girl's dance team celebrate Juneteenth in Austin, Texas.

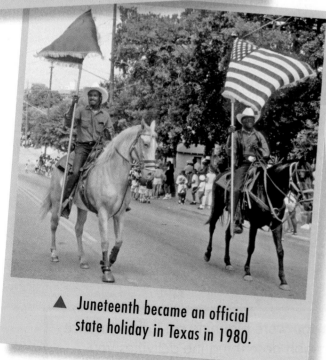

▲ Juneteenth became an official state holiday in Texas in 1980.

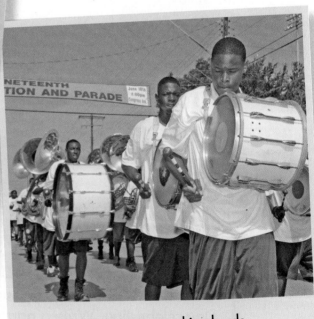

▲ Community marching bands are a highlight of the parade.

◀ Children dance at powwows.

Sharing Heritage

People from many ethnic groups have special days. Mexicans celebrate Cinco de Mayo—the fifth of May. On this day in 1862 the Mexican army won an important battle against the French.

Some Native Americans honor their culture by holding powwows. A powwow is a gathering with dancing and music. The dancers sometimes compete against each other. The National Museum of the American Indian in Washington, D.C., sponsors a powwow in August each year.

QUICK CHECK

Sequence **What events in history were later honored by holidays?**

Check Understanding

1. **VOCABULARY** Write one sentence for each vocabulary word below.
   founder   **holiday**

2. **READING SKILL** Summarize Use your chart from page 124 to write a paragraph that summarizes the reasons communities celebrate.

3. **Write About It** Choose a day your community celebrates. Write a description of how your community celebrates this day.

131

Cultures Around the World

Lesson 5

VOCABULARY

tradition p.133

ancestor p.133

READING SKILL

Summarize
Copy the chart below. As you read, use it to summarize ways cultures celebrate.

Summary

OHIO ACADEMIC CONTENT STANDARDS

H3, PS1, PS2, PS3, GEO4

Dancers in Ghana celebrate the yam festival.

Visual Preview

What are some ways cultures around the world celebrate?

A Food is an important part of many cultural celebrations.

B Some cultural celebrations include special dances.

C Some cultures use puppets at festivals to tell stories.

132

A FESTIVALS AND FOOD

The Chinese Moon Festival celebrates the full moon at harvest time. People in China eat mooncakes during this festival. What do you think mooncakes look like?

Like mooncakes, some foods are a special part of celebrations. Is there a food your family always has for a holiday? Then it is a **tradition**. A tradition is a way of doing something that is passed along by family members over many years. Cultural traditions include foods, music, dances, and other arts.

Celebrating With Food

In the last lesson, you read about a potato festival in our country. Ghana is a country in West Africa that has a celebration called the yam festival. Yams are a very important crop in Ghana. During the festival people sing and dance to celebrate.

In Mexico people celebrate the Day of the Dead, or El Día de los Muertos. On this day Mexicans remember their **ancestors**. Ancestors are early members of your family who have died, such as great-grandparents. The meal at this celebration often includes pan de muerto, or bread of the dead.

▼ Bread made for a Day of the Dead celebration

QUICK CHECK

Summarize **Tell some ways food is part of cultural celebrations.**

133

Dancers doing a reel

B DANCING AT CELEBRATIONS

▲ Girls doing the Sword Dance

Jump up high and kick your legs out to the sides. Be sure to keep your back straight and to point your toes. These are steps in a highland dance from Scotland called the reel. Most highland dances are hard to do—they take a lot of strength and have very difficult movements.

Highland Games

Some communities in Scotland hold celebrations called highland games. These celebrations started in a mountainous area of northern Scotland called the Highlands. Highland games include competitions in dancing. Dancing is part of Scottish culture.

The Scottish tradition of highland dancing has become part of American culture as well. Groups like the Celtic Society of Southern Maryland and the Caledonian Club of San Francisco, California, hold contests in highland dancing.

A Chinese Dance

You can hear the drums. A large dragon winds its way down the street. It looks like the dragon is dancing! You must be at a Chinese New Year parade. Why is a dragon dance part of the celebration? In China the dragon is a symbol of luck and success. People once performed the dragon dance to please the dragon and to ask it for rain during dry times.

A team of dancers carries a dragon made of bamboo, silk, and paper. The dragon could be as much as 100 feet long! The dancers use poles to lift the dragon up and down to the sound of a thumping drum. Today people enjoy watching the dancers perform this tradition at many Chinese celebrations.

▼ These boys work hard to hold up their dragon.

QUICK CHECK

Compare and Contrast How are the reel and the dragon dance alike?

The dragon dance is a traditional Chinese dance. ▼

PUPPETS AROUND THE WORLD

Have you ever made a puppet or put on a puppet show? Many festivals around the world have puppet shows especially for children. Puppets can be part of a country's culture.

◄ Indonesian shadow puppets

Types of Puppets

If you have ever seen your shadow, you have an idea how puppet shows in Indonesia work. Indonesia is a country in Asia. Shadow puppets are popular there. The puppets are made of buffalo or goatskin that is cut into large figures. They are held in front of a light. The audience watches the puppets' shadows on a screen. The puppets tell a traditional story about good and evil.

In England children enjoy Punch and Judy shows. These puppets fit over the hand.

Children watch a puppet show in England. ▼

"Punch" is a hand puppet.

▲ Marionettes in a museum in Italy

Marionettes are puppets that are moved by pulling strings. The name marionette comes from France, but these puppets are used in Italy, too, another country in Europe. In the photo above, even the musicians are puppets! Traditional Italian puppet shows sometimes tell a story about knights in history. Which type of puppet show would you enjoy watching the most?

QUICK CHECK

Main Idea and Details What are some different kinds of puppets?

Check Understanding

1. **VOCABULARY** Write one sentence for each of the vocabulary words below.
   tradition   **ancestor**

2. **READING SKILL** Summarize Use your chart from page 132 to write a paragraph about ways cultures celebrate.

3. **Write About It** Write a letter to a friend about a cultural celebration you have enjoyed.

Map and Globe Skills
Understand Latitude and Longitude

VOCABULARY

grid

latitude

longitude

degree

Every place on Earth has an address, which tells its exact location. To describe the location of a place, geographers use maps with **grids**. Grids are lines that cross each other on a map. Earth's grid has two sets of lines called **latitude** and **longitude**.

Lines of latitude measure how far north or south a place is from the equator. Lines of longitude measure distance east or west of the prime meridian. Lines of latitude and longitude measure distance on Earth's surface in **degrees**. The symbol for degrees is °.

Learn It

- Look at Map A. Lines of latitude north of the equator are labeled **N**. Lines of latitude south of the equator are labeled **S**.

- Now look at Map B. Lines of longitude east of the prime meridian are labeled **E**. Lines of longitude west of the prime meridian are labeled **W**.

- Lines of latitude and lines of longitude can be used to locate any place on Earth. When you locate places on a map, give the latitude first and longitude second.

Map A

Map B

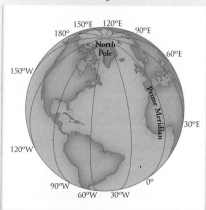

Try It

Use Map C below to answer the questions.

● What line of latitude is at 0 degrees?

● Is Sydney east or west of the prime meridian?

Apply It

● Give the closest latitude and longitude address of Cairo, Egypt.

● Which city is nearest to the address of 30°S, 60°W?

● Find the latitude and longitude closest to San Francisco.

Map C

Ohio Connections

Food in Your Community

Sam wanted to show what he had learned about some of the ethnic groups in his community. So he created a menu for a restaurant that would serve foods from many ethnic groups. Here are steps you can follow to do the same thing.

- Use your library or the Internet to find out about the ethnic groups that live in your community. Find out what types of foods are popular in each of these cultures. Make copies of recipes and photos of different ethnic foods.

- Sam made a menu for his restaurant. He decorated a cover for the menu and listed the menu items on the inside. On the front cover, he wrote the name of his restaurant. He called it "Foods from Around the World."

 For more help with your project visit www.macmillanmh.com

Cultural Activity

Make a Menu

1 Gather your notes and photos.

2 Make a menu for your community's new restaurant. Use markers or colored pencils to make drawings of menu items based on your photos.

3 Decorate the front cover of your menu. Include the name of your restaurant on the cover.

4 Share your menu with the class.

Materials
- construction paper
- white paper
- markers
- crayons
- colored pencils

Tasty Tacos

Excellent Eggrolls

Foods from

Around the World

Scrumptious Sushi

Super Spaghetti

Unit 3 Review and Assess

Vocabulary

Write a sentence or more to answer each question. Use the vocabulary words in your sentences.

1. Describe a **custom** your family has.
2. Explain what **architecture** is.
3. Tell something you do to celebrate your favorite **holiday**.
4. Tell which countries your **ancestors** came from.

Comprehension and Critical Thinking

5. Why are stories important?
6. Why do Americans celebrate Independence Day?
7. **Reading Skill** Why would an immigrant join a community of people who came from the same place that he or she did?
8. **Critical Thinking** Why is it important to learn about customs and celebrations in other cultures?

Skill

Understand Latitude and Longitude

Write a complete sentence to answer each question.

9. Which city is closest to 40 °N, 89 °W?
10. What is the latitude and longitude "address" closest to Galesburg?

Illinois: Latitude and Longitude

Directions: Read the selection.

The Chinese New Year usually lasts fifteen days. On the first day—New Year's Day—children receive red envelopes called Lai-See. The envelopes have money inside and are given for good luck. On the seventh day farmers display their crops. The seventh day is also called "everybody's birthday." On the last day there is a Lantern Festival. On that night people carry lanterns into the street for a parade. The best part of the Lantern Festival parade is the dragon dance. This popular dance is a great way to end the celebration!

Directions: Use the selection to answer questions 1-4.

1. What is the paragraph mostly about?

   ○ A. Lai-See envelopes

   ○ B. Lantern Festival

   ○ C. Chinese New Year

2. When does the Lantern Festival take place?

   ○ A. on the seventh day

   ○ B. on the first day

   ○ C. on the fifteenth day

3. How do you think children feel when they are given Lai-See envelopes?

   Write your answer on a separate piece of paper.

4. Describe what people do during the Lantern Festival.

   Write your answer on a separate piece of paper.

The Big Idea Activities

How do people change communities?

Write About the Big Idea

Narrative Essay

Use the Unit 3 foldable to help you write a narrative essay that answers the Big Idea question, "How do people change communities?" Begin with a topic sentence. Use the notes you wrote on the foldable to include details about ways people change communities. End with a paragraph that summarizes your essay and answers the question.

FOLDABLES™
Study Organizer

Culture and Communities

| Immigrants | Stories | Celebrations |

Projects About the Big Idea

Make a Poster Make a poster that shows food, stories, art, dance, and sports that are part of your culture.

Make a Map You have read about cultural celebrations around the world. Work with a partner to make a map that shows where these different celebrations take place. Make drawings that represent each celebration. Include your drawings on the map. Label each celebration and its location.

National Tom Sawyer Days
Hannibal, Missouri

Highland Games
Scotland

Children's Day
El Paso, Texas

Day of the Dead
Mexico

Independence Day
Washington, D.C.

Chinese New Year
China

EXPLORE The Big Idea

Essential Question
How do people in a community meet their needs?

FOLDABLES Study Organizer

Cause and Effect
Make a Three-Tab Book Foldable to take notes as you read Unit 4. Write the words **Meeting Needs** at the top.

Meeting Needs

LOG ON **For more about Unit 4 go to**
www.macmillanmh.com

Communities at Work

PEOPLE, PLACES, AND EVENTS

Amish at work

Holmes County, Ohio

Amish settle in Ohio

1800s
Approximately 70 percent of the Amish live in Ohio, Pennsylvania, and Indiana. Ohio has the largest number of Amish.

Amish work is done in small groups which turns into a celebration. Cooking a meal together, building a barn, or quilting are useful and enjoyable hands-on experiences.

Today many Amish people live in **Holmes County, Ohio.**

LOG ON For more about People, Places, and Events, visit www.macmillanmh.com

Elijah Pierce

Columbus Museum of Art

Eye Spy Exhibit

1998

The Elijah Pierce Children's Exhibit opens at the Columbus Museum of Art.

Elijah Pierce began his life in Ohio as a barber. He is well known for his wood carvings.

Today you can see many of Elijah Pierce's work at the **Columbus Museum of Art** in Columbus, Ohio.

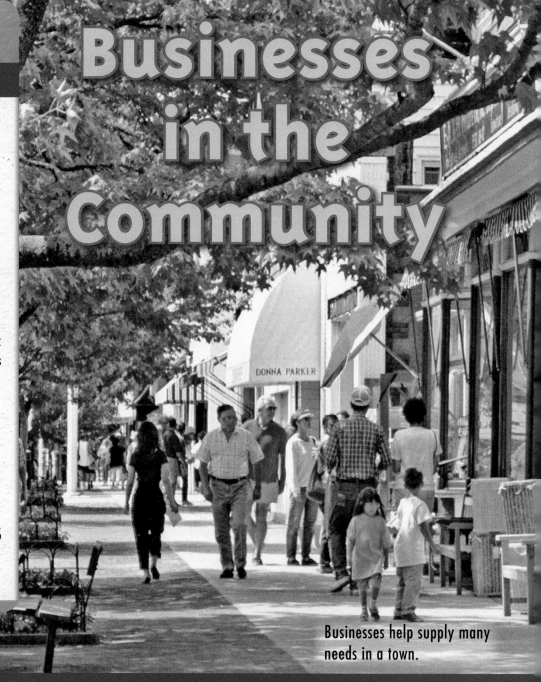

Businesses in the Community

Lesson 1

VOCABULARY

employee p. 149

producer p. 150

consumer p. 150

profit p. 151

economy p. 152

READING SKILL

Cause and Effect
Copy the chart below. List the things that cause prices to go up or down.

Cause	→	Effect
	→	
	→	
	→	

OHIO ACADEMIC CONTENT STANDARDS

E2, E3, E5, E6, SSS3

Businesses help supply many needs in a town.

Visual Preview

How do people and businesses make money?

A People work at many different jobs to earn money.

B Farmers sell their crops to buyers for money.

C Businesses buy from other businesses to supply needs.

D Most people use money to pay for needs and wants.

Ⓐ PEOPLE EARN MONEY

What jobs do people have? Doctors, plumbers, sales people—there are so many different jobs. Some people work outdoors, while others work in an office or a factory.

Almost everyone works at some kind of job. People work to earn money for all the things they need, such as food, clothing, and shelter. They work to have money for fun things like vacations, too. People also work because they enjoy what they do. Working at a job you really like is fun!

Most people work for someone else. They are **employees**. An employee is a person who gets paid to work for someone else—a company or a person—called an employer.

Think about a grocery store. A grocery store is a private business. Who orders the food and puts it on the shelves? Who puts up the price signs? Employees, of course! The owner or manager of the store hires people to do these and other jobs. The owner pays the employees a salary for their work.

QUICK CHECK

Cause and Effect **Why do people work?**

Many people work as doctors or nurses. ▶

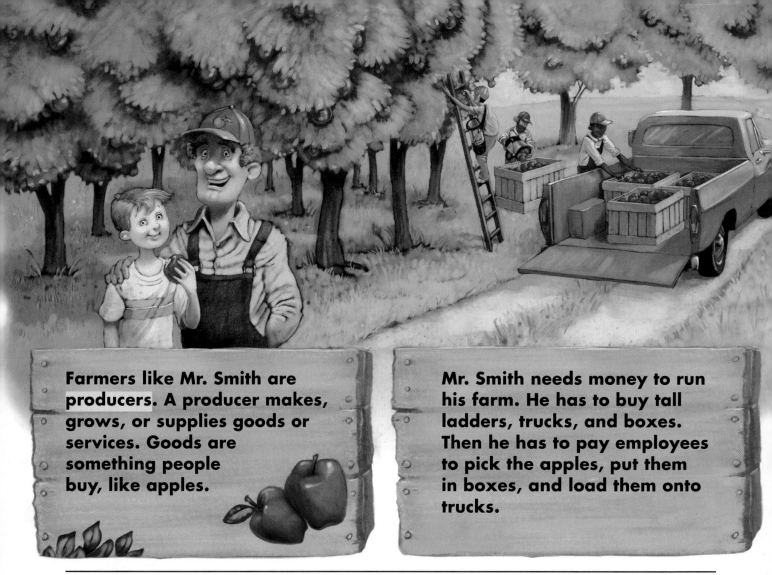

Farmers like Mr. Smith are **producers**. A producer makes, grows, or supplies goods or services. Goods are something people buy, like apples.

Mr. Smith needs money to run his farm. He has to buy tall ladders, trucks, and boxes. Then he has to pay employees to pick the apples, put them in boxes, and load them onto trucks.

Ⓑ SELLING THINGS FOR MONEY

Who grows or makes the things people buy? The apples, pumpkins, lettuce, and carrots sold at a farmers' market are grown on farms. Farmers sell the goods they grow. A farmer might sell a bag of apples for $4.00. How does a farmer decide on a price? The price needs to be high enough so that the farmer can pay for the things he needs to run the business—tools, equipment, and the employees needed to grow the apples.

A farmer also listens to **consumers** when deciding how much to charge. A consumer is a person who buys goods or uses a service. If consumers think a price is too high, they might not buy the product. Then the farmer might decide to lower the price so more people will buy.

Selling Price	$4.00
− Cost of Growing	$3.00
(tools, equipment, employees)	
= Profit	$1.00

Farmers sell their goods to make a profit. Profit is money a business makes after paying for tools, employees, and other costs. At the farmers' market, Mr. Smith has competition—other farmers who are selling apples.

Mr. Smith uses some of his profit to pay for more things he needs for the farm. But he can also use some of it to buy his son a new guitar!

Consumers Decide

Many farmers sell apples. If you are the seller, what can you do to get people to buy from you? You could advertise. You could grow a kind of apple that no one else sells. You might even shine all your apples so they look attractive and people will want to buy them.

What if you are the consumer? How do you decide where to buy an apple? Maybe you will buy from the seller with the lowest price. Perhaps you will buy from a farmer you know and trust. If you do not want to walk very far, you might buy from the closest market.

QUICK CHECK

Summarize **How does a seller decide how much to charge?**

C BUSINESS AND THE COMMUNITY

Think of some things you will use today. Do you picture clothes, food, books, and pencils? These things probably come from stores in your community. These stores are part of your community's **economy**. The economy is the way a place uses its money, goods, natural resources, and services.

Sometimes a community needs goods and services from another community. Restaurants in New York City might depend on farmers in Washington or California to grow fresh ingredients for their meals. The farmers also depend on the restaurants to buy their fruits and vegetables. The two communities are interdependent. Their economies depend on each other. Countries buy and sell from one another as well.

QUICK CHECK

Cause and Effect **Why are some communities interdependent?**

WASHINGTON

New York City

▲ Food grown in Washington state is served in New York City.

Global Connections

A Dollar in Canada

Canada is a soverign nation within the United Kingdom. It has its own money. Canadian coins are made in the same values as United States coins—one cent, five cents, ten cents, twenty-five cents, and fifty cents.

Canada also has a dollar—but there is no dollar bill in Canada. In Canada, the dollar is a coin only. There is even a two-dollar coin. If you want to use paper money in Canada, you would need to trade five Canadian dollar coins for a Canadian five-dollar bill!

When people or businesses in different countries buy and sell to one another, they use different kinds of money. For example, Mexico's money is called the peso. Russia's money is the ruble. The Japanese pay for things with yen.

Canada

Canada's dollar shows Queen Elizabeth II. ▼

The United States dollar shows George Washington. ▼

▲ Japanese yen   ▲ Russian ruble   ▲ Mexican peso

Write About It Write a paragraph describing how Canadian money is similar to and different from United States money.

WHY DO WE USE MONEY?

Before money was invented, people used to barter, or trade. For example, Farmer John raises pigs and Farmer Katie grows carrots. Farmer John would trade a baby pig for Farmer Katie's carrots. But a pig is worth much more than a carrot, so it would take a lot of carrots to equal one pig. Even if Farmer John only needed 5 pounds of carrots, he might get 100 pounds of carrots for his pig. That is a lot of carrots to eat! And what if you had to carry a pig around every time you wanted to buy something?

▼ Before people used money, a farmer might trade to get what he or she needed.

Money Is Easy to Use

To solve the problems caused by bartering, people in Asia invented money. Instead of bartering, Farmer John could sell his pig for money. Then he could use some of the money to buy carrots and spend the rest on other things.

Money is easier in lots of ways. It can be divided into smaller amounts. Money will not fall apart, or run away! Money is easy to carry in your pocket. Using money helps make buying and selling much easier.

▲ Long ago, seashells called cowries were put on a string and used as money. The longer the string, the more it was worth.

QUICK CHECK

Cause and Effect What was the effect of inventing money?

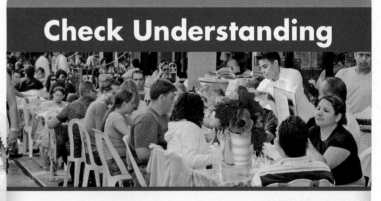

Check Understanding

1. **VOCABULARY** Draw and label a picture to illustrate the vocabulary words below.
   employee   **producer**   **consumer**

2. **READING SKILL Cause and Effect** Use the chart from page 148 to write a paragraph about what causes prices to go up or down.

Cause	→	Effect
	→	
	→	
	→	

 3. **Write About It** Write a paragraph to explain how businesses in a community help people meet their needs.

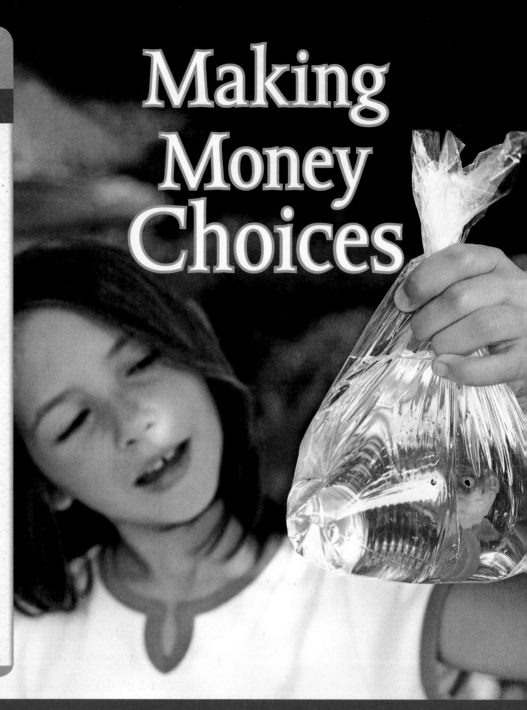

Making Money Choices

VOCABULARY

budget p. 157

income p. 157

expense p. 157

opportunity cost p. 161

savings account p. 162

READING SKILL

Cause and Effect
Copy the chart below. As you read, list how a budget can help you make choices.

Cause	→	Effect
	→	
	→	
	→	

OHIO ACADEMIC CONTENT STANDARDS

E1, E5, CRR1, SSS3

Visual Preview

How do people make choices about saving and spending money?

A People spend money on both needs and wants.

B A budget helps families plan how to spend money.

$15.00 (income)
−10.00 (expenses)
$ 5.00 (savings without popcorn)
× 10
$50.00 (savings over 10 weeks)

C A budget can help people find ways to save money.

D Some people use banks to save for what they need and want.

Suppose you have earned enough money to buy a pet goldfish. Then you remember that you need a new tire for your bike. How do you decide how to spend your money?

People plan how to spend their money by deciding what they need and want. To help them make smart money choices, people often make a **budget**. A budget is a plan for using money.

One thing people include in a budget is **income**—the amount of money someone receives for working. An employee earns income by doing a job. A budget also includes **expenses**. An expense is something people spend money on, such as something they buy or do.

When making a budget, people first plan to pay for the things they need, like food and clothing. With the money left over, they can make choices about buying the things they want, like movie tickets. If you really need that new tire, you may have to wait to buy that pet goldfish you want!

QUICK CHECK

Cause and Effect **How does the amount of income affect what someone can buy?**

Buying a baseball mitt is an expense. Is a mitt a need or a want? ▶

ⓑ EVERYONE BUDGETS

Primary Sources

"The U.S. has never really budgeted for the kinds of unexpected things that go on every year, even though something happens every year. There's an earthquake. There's a fire. There's a hurricane."

Douglas Holtz-Eakin
Director of the Congressional Budget
Office, 2003-2005, February 6, 2006

Write About It Write a paragraph describing the kinds of expenses the United States government might have after a hurricane hits a town.

▲ Members of the United States government make decisions about the country's budget.

Not only people make budgets. Businesses make budgets, too. For example, a company that builds houses spends money on supplies, such as wood and nails. It must pay employees, too. To make sure it does not spend more money than it makes, the company includes its income and expenses in a budget.

Even the government of the United States makes a budget. Read on this page about some of the challenges the government faces in making its budget.

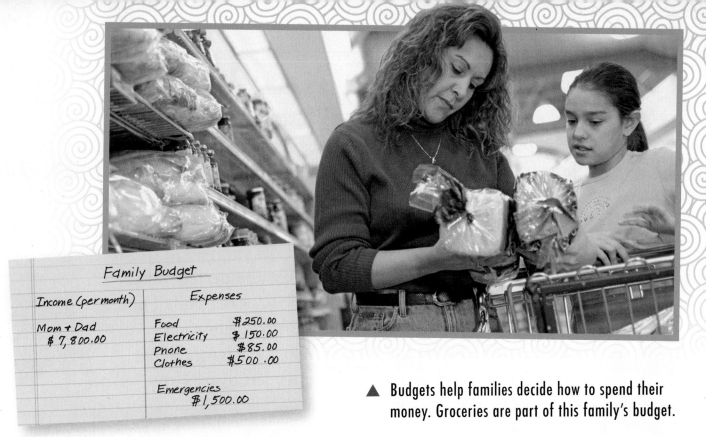

Family Budget

Income (per month)	Expenses	
Mom + Dad $7,800.00	Food	$250.00
	Electricity	$150.00
	Phone	$85.00
	Clothes	$500.00
	Emergencies	$1,500.00

▲ Budgets help families decide how to spend their money. Groceries are part of this family's budget.

A Family Budget

Families need budgets, too. They have to pay for things like food, electricity, and clothing. They also try to save money for the future and for emergencies—things that happen without warning. What if the car needs new brakes or the roof is leaking? A family budget should include money for emergencies such as these.

Making a budget involves decisions. It often means comparing the cost of something with the benefit of having it. A benefit is something that is good or helpful. For example, the special TV movie channel costs extra money each month. Your family loves to watch movies. The service would be a benefit, so your family has to decide if the cost is worth the benefit. If they want the special channel enough, they might even decide to give up something else to have it!

QUICK CHECK

Main Idea and Details **Why do families need to make a budget?**

ⓒ MAKING A BUDGET

Lola is 12 years old. She has a business walking her neighbors' dogs. Each week she earns an income of $15. Lola has expenses, too. Each week she goes to a movie with her friends. After the movie, she buys some treats for the dogs.

While walking the dogs one day, Lola stopped in front of a bike store. In the window, she saw the perfect bike. The price tag said $50. "I can save $50," Lola said. That night Lola made a budget. First she wrote her weekly income at the top of the budget. Then she wrote her expenses below. There was no money left over! How could Lola save money?

▼ Lola walks dogs to earn money.

My Budget $ $ $

Budget A

Income each week $15.00

Expenses each week
Bus ticket	$0.75
Movie ticket	4.25
Popcorn	5.00
Dog biscuits	+ 5.00
Total expenses each week	$15.00

$15.00 (income)
−15.00 (expenses)
  0.00 (savings each week)

Budget B

Income each week $15.00

Total expenses each week
Bus ticket	$0.75
Movie ticket	4.25
Dog biscuits	+ 5.00
Total expenses	$10.00

without popcorn at movie

$15.00 (income)
−10.00 (expenses)
$ 5.00 (savings without popcorn)
 × 10
$50.00 (savings over 10 weeks)

Making Choices

Lola thought hard. Then she thought of a way—if she does not buy popcorn at the movies, she can save $5 a week. After ten weeks, she will have saved $50!

By choosing to save money to buy a bike, Lola also chose to stop buying a snack at the movies. This was her **opportunity cost**. An opportunity cost is the value of the thing you give up when you choose one thing instead of another. In saving for a bike, Lola's opportunity cost was not getting to eat popcorn at the movies.

QUICK CHECK

Summarize How did making a budget help Lola?

D SAVING MONEY

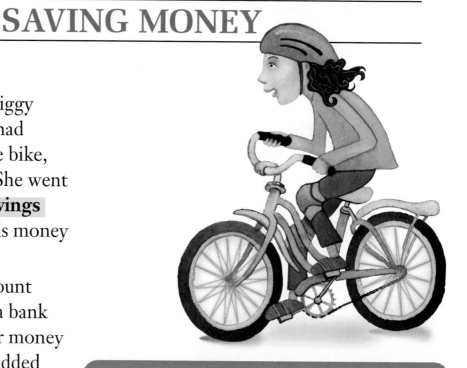

Money in the Bank

Lola put money into her piggy bank each week. After Lola had saved enough money for the bike, she decided to keep saving. She went to the bank and opened a **savings account**. A savings account is money a person keeps in a bank.

Lola knew her savings account would earn interest, money a bank pays people for keeping their money in the bank. The interest is added to the money Lola saves. The more money Lola saves, the more interest she earns.

Many people use banks to help them save for things they want. Benjamin Franklin, a famous American leader, knew the importance of saving. He once said,

"If you would be wealthy, think of saving as well as getting."

QUICK CHECK

Main Idea and Details Why is it a good idea to put money into a savings account?

Check Understanding

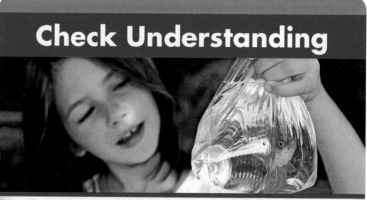

1. **VOCABULARY** Write a letter to a friend about how you spent money this week. Use the following words.

   budget   income   expense

2. **READING SKILL Cause and Effect** Use your chart from page 156 to write a paragraph on how a budget can help you decide how to spend money.

Cause	→	Effect
	→	
	→	
	→	

 3. Write About It Make a list of some ways that you could save money.

Citizenship

Points of View

How do we make decisions about spending money?

Every time we buy something we make choices. Sometimes we must give up one thing to buy something else. Read three points of view on making money choices.

"Saving your money until you have enough to buy what you want is better than spending your money to get things you can afford right now. It is better to just not buy anything."

Jenny
Athens, Ohio

"I get a weekly allowance that I try to make last all week. You never know if something is going to come up that you didn't expect, like a night out with friends or something."

Marcus
Columbus, Ohio

"You should think about and plan before you spend your money. I had to choose between buying a new skirt and going to the movies. I picked the skirt because I could wear it a lot, which lasts longer than a movie. I could go to the movies another time."

Kayla
Youngstown, Ohio

Write About It Write a paragraph about choosing to buy one thing over another.

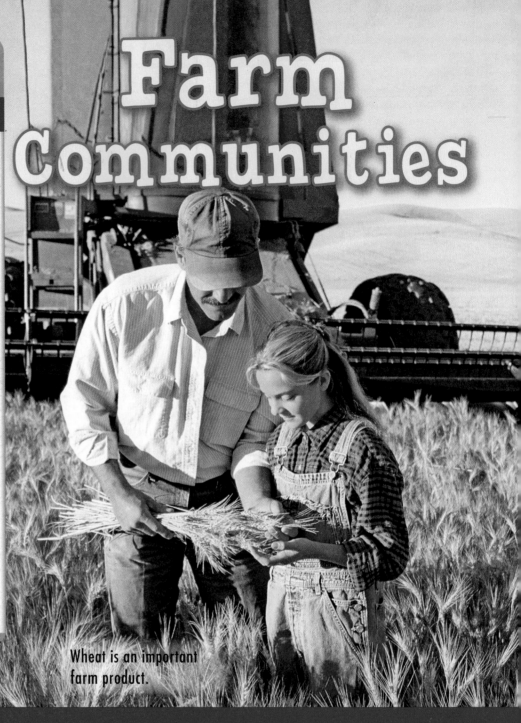

Farm Communities

Lesson 3

VOCABULARY

human resource p. 165

capital resource p. 165

demand p. 168

supply p. 168

scarcity p. 168

READING SKILL

Cause and Effect
Copy the chart below. As you read, list the ways that supply affects price.

Cause	→	Effect
	→	
	→	
	→	

OHIO ACADEMIC CONTENT STANDARDS

H1, E2, E6, E7, SSS3, SSS4, SSS5

Wheat is an important farm product.

Visual Preview

How do farmers produce goods for the economy?

A Farmers use many resources to grow crops.

B Different crops grow in different regions of the country.

C The price of a crop depends on how much of it there is.

THE BUSINESS OF FARMING

Beautiful, golden grains of wheat! Somewhere a farmer worked hard to grow the wheat to make your bread, rolls, and muffins.

Agriculture is an important part of the United States economy. Agriculture is the business of growing crops or raising animals for food. From apples to corn to wheat to zucchini, a lot of work is involved in getting the food we buy to market.

Farmers use natural resources—soil, water, and sunlight—to grow crops. They also need **human resources**, the people, both employers and employees, who work for a business. **Capital resources** are needed, too. Capital resources are the tools, machines, and buildings people use to produce goods.

Tractors and computers are some capital resources farmers use. Stores sell farmers the resources and supplies they need. Farmers sometimes borrow money from banks to buy capital resources. They make an agreement with the banks to pay the money back.

QUICK CHECK

Cause and Effect Why do farmers sometimes borrow money from banks?

This tractor is a capital resource. ▶

165

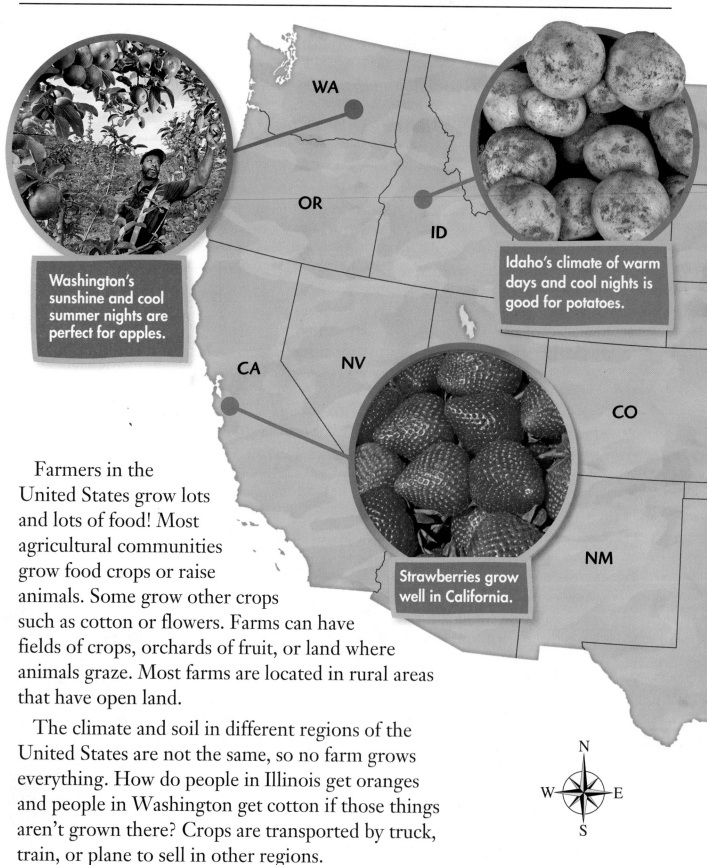

Washington's sunshine and cool summer nights are perfect for apples.

Idaho's climate of warm days and cool nights is good for potatoes.

Strawberries grow well in California.

Farmers in the United States grow lots and lots of food! Most agricultural communities grow food crops or raise animals. Some grow other crops such as cotton or flowers. Farms can have fields of crops, orchards of fruit, or land where animals graze. Most farms are located in rural areas that have open land.

The climate and soil in different regions of the United States are not the same, so no farm grows everything. How do people in Illinois get oranges and people in Washington get cotton if those things aren't grown there? Crops are transported by truck, train, or plane to sell in other regions.

New York's thick grass is food for cows.

ME

VT

NH

NY

MA

CT

RI

MN

MI

OH

IN

NJ

DE

Rich soil in the Midwest helps corn, wheat, and soybeans grow.

KS

KY

OK

TN

AR

MS

AL

Farms in the warm Southern states grow cotton.

TX

LA

FL

Florida's warm climate is good for growing oranges.

Quick Check

Main Idea and Details What things make specific regions in the United States good for growing different crops?

C BUYING AND SELLING

Everyone needs to eat, so there is always a high **demand** for food. Demand is the number of people who want certain goods or services.

Suppose corn is for sale at a farmers' market. If only one farmer is selling corn, there is a low **supply**. Supply is the amount of goods or services that are available. A small supply of corn leads to **scarcity**. Scarcity means a shortage of certain goods or services.

If lots of people want to buy corn, then there is a high demand. As people line up to buy the corn, the farmer may raise the price. Since the demand is high and only one farmer is selling it, many people are willing to pay the higher price.

High demand means the farmer can charge more for his corn. ▶

EVENT

Every fall Circleville, Ohio holds a **Pumpkin Show.** There, farmers display more than 100,000 pounds of pumpkins, squash, and gourds. In 2007 the largest pumpkin weighed 1,524 pounds!

Circleville Pumpkin Show

Making Choices

What if the demand for corn is high, but there is a scarcity of human resources to pick the corn? A farm owner might have employees who usually do other jobs pick corn instead. Then the farmer will have enough corn to meet the high demand. When human resources or capital resources are low, farm owners need to make choices about how they use their resources.

Some people might not pay the high price for the corn. They may go to a grocery store to look for cheaper corn, or even buy something else. This is how our free enterprise economy works. Free enterprise is the freedom to run your business the way you decide. It is also the freedom to buy from whomever you want.

▲ Grocery stores buy a lot of corn, so they often sell it at lower prices.

QUICK CHECK

Summarize **What is a free enterprise economy?**

Check Understanding

1. **VOCABULARY** Write a sentence to explain each vocabulary term below.
   human resource   **capital resource**
   supply   **scarcity**

2. **READING SKILLS Cause and Effect** Use your chart from page 164 to write a paragraph about how supply affects price.

 3. Write About It Write a letter explaining why you decided to buy something at a certain place.

169

Chart and Graph Skills
Use Line Graphs

VOCABULARY

line graph

Suppose you are reading a book about farms in Ohio. You come to a diagram like the one below. It is a **line graph**. A line graph shows information that changes over time. Let's see how to get information from a line graph.

Learn It

- Read the title. The graph title tells you that this graph is about farmland in Ohio from 1950 to 2000.

- The numbers on the left show the acres of farmland. The years are shown at the bottom.

- To read the graph, find the dot above each year. Put your finger on the dot, then move it to the left to find the amount of farmland for that year.

- The dots are connected to make a line. The line shows that the amount of farmland has gone down since 1950.

Farmland in Ohio, 1950 to 2000

Acres of Farmland in millions

25
20
15
10
5
0

1950 1960 1970 1980 1990 2000

Year

Try It

Look at the graph at right.

- What does this graph show?

- What do the numbers on the left show?

- How did the amount of land used for farming change between 1950 and 2000?

Farmland in the United States, 1950 to 2000

Apply It

Now make your own line graph. Use this information about a third-grade class that printed and sold T-shirts.

Week 1, 10 T-shirts sold
Week 2, 20 T-shirts sold
Week 3, 50 T-shirts sold
Week 4, 25 T-shirts sold

- What title will you give your graph?

- What information will you put at the bottom of the graph? What will you put along the side?

- What does the graph tell you about the class's T-shirt sale?

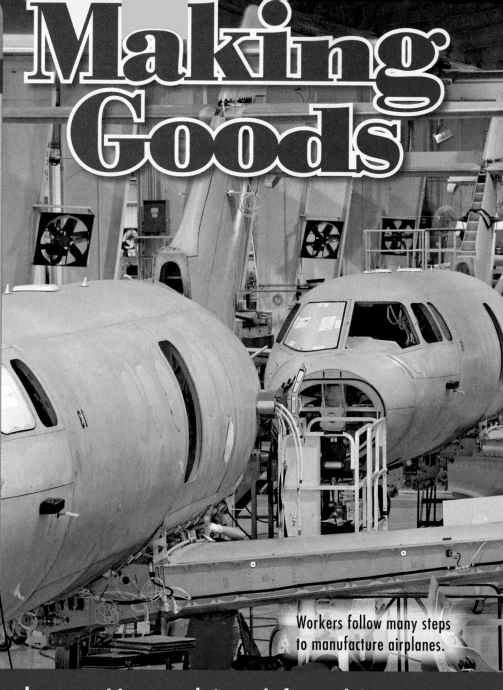

Making Goods

Lesson 4

VOCABULARY

factory p. 173

specialize p. 176

import p. 178

export p. 179

READING SKILL

Cause and Effect
Copy the chart below. As you read, list ways the growth of the auto industry affected other industries.

Cause	→	Effect
	→	
	→	
	→	

OHIO ACADEMIC CONTENT STANDARDS

E4, SSS3

Workers follow many steps to manufacture airplanes.

Visual Preview

How do communities meet their needs for goods?

A New methods helped produce goods quickly and more cheaply.

B Many factories and towns were built to produce manufactured goods.

C People can buy products that are made in other nations.

D The United States trades with other nations to get the products it needs.

As the line of cars moves along, workers and machines put them together. Your job is to put the doors on. When the car reaches the end of the line, it is complete.

In 1885 the first automobile was built in Europe. By 1900 companies in the United States had started manufacturing autos, too. Manufacturing, or the making of goods by machines, is an important part of the United States economy. A place where goods are manufactured is called a **factory**.

In 1903 Henry Ford started the Ford Motor Company in Detroit, Michigan. At first each car was built from start to finish by one or two people. Each car took a long time to build, so cars were very expensive. By 1913 Ford began using assembly lines in his factories. On an assembly line, each worker has a specific job to do, like putting on wheels or windows. Building cars this way is much faster and costs less money.

QUICK CHECK

Cause and Effect **How did Henry Ford change car manufacturing?**

Factories today still use assembly lines to manufacture many products. ▶

In the late 1880s, steel factories were built in Pittsburgh, Pennsylvania; Gary, Indiana; and Chicago, Illinois, because these places were near coal mining areas.

Many people came to work in the steel mills. The towns around the mills grew rapidly.

Ⓑ GROWTH OF MANUFACTURING

As the price of cars came down, many more people could afford one. That meant the demand for cars went up, so manufacturers opened more factories and hired more employees to meet the demand. Automobile manufacturing became a huge part of the United States economy.

Today steel is made in new, less expensive ways. One new way uses scrap steel recycled from old bridges, refrigerators, and cars.

Steel manufacturing has made it possible for the United States to make many goods, including machines, tools, bridges, and railroad tracks.

Steel Manufacturing

To make cars, factories needed steel. Lots of steel! That meant the steel industry grew, too. Making steel uses both iron ore and coal, so steel factories were built near where these natural resources were found. The United States still makes many kinds of steel for many different steel products, from playground equipment to pots and pans.

QUICK CHECK

Cause and Effect **What made the steel industry grow?**

Some businesses or regions make certain products better than others. When businesses or regions have people who are good at making something, they can **specialize** in that product. To specialize means to make one thing very well. Perhaps a region is located near natural resources that are needed to make something. The businesses there can specialize in certain products because they have the resources they need to make them.

Specialized Products

In the 1940s, the United States specialized in making steel and steel products. Why? It was because the United States had plenty of iron ore and coal. Pittsburgh, Gary, and Chicago became known as "steel towns."

Other countries specialize, too. Spain and Greece specialize in producing olive oil. Switzerland is famous for making watches. Japan is known for electronics. China produces many types of clothing. These countries have what they need to make these products faster, better, or at a lower cost.

Canada
paper

NORTH
AMERICA

United States
airplanes

Mexico
ceramics

Brazil
books

SOUTH
AMERICA

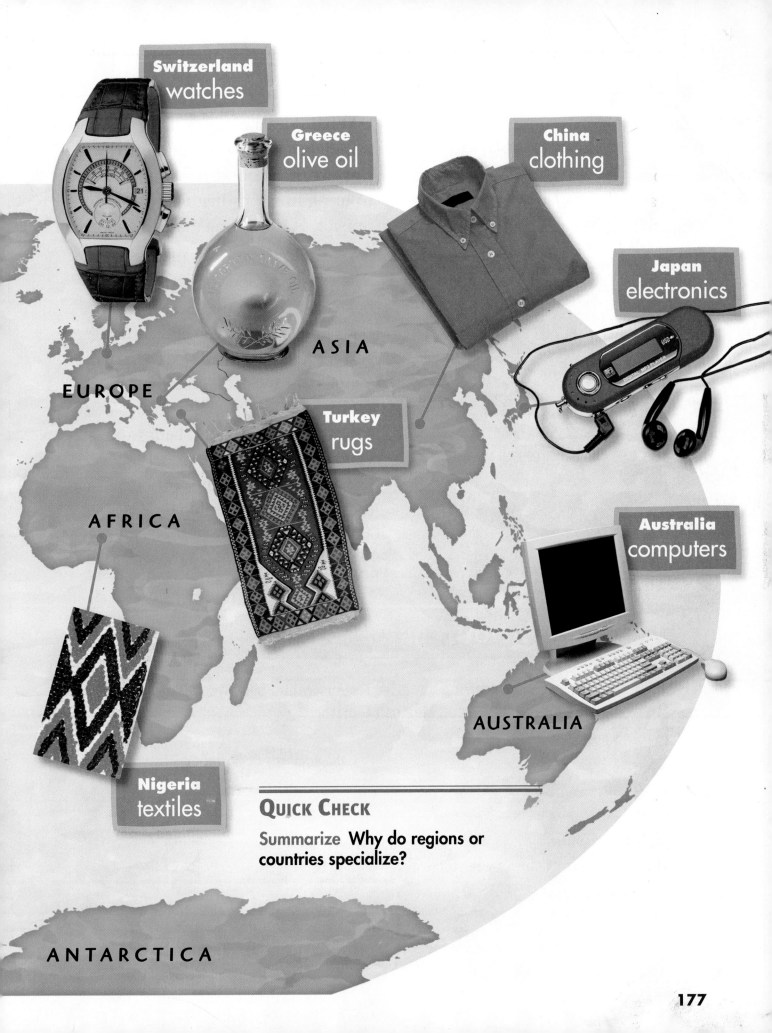

Switzerland
watches

Greece
olive oil

China
clothing

Japan
electronics

ASIA

EUROPE

Turkey
rugs

AFRICA

Australia
computers

AUSTRALIA

Nigeria
textiles

QUICK CHECK

Summarize **Why do regions or countries specialize?**

ANTARCTICA

D GOODS IN AND OUT

What does a country do when it does not make or grow something? It will **import** those goods. To import means to bring in goods made or grown outside of the country for sale or use.

The climate in most of the United States is not good for growing coffee beans. So the United States imports coffee beans from Central America and South America. It imports many fruits from these places, too. The United States also imports toys and shoes from China, and beef from Canada. Read the quote below to learn about some other products that the United States imports.

◀ Most of the bananas sold in the United States are imported.

Primary Sources

"Americans are growing hungrier for Australian beef, Canadian pork, Chilean plums, and Mexican tomatoes."

A quote from the *Arkansas Democrat-Gazette*, April 16, 2006

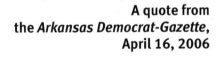

Write About It Write a paragraph about why you think Americans are "growing hungrier" for these products.

▲ Large ships carry imports and exports all over the world.

When a country makes a lot of something, it can **export** that product. To export means to send goods out of a country to be sold somewhere else. The United States exports many things, such as cars to Canada and wheat to Japan. Importing and exporting helps the economies of both countries.

QUICK CHECK

Main Idea and Details What can a country do to get products that it does not produce?

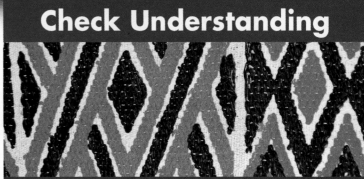

Check Understanding

1. **VOCABULARY** Use the words below to write a paragraph about making goods.
   factory   **specialize**   **export**

2. **READING SKILL Cause and Effect** Use your chart from page 172 to write a paragraph about how the growth of the auto industry affected other industries.

Cause	→	Effect
	→	
	→	
	→	

3. **Write About It** Write a paragraph to explain why countries import goods.

179

WORKING TOGETHER

VOCABULARY

international trade p. 182

domestic trade p. 184

cooperate p. 186

READING SKILL

Cause and Effect
Copy the chart below. As you read, list ways communities work together.

Cause	→	Effect
	→	
	→	
	→	

OHIO ACADEMIC CONTENT STANDARDS

H3, PS2, E2, E3, E6, CRR1, CRR2, CRR3, SSS1, SSS3

Working on the International Space Station

How do communities work together?

A People from many countries help each other.

B Countries all over the world buy and sell goods to one another.

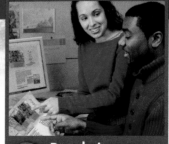

C People in different states work together to make goods like this book.

D Cities in the United States form ties with cities in other countries.

A COUNTRIES WORK TOGETHER

It is November 2000. You are aboard the space shuttle with United States astronauts and Russian cosmonauts. There is much work to do, and everyone must work together!

Countries often work together so they can learn from one another. The United States, Russia, and other countries shared ideas to build the International Space Station. Astronauts from different countries continue to live and work at the space station today. They do experiments and research to help improve life on Earth and to search for possible life on other planets.

Countries also work together on Earth to help those in need. Some doctors and nurses work for an international group called Doctors Without Borders. They travel around the world to care for sick people. Groups like this one, which started in France, work to improve hospitals and health services in many countries.

QUICK CHECK

Cause and Effect **What are some reasons countries sometimes work together?**

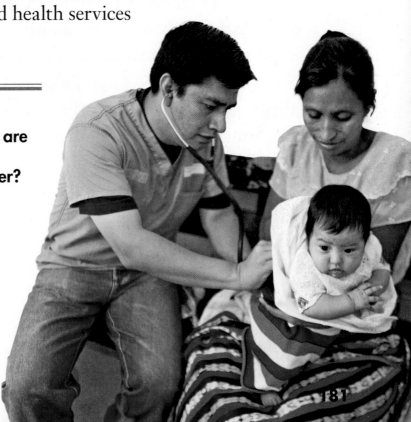

A doctor gives a baby a health checkup. ▶

181

🅑 TRADING TOGETHER

Another way countries work together is to exchange goods. What if there are goods that the United States needs that are not made or grown here? Then the United States trades with other countries to get what it needs. Trade between different countries is called **international trade**. For example, the United States exports cars to Canada and imports Canadian wood.

Countries import goods they need and export goods they specialize in making. Trading with each other helps the economies of both countries.

Saudi Arabia, a country in the Middle East, does not make cars. It buys them from other countries, including the United States. The United States needs more oil than it can produce, so it imports oil from Saudi Arabia.

PEOPLE

Vivienne Tam is a clothing designer in New York City. She also works with young designers in Hong Kong and China, her home country. People all over the world wear Vivienne Tam's clothing.

Vivienne Tam

The United States exports cars to many other countries. The United States also imports cars that other countries make. You can see information about this international car trade in the Datagraphic below.

QUICK CHECK

Summarize **How does trading together help both countries?**

DataGraphic
Trading Partners

The United States does a lot of business in cars! The graph and map show you the major countries for this car exchange.

U.S. Car Imports, 2005

Canada	🚗🚗🚗🚗🚗🚗 🚗🚗🚗🚗🚗🚗 🚗🚗🚗🚗🚗🚗 🚗🚗🚗🚗
Germany	🚗🚗🚗🚗🚗🚗 🚗🚗🚗🚗🚗🚗
Japan	🚗🚗🚗🚗🚗🚗 🚗🚗🚗🚗🚗🚗 🚗🚗🚗🚗🚗🚗 🚗🚗🚗🚗🚗

🚗 = $2 billion in car sales

U.S. Car Exports, 2005

CANADA

UNITED STATES

MEXICO

🚗 = $2 billion

Source: Bureau of Economic Analysis, U.S. Department of Commerce, 2006

Think About Imports and Exports

1. How many billions of dollars worth of cars does the United States import from Germany?

2. With which country does the United States both buy and sell cars?

C STATES WORK TOGETHER

Most states in the United States specialize in making something. States are proud of their products and may put labels on them, like Florida oranges or Washington apples.

States also trade their goods and services. Wherever you live, you can buy goods made in other states. This is **domestic trade**. Unlike international trade, domestic trade is trade that takes place within the borders of a country.

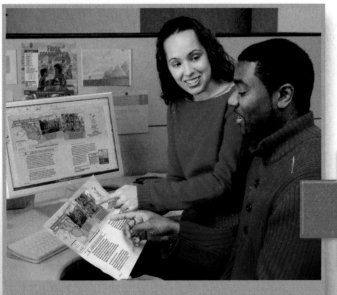

New York City, New York

1 The pages of your textbook are written in New York City, New York. Once the writing and corrections are done, the pages are sent to be printed.

Willard, Ohio

2 In Willard, Ohio, the pages of your textbook are printed and bound together to make a book. Thousands of textbooks are printed here.

People in several states worked together to produce your textbook. It was written in one state and printed in another. The paper it was printed on came from still another state. Look at the map and boxes on these pages to see how people in different states worked together to make your textbook and get it to classrooms like yours.

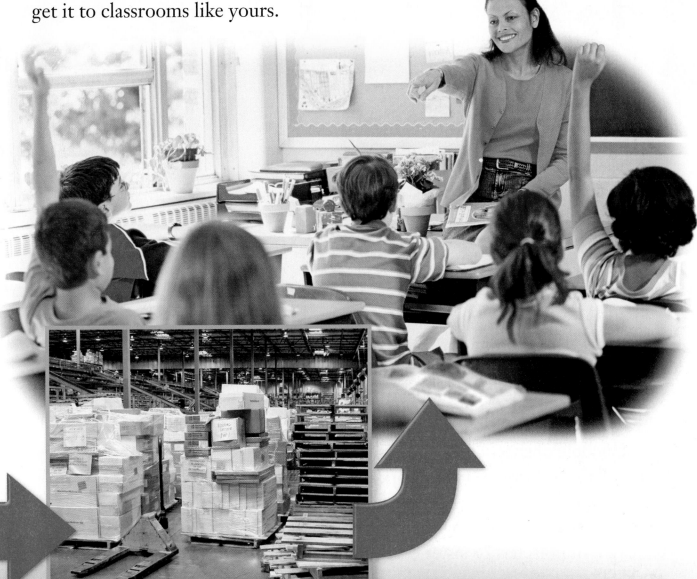

DeSoto, Texas

3 The finished textbooks are shipped to a warehouse in DeSoto, Texas. A warehouse is a building where goods are stored until they are sold.

QUICK CHECK

Summarize **How is domestic trade different from international trade?**

Chicago's Sister Cities

Chicago, United States

Mexico City, Mexico

Map Skill

LOCATION Which of Chicago's sister cities are shown on the map?

D SISTER CITIES

In 1956 President Dwight D. Eisenhower set up a program so that cities in the United States could form partnerships with "sister" cities in other countries. People in sister cities agree to learn about culture, trade, and government in each other's community.

The people of sister cities **cooperate** with each other. To cooperate means to work together. Sister cities cooperate by helping people in need, opening new businesses, and sharing their cultures. Chicago, Illinois, has 21 sister cities all over the world. The people of Chicago learn about different cultures by sharing with people in their sister cities.

EVENT

The yearly **North Carolina International Festival** is held in Raleigh. At this event, the community celebrates world cultures through art, storytelling, food, and dance.

North Carolina International Festival

Galway, Ireland

Moscow, Russia

Paris, France

Osaka, Japan

Durban, South Africa

Traveling and Learning

Students from Lake View High School in Chicago traveled to Paris, France—one of their sister cities. They had a wonderful time talking with French students and seeing sights like the Eiffel Tower. Yury G., one of the Chicago students, said,

" They were so nice and friendly to us. Even though sometimes we couldn't find the right word in English or French, we managed to communicate. "

QUICK CHECK

Main Idea and Details **How do sister cities cooperate?**

Check Understanding

1. **VOCABULARY** Write a sentence for each of the vocabulary words below.
   international trade   domestic trade cooperate

2. **READING SKILL Cause and Effect** Use your chart from page 180 to write a paragraph about ways communities work together.

Cause	→	Effect
	→	
	→	
	→	

3. **Write About It** Write a paragraph telling how communities benefit from having sister cities.

Ohio Connections
Businesses in Your Community

Peter learned about businesses in his community by interviewing people. When Peter got home, he made an accordion book about what he found out. Here's what you can do to learn about businesses in your community:

- Make a list of businesses or jobs in your community that interest you.

- Think of questions you would like to ask people about working in those businesses.

- Have an adult come with you to interview people at three different businesses. Bring a pencil and notebook. Write down what each worker tells you. If you have a camera, ask if you can take pictures of them at work.

For more help with your project visit www.macmillanmh.com

Economics Activity

Make an Accordion Book

1 Gather the notes and photos you took during the interviews.

2 To make your book, start with a large piece of stiff paper. Paper that is 36" long by 8" wide is a good size. Fold the paper into even parts.

3 On each page, write the name of a worker you interviewed and paste a photo of the person. Summarize the things the worker told you, and write them below the photo or on the back. Make a cover for your book, and give your book a title.

4 Share your book with your classmates.

Materials
- notebook
- pencil or pen
- camera
- poster board
- markers
- scissors
- glue

1. Construction Worker
2. Librarian
3. Banker
4. Shop Owner
5. Police person

Vocabulary

Write a sentence or more to answer each question.

1. If you ran a business, how could you be sure you made a **profit**?

2. What are examples of **expenses** a family has?

3. Which do you think are more important in running a business, **human resources** or **capital resources**?

4. Find something in your home that was **imported** from another country and tell where it is from.

Comprehension and Critical Thinking

5. How does a business figure out if it made a profit?

6. How does the United States get the goods it needs?

7. **Critical Thinking** What kinds of things would you include in a family budget?

8. **Reading Skill** What usually happens to the price of something when there is a scarcity of that thing?

Skill

Use Line Graphs

Write a complete sentence to answer each question.

9. What was the population of the United States in 1970?

10. Did the United States have more people or fewer people in 2000 than it did in 1970?

Population of the United States, 1970 to 2000

Ohio Achievement Test Preparation

Directions: Read the selection.

Jenny wanted to buy a new MP3 player. She saw one that cost $50. Her parents told her that she needed to earn enough money to pay for the player herself. Jenny decided to pack her lunch every day instead of buying the school lunch. This saved her $6 a week!

She also decided to open a savings account to put the money she saved away in a safe place. The savings account earned interest. Jenny saved enough money after 9 weeks. She decided to keep saving so that she had enough money to buy a case and some songs for her new player. The longer the money was in the savings account, the more interest she earned. The longer Jenny waited, the more money she had in her savings account.

Directions: Use the selection to answer questions 1–3.

1. What did Jenny give up in order to buy her MP3 player?

   ○ A. buying lunch at school

   ○ B. packing her lunch

   ○ C. buying new songs for her MP3 player

2. What is the main idea?

   ○ A. Jenny earned interest in her savings account.

   ○ B. Jenny saved for a new MP3 player.

   ○ C. Jenny packed her lunch.

3. Describe how Jenny saves the money she needs to buy the MP3 player.

   Write your answer on a separate piece of paper.

The Big Idea Activities

How do people in a community meet their needs?

Write About the Big Idea

Expository Composition

Think about what you learned in Unit 4 about the ways people meet their needs. Use the notes you made on your foldable to write an essay to answer the Big Idea question.

Be sure to begin with a sentence that tells the topic of the composition. Include one paragraph for each way that people meet their needs. Include causes and effects, and give examples from your own community. End with a concluding paragraph.

FOLDABLES
Study Organizer

Meeting Needs

Projects About the Big Idea

Make a Budget Suppose you are starting a lemonade business. Make a budget that shows your expenses and your income. Include in your budget the costs of different ways of making lemonade. Then decide which way would be the best for your business.

Make a Poster You just heard that a new, bigger baseball park is being built in your community. How will this change your community and its economy? What will the new park replace? Make a poster showing why you think the decision to build this baseball park is good or bad for the community.

Income per week:		Cost of lemons and sugar:	
sell 1 cup of lemonade	$1.00	12 lemons	$2.00
sell 15 cups in 1 week	$15.00	1 box sugar	$1.00
Expenses per week:		Cost of lemonade mix:	
cups	$3.00	Brand A	$4.00
lemons and sugar	$3.00	Brand B	$5.00

lemonade from lemons and sugar?

Use lemonade mix and lemons?

Brand B mix costs more but it tastes better than Brand A—is it worth it?

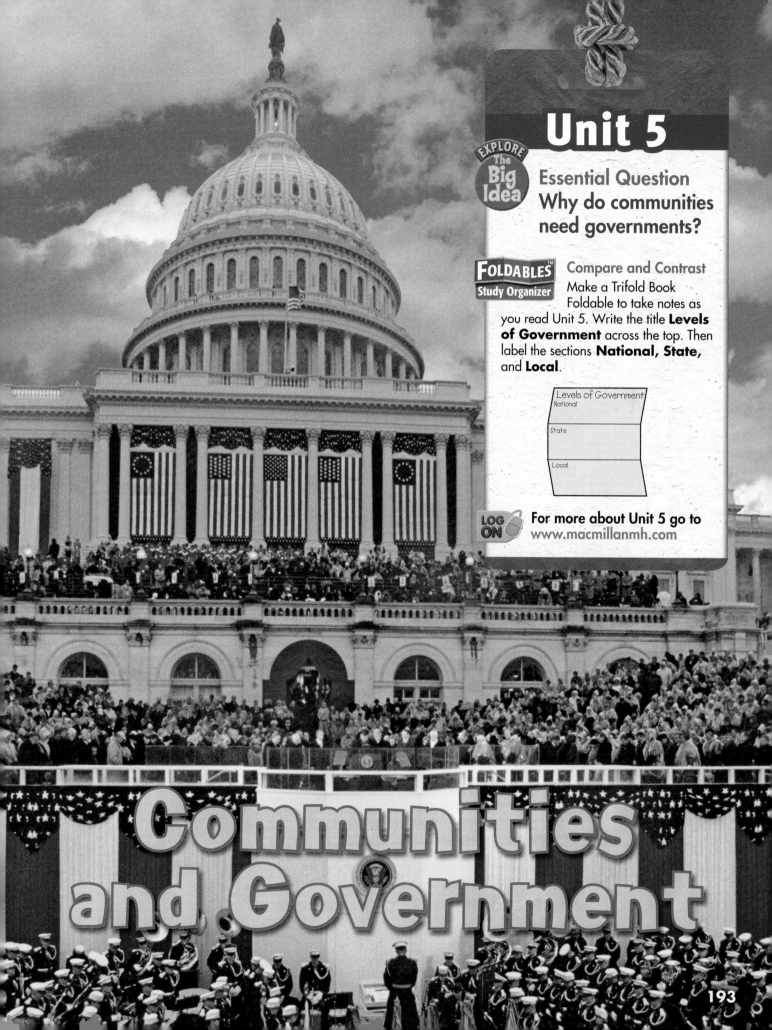

Unit 5

EXPLORE The Big Idea

Essential Question
Why do communities need governments?

FOLDABLES Study Organizer

Compare and Contrast
Make a Trifold Book Foldable to take notes as you read Unit 5. Write the title **Levels of Government** across the top. Then label the sections **National, State,** and **Local**.

Levels of Government
National

State

Local

LOG ON For more about Unit 5 go to www.macmillanmh.com

Communities and Government

PEOPLE, PLACES, AND EVENTS

William McKinley

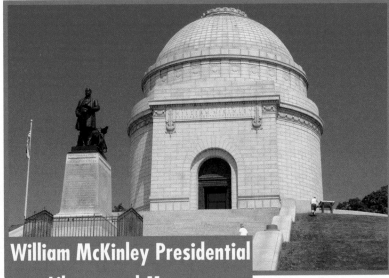

William McKinley Presidential Library and Museum

Inaugural Address

1897
William McKinley was sworn in as the 25th President at the Capitol in Washington, D.C.

William McKinley was born in Niles, Ohio in 1843 and **became President** in 1897. He was one of eight Presidents from the state of Ohio.

Today you can learn more about William McKinely by visiting the museum in Canton, Ohio.

LOG ON For more about People, Places, and Events, visit
www.macmillanmh.com

John Glenn

John and Annie Glenn Historic Site

Journey Into Space

1998

John Glenn became the oldest person ever to journey into space at the age of 77 aboard the space shuttle *Discovery*.

John Glenn was one of the first astronauts in NASA and the first American to orbit Earth before becoming a United States senator in 1974.

Today you can visit the John and Annie Glenn Historic Site and Exploration Center in New Concord, Ohio.

National Government

VOCABULARY

citizen p. 197

executive
branch p. 198

legislative
branch p. 199

judicial branch p. 199

READING SKILL

Compare and Contrast
Copy the diagram below.
As you read, use the
diagram to show how two
branches of government
are alike and different.

Different   Alike   Different

**OHIO ACADEMIC
CONTENT STANDARDS**

GOV5, GOV6, CRR1, CRR2, CRR3

**VISUAL
PREVIEW**

What is important to know about our national government?

A The United States
government
protects the rights of
citizens.

B The national
government has
three branches that
share power.

C "The Star-
Spangled
Banner" is a symbol
of our country.

D America has
other symbols
that stand for our
country's values.

PROTECTING RIGHTS

Does your class have a list of classroom rules? Why do you think there are rules? What would you do if you thought a classroom rule was unfair?

Why do countries have governments? The United States government works to protect the rights of its **citizens**. A citizen is a person who lives in a community and has certain rights and responsibilities, or duties. Our government makes laws to protect our rights, to be sure all people are treated fairly, and to keep us safe.

All citizens have the right to gather peacefully. ▼

American Freedoms

The United States Constitution is our most important law. The Constitution protects our five basic rights, or freedoms. They are the freedom to practice any religion, the freedom to meet peacefully in groups, the freedom to say what we think, the freedom to write what we think, and the right to ask the government for help if we think we are treated unfairly. All the laws our government makes must protect these rights. In return, citizens are asked to take part in government by voting in elections and by paying taxes.

QUICK CHECK

Compare and Contrast How are rights different from responsibilities?

B SHARING POWER

The leaders who wrote the Constitution did not want any one part of the government to have all the power. So they divided the government into three parts, or branches. Each branch has a job to do. Each branch works in its own building in our nation's capital, Washington, D.C.

The White House

The President is the head of the **executive branch**, the part of government that carries out laws. The executive branch cannot make the laws, but the President must say yes or no to each new law that Congress makes. This power to say no to a law is called a veto.

Library of Congress

Lincoln Memorial

Washington Monument

The Capitol

The legislative branch, called Congress, is the part of government that writes laws. This branch has two parts—the House of Representatives and the Senate. Members of the two parts come from all 50 states. To pass a law, both parts must agree.

The Supreme Court

Sometimes laws that are passed may not be fair. The judicial branch decides if laws are fair and follow the Constitution. This branch is made up of our courts and judges. The Supreme Court, with nine judges, is the country's most powerful court.

Natural History Museum

National Gallery of Art

Smithsonian Castle

Air and Space Museum

QUICK CHECK

Compare and Contrast What are the jobs of each branch of government?

C A SONG ABOUT FREEDOM

"The Star-Spangled Banner" is America's national anthem, or official song, and a well-known symbol of our country. You can read the words and music to "The Star-Spangled Banner" on the next page.

The Song Tells a Story

In 1814 the United States was fighting a war against the British. One rainy night, a man named Francis Scott Key watched British ships firing on an American fort. An American flag flew over the fort, but soon it got too dark for Key to see the flag.

Key knew that if the British captured the fort, they would take down the American flag. In the morning Key saw that the flag was still there! He knew then that the Americans had won the battle.

Key wrote a poem about what he had seen. In time people began to sing the poem to the tune of an old British song. In 1931, more than 100 years later, the song became our national anthem.

QUICK CHECK

Summarize **What was Key describing when he wrote "The Star-Spangled Banner"?**

The Star-Spangled Banner

Music Attributed to J.S. Smith
Words by Francis Scott Key

Oh,— say, can you see, by the dawn's ear-ly light,

What so proud-ly we hailed at the twi-light's last gleam-ing?

Whose broad stripes and bright stars, through the per-il-ous fight,

O'er the ram-parts we watched were so gal-lant-ly stream-ing?

And the rock-ets' red glare, the bombs burst-ing in air,

Gave proof through the night that our flag was still there.

Oh, say, does that_ Star-Span-gled Ban-ner_ yet_ wave_

O'er the land__ of the free and the home of the brave?

As you've just read, "The Star-Spangled Banner" is an important symbol of our country. Another important symbol is the flag itself. The United States flag reminds us of the freedom and values we share as Americans. We display it on national holidays and on many other special occasions. Americans show respect for the flag and the ideas it represents by reciting the Pledge of Allegiance. Read the Pledge below.

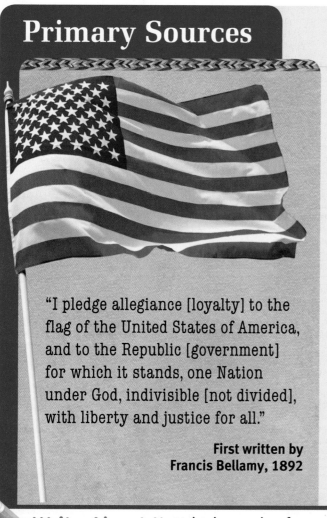

Primary Sources

"I pledge allegiance [loyalty] to the flag of the United States of America, and to the Republic [government] for which it stands, one Nation under God, indivisible [not divided], with liberty and justice for all."

**First written by
Francis Bellamy, 1892**

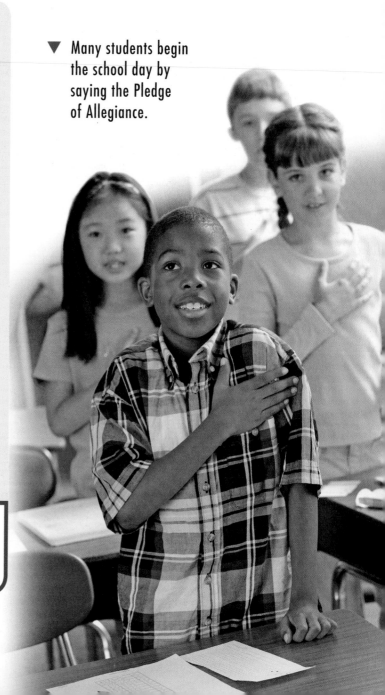

▼ Many students begin the school day by saying the Pledge of Allegiance.

Write About It Which words of the Pledge of Allegiance describe rights people have?

▲ The words on the bell say, "Proclaim Liberty throughout all the Land. . . ."

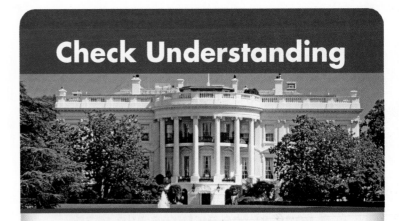

▲ The bald eagle, our national bird, is another symbol of our country.

The Liberty Bell

The Liberty Bell has rung for many important events. Its most famous ringing was on July 8, 1776, when it called citizens of Philadelphia to hear the reading of the Declaration of Independence. Later, in 1837, a group that worked to end slavery used the bell as a symbol of liberty.

Because it is cracked, the Liberty Bell can no longer be rung. But each year on the Fourth of July it is gently tapped 13 times by descendants of the Declaration's signers.

QUICK CHECK

Summarize **What do many American symbols represent?**

Check Understanding

1. **VOCABULARY** Write a sentence to explain each term below.
   executive branch   judicial branch
   legislative branch

2. **READING SKILL Compare and Contrast** Use your diagram from page 196 to write a paragraph about how two branches of national government are alike and different.

3. **Write About It** Write a letter to tell a friend something important you learned about our national government.

Chart and Graph Skills
Use Flow Charts

VOCABULARY
flow chart

Suppose your class decides to elect a class president. There are several steps to follow. These steps have to be done in a certain order. A **flow chart** shows the different steps to complete a process. A flow chart can help you understand and remember the steps in the right order.

Electing a Class President

Learn It

Look at the chart as you read.

- **Read the title.** This flow chart shows the steps for electing a class president.

- **Look at the pictures and read the captions.** Both pictures and captions give information.

- **The arrows and numbers show the order of the steps.** Start at the top and follow the arrows. The steps are done in order. Flow charts are read from top to bottom, like this one, or from left to right.

Students tell why they should be chosen class president.

Students vote for the person they think will do the best job.

Someone fair counts the votes.

The student with the most votes becomes the class president.

Try It

Now read the flow chart on this page and answer the questions.

- What does the chart show?

- What is the first step? What is the last step?

- What happens just before the President signs the bill?

- Does Congress vote on the bill before or after the President signs it?

Apply It

Do you know how to make a sandwich, plant a garden, or make papier-mâché?

Make your own flow chart to show the steps. Make a list of steps. Tell them in order. Draw a picture to show each step. Use arrows and numbers to show the order of the steps. Give your chart a title.

Share your flow chart with your classmates.

An Idea Becomes a Law

People get an idea for a new law.

A representative presents the idea to Congress. The idea is called a bill.

Congress votes "yes" on the bill.

The president signs the bill into law.

VOCABULARY

governor p. 207

capitol p. 207

READING SKILL

Compare and Contrast
Copy the diagram below. As you read, use it to show how state and national governments are alike and different.

Different   Alike   Different

OHIO ACADEMIC CONTENT STANDARDS

GEO1, GEO3, GOV1, GOV3, GOV4, CRR1, SSS1, SSS4, SSS5

State Government

Ohio Governor
Ted Strickland

VISUAL PREVIEW

How do state governments help the community?

A Our state governments have three branches that share power.

B States use tax money to pay for services such as schools and highways.

C States provide services such as law enforcement and parks.

A THREE BRANCHES

Did you know that each state has its own government? How is state government like national government? Let's look at state government in Ohio.

Like our national government, state governments are divided into three branches. A **governor** is a person elected to be head of a state's executive branch. In 2006 the citizens of Ohio elected Ted Strickland to be their governor. A governor helps carry out state laws.

Ohio has a legislative branch, too. Members of the legislative branch write laws. The judges in Ohio's judicial branch make sure state laws agree with Ohio's constitution. All three branches of Ohio government work in Columbus, the state capital. As in national government, all branches of Ohio government work together for the people in our state.

PLACES

A **capitol** is a building in which the state or national government meets. The capitol of Ohio is located in Columbus. It is called the Ohio Statehouse. The original Statehouse was built in 1861. The governor's and judicial offices are located in the Ohio capitol.

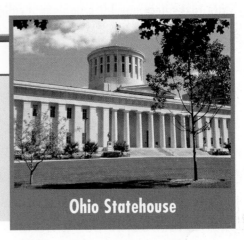

Ohio Statehouse

QUICK CHECK

Compare and Contrast **How is the executive branch of a state government like the executive branch of national government?**

State government provides services, such as schools, parks, and highways. All these things cost money! Did you ever wonder how the government pays for these services? It uses tax money collected from its citizens.

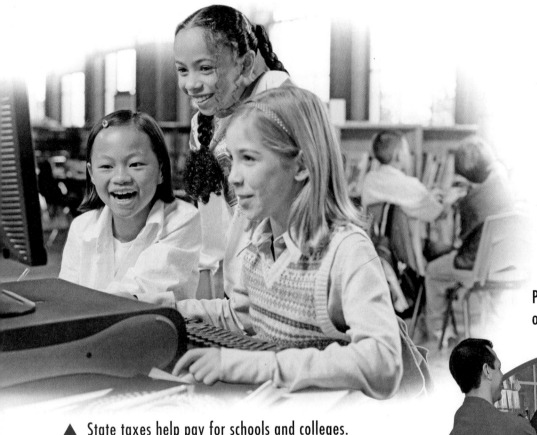

People pay sales tax on things they buy. ▼

▲ State taxes help pay for schools and colleges.

Different Kinds of Taxes

There are many kinds of taxes. Some are federal, or national, taxes. People who work pay income tax to the federal government. Many states have an income tax, too. Some states, like Arizona, also have a sales tax. That means people pay a little extra on some things they buy. A price tag on a shirt says $14.00, but you might pay $14.79. The extra 79 cents is the sales tax. This money goes to the state government.

Taxes in Arizona

Citizens of Arizona pay taxes to their state government. The taxes help pay for government services. The graphs below show how Arizona spent its tax money.

DataGraphic
Arizona Tax Money

Study the two graphs. Then answer the questions.

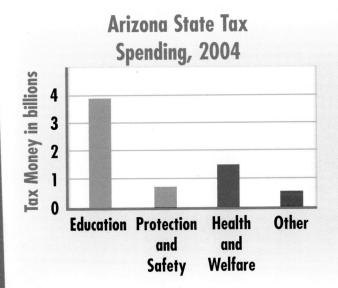

Arizona State Tax Spending, 2004

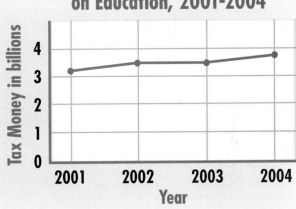

Arizona State Tax Spending on Education, 2001-2004

Source: *Arizona Office of Finance and Budgeting, 2006*

Think About Arizona Tax Dollars

1. Which item got the most of Arizona's tax money in 2004?

2. Did the amount of money spent on education in Arizona go up or down from 2001 to 2004?

QUICK CHECK

Summarize **What are some things that tax money is used for?**

State governments provide many services. States build and take care of state highways. States run health programs, and build colleges. State governments also give money to help local schools.

States make license plates for cars and trucks. States issue licenses to people, too. A license shows that you have the skill to do something, such as drive a car, or that you have permission for an activity, such as hunting or fishing.

▲ Doctors must have a license from their state government to take care of people.

State governments hire police officers to keep state highways safe. ▼

▲ Kartchner Caverns State Park opened in 1999. The men who found the cave kept it a secret until they were sure it would be protected.

Protecting the Environment

State governments also work to protect the environment. States set aside land to keep plants, animals, and other natural resources safe. In 1974, two men discovered an unique cave with unusual colors and rock formation in the mountains near Benson, Arizona. The state government bought the cave and the land around it to protect it. The area is now Kartchner Caverns State Park.

QUICK CHECK

Summarize **What are some services that state governments provide?**

Check Understanding

1. **VOCABULARY** Research your state's governor. Then write a sentence about him or her using the following words.
   governor   **capitol**

2. **READING SKILL**
   Compare and Contrast
   Use your diagram from page 206 to write a paragraph about how state and national governments are alike and different.

   Different   Alike   Different

3. **Write About It** Write a letter to your state's governor. Give your opinion about something you think is important in your state.

Map and Globe Skills
Use Road Maps

VOCABULARY

road map

interstate
  highway

state highway

Suppose you and your family are driving in Indiana. How would you know which roads to take? A **road map** could tell you. Road maps show the roads you can use to get from one place to another.

You can find road maps in a highway atlas. You can also buy a road map that shows just one state.

Learn It

Look at the map on page 213. Read the steps for using a road map.

- Read the map title. This map shows some roads in Indiana.

- Look at the map key to understand the symbols. An **interstate highway** connects two or more states. U.S. highways are older roads that pass through towns. A **state highway** begins and ends within a state.

- Identify directions. Roads that run east and west usually have an even number, such as 50 or 70. Roads that run north and south usually have an odd number, such as 69 or 65. This helps drivers figure out in which direction they are driving.

Try It

Use the map on page 213 to answer the questions.

- Which highway could you drive from Gary to Indianapolis?

- Which highway would you take from Indianapolis to visit Hoosier National Forest?

- Which U.S. highway connects South Bend and Indianapolis?

- In which direction does State Highway 50 run?

- Which interstates run east and west, and pass through Indianapolis?

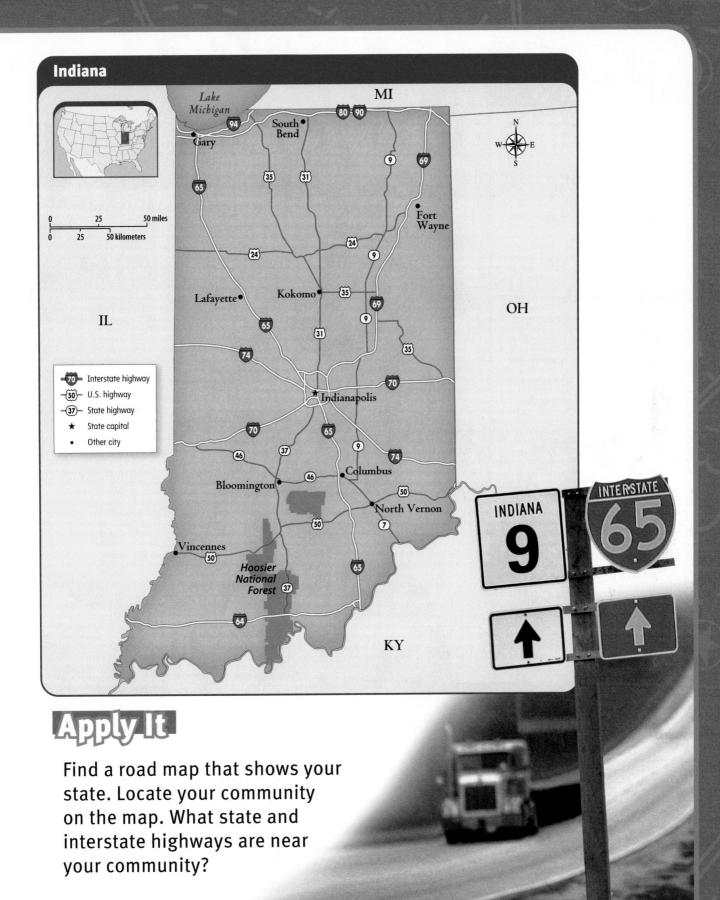

Indiana

Apply It

Find a road map that shows your state. Locate your community on the map. What state and interstate highways are near your community?

Local Government

VOCABULARY

local government p. 215

mayor p. 215

council p. 216

sovereign p. 219

READING SKILL

Compare and Contrast
Copy the diagram below. As you read, use it to show how the jobs of the mayor and city council are alike and different

OHIO ACADEMIC CONTENT STANDARDS

GOV1, GOV2, GOV3, GOV4, CRR3

Local fire departments help keep communities safe.

VISUAL PREVIEW

How does local government help the community?

A A mayor and city workers are all part of local government.

B Town and city governments provide many different local services.

C Native American communities have their own local governments.

Your class is visiting the local firehouse. A loud bell sounds—the firefighters fly into action. With sirens blaring, they climb onto the fire truck and race to the rescue!

Who hires the firefighters and the police? Who makes sure the trash is picked up, and checks that traffic lights work properly? **Local government** does! Local government is the people who run a town or a city. Local government is the level of government that most closely touches our everyday lives.

Let's look at Sylvania, Ohio, to see how its local government works. Craig Stough became **mayor** of Sylvania in 1996. Many towns and cities have a mayor as the head of local government. Each week Mayor Stough goes to meetings, tries to solve city problems, and makes sure city laws are followed. What branch of government does this sound like? If you said the executive branch, you're right!

QUICK CHECK

Compare and Contrast How is a mayor's job different from a governor's job?

City workers repair streets and roadways. ▶

215

Mayor Stough works with the city **council** to plan for the future of Sylvania. A council is a group of people who make the laws for a community. The council is elected by the citizens of the community. It is the legislative branch of local government. Local governments have a judicial branch, too. The local courts rule on offenses such as traffic tickets.

Community Services Meet Needs

Citizens and businesses pay taxes to local governments. Local governments then use tax money to provide services. They hire people to fix road signs, collect trash and recyclables, and run the library. They pay government employees such as police officers and firefighters. The pictures on the right show some services that most local governments provide.

Towns in other countries have governments, too. You will read about the government of Adelaide, Australia, on page 218.

The town library provides books, newspapers, and computers.

Police officers keep the community of Sylvania safe.

Firefighters protect Sylvania from fires.

QUICK CHECK

Compare and Contrast How is a city council different from a state's legislative branch?

Local government takes care of parks.

The highway department helps keep the roads of Sylvania safe.

Mayor Stough and the Sylvania city council

People visit Sylvania Historical Village to learn about the history of their community.

217

Global Connections

Local Government of Adelaide, Australia

Back in 1840 the city of Adelaide, Australia, was very small. That was the year the city elected its first mayor. Today Adelaide is one of Australia's largest cities.

Every three years the people of Adelaide elect a mayor and a city council. These government leaders work to keep the city beautiful. The city's many employees take care of Adelaide's libraries, roads, parks, and beaches.

Adelaide is known as "Festival City." Every two years the local government holds the Adelaide Festival of Arts. People from all over the world go to Adelaide for this celebration. Another important Adelaide event is a bicycle race called the Tour Down Under.

▲ Adelaide City Hall

Adelaide

◀ Adelaide's city council sponsors many local events, including a bicycle race.

Write About It Write a paragraph describing how Adelaide's local government is similar to Sylvania's.

Native Americans are citizens of two **sovereign** governments—the United States, and their own tribal group, or nation. Sovereign means independent, or self-governing. Native Americans vote in local, state, and national elections. In addition, they may also vote in tribal elections. Each tribal group can make its own laws and choose its own leaders.

There are more than 500 Native American governments in the United States. These governments all share the same goal—they work for their people. For example, the Navajo Nation makes laws that protect Navajo people and Navajo culture.

Tribal governments work with the national, state, and local governments. They also work with other tribal governments and cooperate on many issues that are important to their tribes.

QUICK CHECK

Summarize Native Americans are citizens of what governments?

▲ Ben Nighthorse Campbell was a United States senator. Now he serves in the government of the Northern Cheyenne Nation.

Check Understanding

1. **VOCABULARY** Write one sentence for each of these vocabulary words.
   mayor   council   sovereign

2. **READING SKILL**
   Compare and Contrast
   Use your diagram from page 214 to write a paragraph comparing a mayor and a city council.

3. **Write About It** Make a list of some ways people can take part in local government.

Rules and Laws

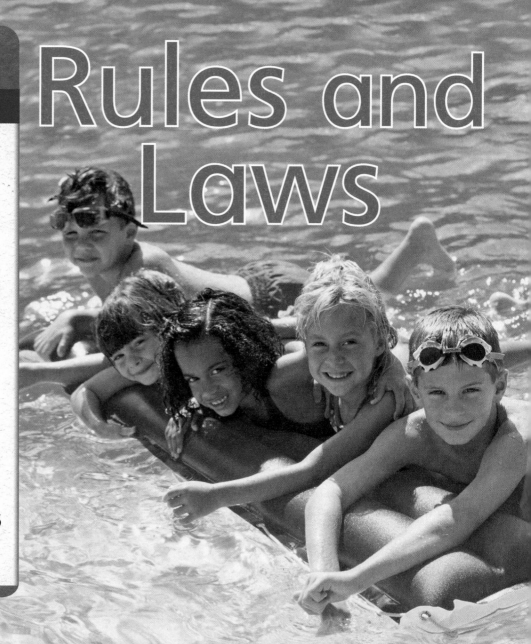

Rules help keep us safe.

VISUAL PREVIEW

How does having rules and laws help communities?

A Rules and laws protect us and help us get along.

B Laws are made to protect our rights, and for the good of all.

C Government lawmakers must follow the laws, too.

D Native Americans make laws for their own communities.

RULES AND LAWS HELP PEOPLE

You are at the swimming pool. Your friend wants you to dive in, but just then you see a sign that says "No diving." You know the rule is meant to keep people safe.

Rules not only help keep people safe, rules also help people in a community get along. Have you ever been in a room where everyone was talking at once? It is a lot easier to discuss things when people take turns. Taking turns is a rule that helps people work together.

Laws Are Rules

You know cars must stop at a red light. That's the law. A law is a rule the government makes for all people in a town, state, or country. What would happen if drivers didn't obey this important traffic law? Someone could have an accident, and people might get hurt. If a driver doesn't stop at a red light, a police officer may give the driver a ticket. Then the driver will have to go to court and pay a fine.

Rules help us be fair. ▼

Other laws protect our property. For example, it is against the law for someone to take something of yours without permission. People who break laws are punished. They may have to pay a fine or even go to jail.

QUICK CHECK

Compare and Contrast **What would it be like if there were no traffic laws?**

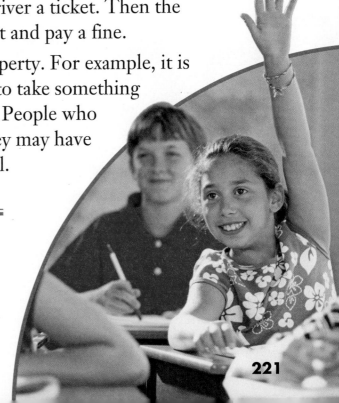

221

Ⓑ GOOD FOR ALL

Many communities have a law against littering. You might think, "One little wrapper won't matter—I'll just drop it." But what if everyone did that? The streets would be a mess! Putting trash where it belongs is an example of working for the **common good**, or doing whatever helps the most people in the community. Good citizens do things for the common good.

Good Citizens

Governments make laws for the common good. One law says not to chain a bicycle to a fire hydrant. This is for everyone's good, because firefighters need to get to fire hydrants easily. Obeying laws is one way of being a good citizen.

Another way of being a good citizen is to serve on a **jury**. A jury is a group of citizens who listen to the facts in a court trial and make a decision based on the law.

Have you ever voted in a classroom or school election? Good citizens vote for leaders at every level of government—national, state, and local. Voters choose leaders that they believe will work for the common good.

▲ Picking up litter helps everyone.

Voting is one way to be a good citizen. ▼

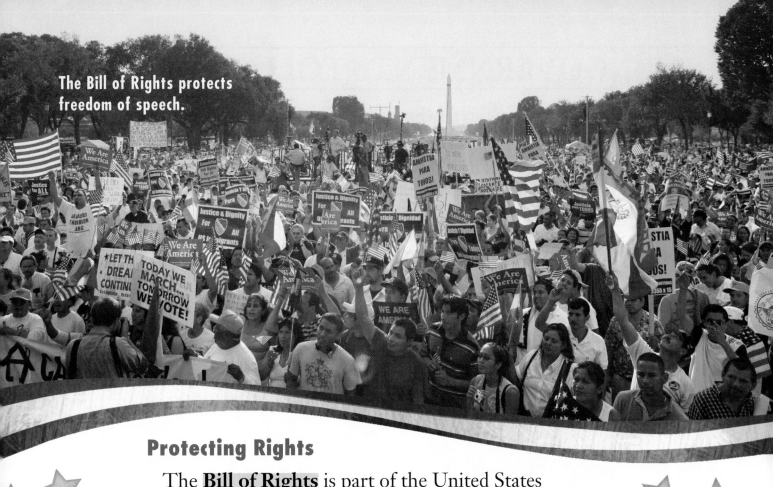

The Bill of Rights protects freedom of speech.

Protecting Rights

The **Bill of Rights** is part of the United States Constitution. It protects our most important rights. In some countries, people can be put in jail just for saying they disagree with the government. In the United States you cannot be arrested for disagreeing. The Bill of Rights makes sure we have the freedom to say and write what we want. It protects other rights, too.

QUICK CHECK

Summarize What are some ways to be a good citizen?

PEOPLE

In the past, African Americans were often treated unfairly. During the 1960s, **Dr. Martin Luther King, Jr.**, led the fight for equal rights for all Americans. Dr. King made speeches and led peaceful marches to help change unfair laws.

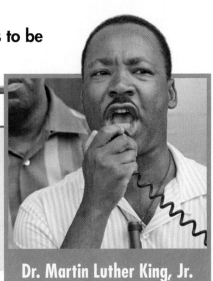

Dr. Martin Luther King, Jr.

GOVERNMENTS FOLLOW RULES

Good citizens aren't the only ones who follow rules and laws. Governments and government leaders must follow the law, too. The highest, or most important, law in our country is the United States Constitution.

We elect the leaders who will speak and act for us in government. The people who we elect promise to obey the Constitution. This means they cannot pass a law that goes against any laws already in the Constitution.

▼ These lawmakers were elected by members of their communities.

▲ In 2006 Hopi, Navajo, and United States leaders signed an agreement to end a dispute over land.

Tribal Government

Many Native American tribal groups, such as the Hopi and the Navajo, have their own tribal governments. Leaders in these tribal governments create laws for their group. They also work with other local, state, and national governments.

Many Hopi live on the Hopi Reservation in Arizona. A reservation is land set aside for use by Native Americans. The Hopi Tribal Council meets in Kykotsmovi Village, but each of the villages on the reservation also has its own traditional Hopi government. In traditional Hopi government, decisions are not made by voting. Instead problems are discussed until everyone in the community agrees on each decision.

QUICK CHECK

Summarize **Why must governments follow the law?**

Ⓓ HOPI GOVERNMENT

▲ A Hopi police officer on patrol

Each Hopi village sends members to the Hopi Tribal Council. The Council members work for the common good of the Hopi and to help each other in times of need.

A few years ago, the Council formed a water team. The team works with state and national leaders to protect Hopi water rights. Hopi Tribal Chairman Wayne Taylor, Jr., said,

> ❝ Of all the [things] necessary for economic development, none is more important than water.... ❞

QUICK CHECK

Summarize What does the Hopi Tribal Council do?

Check Understanding

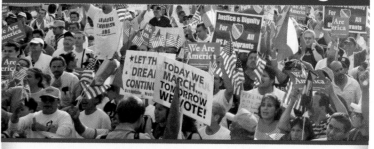

1. **VOCABULARY** Write a sentence to explain each vocabulary term.
   common good   **Bill of Rights**

2. **READING SKILL**
   Compare and Contrast
   Use your diagram from page 220 to write a paragraph describing how rules are different from laws.

   3. **Write About It** Write a paragraph about some of the things people in your community do that are for the common good.

Citizenship

Democracy in Action

Being Informed

Students in Claysville, Pennsylvania, noticed a lot of trash outside their school. No wonder! There were no trash cans! The class decided to do something. They found out who to ask for help and how to get what they wanted. Now the playground is cleaner. Read the steps below to learn how to become informed.

Being Informed

1. **Identify the problem.** Make a list of what you already know, and what you need to find out.

2. **Get information.** Read local newspapers, search the Internet, watch television, or talk to people who know about the problem.

3. **Examine the information.** Try to decide which information is fact and which is opinion.

4. **Find out who is in charge.** Some problems are the responsibility of government leaders. Find out which leader is in charge of the problem you're interested in.

Write About It Gather information about a problem in your school or community. Write a paragraph telling what you think should be done.

Lesson 5

Taking Action

VOCABULARY

volunteer p. 229

nonprofit p. 230

bill p. 231

READING SKILL

Compare and Contrast
Copy the diagram below. As you read, list how lawmakers and volunteers are alike and different.

Different   Alike   Different

OHIO ACADEMIC CONTENT STANDARDS

GOV1, GOV2, CRR1, CRR2, CRR3, SSS1, SSS6

A beautiful community makes everyone happy.

VISUAL PREVIEW — **What are some ways people get involved in their community?**

A People can do many things to help their community.

B Some people work with others to help people in their community.

C People vote for lawmakers who will best help their community.

D Voting is the right of every United States citizen.

A GETTING INVOLVED

People in your neighborhood have permission to turn an empty lot into a little park. Everyone works on the clean-up. You offer to help paint a mural for the new park.

If you **volunteer** to help, you are being a good citizen. A volunteer is a person who chooses to do a job without getting paid. Volunteers do many things. They might clean a park or collect clothing for the homeless. They work for the common good of their community.

What Can People Do to Help?

People can volunteer to do many different things. Volunteers who clean up public parks make them better for everyone. Some people collect canned food to help people who do not have enough to eat. Planting flowers can make a community more beautiful. In some schools, volunteers help other students with their schoolwork.

EVENT

National & Global Youth Service Day teaches children the importance of volunteering. Young people can volunteer to pick up trash, clean schools, or teach others about the environment.

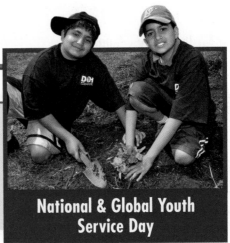

National & Global Youth Service Day

QUICK CHECK

Compare and Contrast **How is a volunteer different from an employee?**

HELPING THE COMMUNITY

People often volunteer by joining **nonprofit** groups. A nonprofit group does not make money from the work it does. The Red Cross is a nonprofit group that helps communities during disasters, such as hurricanes or tornadoes.

In 2005 Jackie, Melissa, and Jenna Kantor were just 14, 11, and 8 years old. They decided to help families affected by Hurricane Katrina. They started Project Backpack. They collected school supplies, toys, and books and sent them in backpacks to kids who needed help.

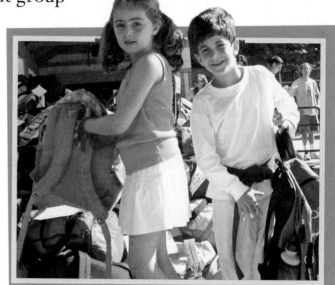

▲ Kids started a nonprofit group called Project Backpack.

Building Homes

Habitat for Humanity is a nonprofit group that helps people build homes for themselves. Families who need houses work with Habitat volunteers to build their own homes. This nonprofit group allows people in a community to help their neighbors.

▼ Habitat for Humanity volunteers help build houses.

Make a Difference

Have you ever wondered if you can really make a difference? You can—no matter how old you are. In New Hampshire, a group of third and fourth graders wrote a **bill** saying that the pumpkin should be the state fruit. A bill is a written idea for a law. Why did they choose the pumpkin? Student Reanna Parker said, "It's strong and sturdy like the people of New Hampshire."

The students got their representative in the state government to present the bill to other lawmakers. In April 2006, the New Hampshire House of Representatives and Senate made the bill a law.

▲ Third and fourth graders took their idea to state lawmakers.

Children in Illinois wanted to make a difference in another way. They held car washes and ran bake sales to raise money for hurricane victims. One school raised over $5,000 by selling lemonade! The kids who worked on these projects felt great knowing that their actions made a difference to people who needed help.

QUICK CHECK

Summarize **How do people make a difference in their communities?**

Lemonade
50¢
All money goes to help rebuild after hurricanes.

C GOVERNMENT LEADERS HELP

Have you ever dreamed of running for government office? You can start by getting involved in your school government. As you grow up, you can stay involved in government. Being a government leader is one way people help their community.

Government leaders have a responsibility to help pass laws that will aid people in their city, state, and country. Senator Shirley Smith works in the Ohio State Senate. She is interested in helping people who live in her state get the health care they need. Leaders like Senator Smith work to pass laws that make sure children have programs to keep them safe and healthy.

▲ Ohio Senator Shirley Smith

▼ Lawmakers make sure students can eat a healthy lunch.

Get Out and Vote

As you have learned, government leaders such as Senator Smith are elected by the people. If people think Senator Smith does a good job, they let her know by voting for her again. If you are a citizen, one day you will be able to vote. The people you vote for will make the laws that affect you.

In the past, not everyone could vote. When the Constitution was first written in 1789, only white men were allowed to vote. Read on to find out how voting rights have changed since then.

▲ Some government leaders help support after-school sports programs.

PEOPLE

Elizabeth Cady Stanton and **Lucretia Mott** spoke in 1848 at the Seneca Falls Convention in New York. They spoke about the importance of women's rights, including the right to vote.

Elizabeth Cady Stanton and Lucretia Mott

QUICK CHECK

Main Idea and Details How do government leaders help communities?

1848 Elizabeth Cady Stanton and Lucretia Mott leads a meeting in New York, called the Seneca Falls Convention, to discuss women's rights.

1870 The Fifteenth Amendment gives African American men the right to vote.

Ⓓ HISTORY OF VOTING RIGHTS

In the late 1700s, when the United States government was just beginning, only white men could vote. African American men and all women were not allowed to vote. They did not have a say in how the government was run. People worked hard to change this, and over the years, more and more people won the right to vote.

Fighting for Change

In 1866 Elizabeth Cady Stanton and Susan B. Anthony formed the American Equal Rights Association. This group worked to win the right to vote for all men and women. Soon other groups formed. They tried to convince the government to change the laws. People made signs and organized meetings and parades. Some even went to jail for their actions.

Today Today every United States citizen who is eighteen or older has the right to vote.

1920 The Nineteenth Amendment gives women the right to vote.

Voting Today

It took many years, but the law was finally changed. The United States Constitution was amended, or changed, to include more people who could vote. Today it is against the law to prevent any citizen from voting.

QUICK CHECK

Compare and Contrast **How is voting today different than voting before 1870?**

Check Understanding

1. **VOCABULARY** Write three or four sentences explaining ways to be a good citizen. Use these vocabulary words.
   volunteer   **nonprofit**

2. **READING SKILL**
   Compare and Contrast
   Use your diagram from page 228 to write a paragraph on how volunteers and lawmakers are alike and different.

   Different   Alike   Different

3. **Write About It** Write a letter to your local government about a change you would like to see in your community.

Ohio Connections

Symbols and Landmarks in Your Community

Nadia learned about her community's symbols, landmarks, and city seal. Then she decided to make her own city seal. You can make a city seal for your community, too. Here is what to do:

- Go to your city hall, your local library, or look on the Internet to find out about your city or town's seal and local landmarks.

- Think about other people, places, or things that are symbols of your community. Which of these could you put on a seal? What is your city known for? What animals live nearby? Were any famous people born in your community? What is produced in your area?

- Find photographs of your community's symbols and landmarks that will help you make your own city seal.

The Pro Football Hall of Fame in Canton, Ohio

 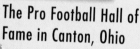
For more help with your project visit
www.macmillanmh.com

Government Activity

Make a City Seal

1. Look at your notes and pictures. Choose one or more things you would like to put on your city seal.

2. Try out many ideas on notebook paper until you make a design you really like. Some city seals show just one place or thing. Others include three or four symbols.

3. Draw your best design on poster board.

4. Include your city's name on your seal. You may also want to include the year it was founded, or a nickname for the city.

5. Share your city seal with your classmates.

Materials
- photographs
- notebook
- markers, colored pencils, or crayons
- poster board

Unit 5 Review and Assess

Vocabulary

Write the sentences. Choose the correct term to fill in the blank.

governor   **Bill of Rights**

council   **nonprofit**

1. The town _____ makes laws in local government.

2. The _____ is part of the Constitution.

3. The head of a state's executive branch is the _____.

4. Many people volunteer to work for a _____ group such as the Red Cross.

Skill

Use Road Maps

Write a complete sentence to answer each question.

9. What kind of road is Highway 84?

10. Which roads would you drive on if you traveled from Enfield to New Haven to Norwalk?

Comprehension and Critical Thinking

5. What are the five basic rights protected by the Constitution?

6. What is an example of something that is done for the common good?

7. **Reading Skill** Why might local government affect citizens more than state or national governments do?

8. **Critical Thinking** Why is it important to vote?

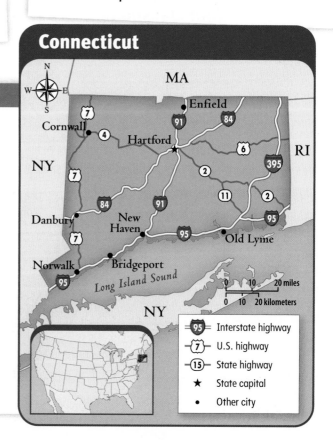

Connecticut

MA

Enfield

Cornwall

Hartford

RI

NY

Danbury

New Haven

Old Lyme

Norwalk

Bridgeport

Long Island Sound

NY

0   10   20 miles
0   10   20 kilometers

🛡95🛡 Interstate highway
🛡7🛡 U.S. highway
🛡15🛡 State highway
★ State capital
• Other city

Directions: Read the selection.

Counties are divided into smaller areas called **townships**. In Ohio there are more than 1,000 townships. Townships are usually located in rural areas. Each one is run by a group of people called **trustees**. Trustees do not make laws. Instead, they make sure that people living in their township have the services they need. These services may include snow plowing and road maintenance.

What if there was a fire out in the country, far from a fire station? Townships usually own fire trucks and have volunteer fire departments. The volunteers take classes and practice fighting fires.

Directions: Use the selection to answer questions 1–4.

1. Where are townships usually located?

   ○ A. in the suburbs

   ○ B. in the city

   ○ C. in the country

2. What does a **trustee** do?

   ○ A. makes laws

   ○ B. makes sure people in a township have services they need

   ○ C. makes sure that the laws are obeyed in a township

3. Describe the services a township might need.

   Write your answer on a separate piece of paper.

4. How does a person become a fire fighter in a township?

   Write your answer on a separate piece of paper.

The Big Idea Activities

Why do communities need governments?

Write About the Big Idea

Write an Essay

Think about what you have learned in Unit 5. Use your foldable to help you write an essay that answers the Big Idea question. First write an introduction. Then write one paragraph about each level of government. Tell what the government does at each level, and explain why communities need government. For local government, include examples from your own local government. Then write a conclusion to your essay.

FOLDABLES
Study Organizer

Levels of Government
National

State

Local

Projects About the Big Idea

Plan a School Project Think about your school community. Is everything just the way you want it, or is there something you would like to change? Work with other students to plan a project that will bring about a change for the common good.

Make a Poster Make a poster that shows the elected members of your local government. Include the services your local government provides to your community.

Reference Section

The Reference Section has many parts, each with a different type of information. Use this section to look up people, places, and events as you study.

**Unit 1 Reading Skill:
Main Idea and Details** R2

Unit 2 Reading Skill: Sequence R4

Unit 3 Reading Skill: Summarize R6

Unit 4 Reading Skill: Cause and Effect . . R8

**Unit 5 Reading Skill:
Compare and Contrast** R10

Geography Handbook GH1

Atlas GH14

Glossary REF1

Index REF6

Credits REF16

Main Idea and Details

The **main idea** is what the paragraph is about. It is what the author wants you to understand about the subject. Often the main idea is in the first sentence of a paragraph. The other sentences have **details** that tell more about the main idea. Finding the main idea and details will help you understand what you read.

Learn It

- **Read the paragraph.** Think about what the paragraph is about. See if there is a sentence which states the main idea.

- **Now look for details.** Sentences with details give more information about the main idea.

Main Idea The first sentence states the main idea.	• There are many interesting things to do in Pittsburgh. If you are interested in science, you can go to the Carnegie Science center. There you can board a real submarine. If you like animals you can visit the zoo. You can visit the
Details These details tell some of the fun things to do in Pittsburgh.	Children's Museum where you can work with paint and clay.

Try It

Copy and complete the chart. Write the main idea and the details of the paragraph on page 1 in the boxes.

Main Idea	Details

Apply It

● Review the steps in Learn It.

● Read the paragraph below. Then make a main idea and details chart for the paragraph.

It takes many people to build a new building. An architect makes a plan that tells how the building will be made. Steelworkers put up the framework. Other workers pour concrete. Others may lay bricks to make the walls. Electricians put in wires and lighting.

Unit 2 • Reading Skills

Sequence

The paragraph below tells some events during Christopher Columbus's first journey to the Americas. When you read, think about the **sequence**, or order, of events. Thinking about the order of events will help you understand and remember what you read.

Learn It

- Look for clue words such as first, next, later, and last. These words can help show the order of events.

- Look for dates that tell exactly when things happened.

First Event
Columbus left Spain.

Clue words
These words help you recognize other events. sequence.

Dates
Dates help you keep events in order.

Christopher Columbus and his crew left Spain on August 3, 1492. The first stop was the Canary Islands. There they got fresh supplies. Five weeks later, Columbus and his crew landed on an island in what is now the Bahamas. Both Columbus and his crew were glad to be on land! Next, Columbus explored the coast of Cuba and the coast of Hispaniola. By January 1493, Columbus began sailing back to Spain.

Try It

Copy and complete the chart below. Write the events from the paragraph on page 1 in the correct sequence. You may need to add boxes to the chart to show more events.

First
↓
Next
↓
Last

How did you figure out the sequence of events?

Apply It

● Review the sequencing steps in Learn It.

● Read the paragraph below. Then create a sequence of events chart to show the order of events.

In August 1620 the Pilgrims left England to go to America. They started out on two ships, the Speedwell and the Mayflower. The Speedwell began leaking, so both ships returned to land. All the Pilgrims crowded onto the Mayflower. The Pilgrims began their journey once again. They sailed for many weeks. On November 11th, the Mayflower reached America.

Summarize

How do you tell a friend about a book or movie? You might retell the story in your own words. Of course, you don't tell every single thing that happened. You tell the important parts. To retell a story this way is to summarize. **Summarizing** what you have read can help you remember information in social studies.

Learn It

- Read the whole selection. Try to state what the selection is about in your own words.

- Find important supporting details and combine them.

- Write one or two sentences to summarize what the whole selection is telling you.

Details
These details support the main idea. They can be combined.

Main Idea
This is a main idea. Use it to begin your summary.

Some holidays honor heroes, such as Martin Luther King, Jr. Others are special to the different ethnic groups in our country. For example, Irish Americans wear green to honor St. Patrick on St. Patrick's Day. Mexican Americans celebrate Cinco de Mayo. Some holidays honor Americans who fought in wars to defend our country. Veteran's Day, November 11, honors people who served in our armed forces. On Memorial Day, we remember men and women who died in wars. There are many reasons Americans celebrate holidays.

Try It

Now copy the chart. Fill in the boxes to summarize the paragraphs on page R6.

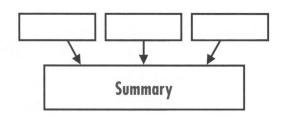

Summary

Write a summary of the selection on page R6.

Apply It

- Review the summarizing steps in Learn It.

- Make a chart like the one above. Use it to summarize the paragraphs below.

People in Barbourville, Kentucky, hold a Daniel Boone Festival to honor the explorer Daniel Boone. The festival has a parade, a fishing competition, and a quilt show. The town of Akeley, Minnesota, has a celebration called Paul Bunyan Days to honor the legend of Paul Bunyan.

Mark Twain was an American writer. People in Hannibal, Missouri, hold a festival to celebrate his stories, called National Tom Sawyer Days. It is named for character in one of Twain's books. During the festival there is a fence-painting contest and a frog-jumping contest.

Cause and Effect

Think about the last time you spent money. You had a reason. A **cause**, or reason, is why something happens. An **effect** is what happens. Thinking about causes and effects will help you understand events you read about.

Learn It

- To find a cause, ask, "Why did it happen?"

- To find an effect, ask, "What happened?"

- Look for words such as because, as a result, and so. These words often link causes and effects.

- Now look for causes and effects in the paragraph.

Cause
This sentence tells why Ana had money.

Effect
This is an effect.

Clue words
The words "as a result" and "so" are clue words. These words often link causes and effects.

Ana's grandparents and aunts gave her money for her birthday this year. As a result, Ana has $70. She decided to save $50 of the money, so she opened a savings account. So now she has $20 left to spend on things she wants.

Try It

Copy the cause and effect chart below. Then complete the chart with causes and effects from the paragraph on page R8.

Cause	→	Effect
	→	
	→	
	→	

Apply It

● Review the steps for understanding cause and effect in Learn It.

● Read the paragraph below. Then make a chart to show the two causes and two effects.

Because he wanted to buy something special, Danny saved all the money he made delivering newspapers. He wants to get a new computer game. He'd like a new baseball glove, too. Danny only has enough money for one or the other. So he needs to make a decision.

Unit 5 • Reading Skills

Compare and Contrast

Compare means to see how things are alike. **Contrast** means to see how things are different. Comparing and contrasting will help you understand what you read in social studies.

Learn It

- To compare two things, look for how they are alike.

- To contrast two things, look for ways they are different.

  Now read the passage below. Think about how the Washington Monument and the Lincoln Memorial are alike and different.

Alike
Both honor Presidents.
Both are on the Mall.

Different
The Lincoln Memorial is a wide, low building. It has a statue of Lincoln.

The Washington Monument is tall. It does not have a statue.

The Washington Monument and the Lincoln Memorial honor two of our country's greatest Presidents. Both structures are located on the Mall in Washington, D.C. and both are famous buildings. The Lincoln Memorial is a low, wide building. It has a large statue of Abraham Lincoln inside. The Washington Monument looks like a tall needle. There is no statue of Washington in the building. The building does have an elevator that carries visitors 500 feet to the top so they can look out over the city.

Try It

Copy the Venn Diagram. Then fill in the left-hand side with details about the Washington Monument. Fill in the right side with details about the Lincoln Memorial. Fill in the center with ways the two buildings are alike.

What did you look for to find how they were alike and different?

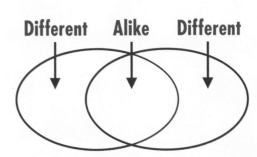

Different   Alike   Different

Apply It

- Review the steps for comparing and contrasting in Learn It.

- Read the paragraph below. Then make a Venn Diagram to compare and contrast the two eagles.

The bald eagle lives in North America near the ocean, or near lakes and rivers. It eats mostly fish. The bald eagle is not really bald--it has white feathers on its head. It is our national bird. The golden eagle is smaller than the bald eagle and lives in the West, in wide open spaces. The golden eagle is dark brown, but has lighter feathers on its head and neck that look golden. Both eagles have great eyesight and can fly very high.

Geography Handbook

Geography and You GH1

Six Essential Elements GH1

Five Themes of Geography GH2

Dictionary of Geographic Terms . GH4

Reviewing Geography Skills GH6

    Looking at Earth GH6

    A Map of the World GH7

    Reading a Map GH8

    Finding Distance and Direction GH10

    Special Maps: Landform Map GH11

    Road Map/Grid Map GH12

    Historical Map GH13

Atlas GH14

    United States: Political GH14

    United States: Physical GH16

    World: Political GH18

    North America: Political GH20

    North America: Physical GH21

    Ohio: Political GH22

    Ohio: Physical GH23

    The Fifty United States GH24

Geography and You

Geography is the study of Earth and the people, plants, and animals that live on it. Most people think of geography as learning about cities, states, and countries, but geography is far more. Geography includes learning about land—mountains, and plains—and bodies of water—oceans, lakes, and rivers.

Geography includes the study of how people adapt to living in a new place. Geography is about how people move around, how they move goods, and how ideas travel from place to place.

Geography includes so many things that geographers have divided this information into six elements, or ideas, so you can better understand them.

Six Essential Elements

The World in Spatial Terms: Where is a place located and what land or water features does this place have?

Places and Regions: What is special about a place and what makes it different from another place?

Physical Systems: What has shaped the land and climate of a place, and how does this affect the plants, animals, and people there?

Human Systems: How do people, ideas, and goods move from place to place?

Environment and Society: How have people changed the land and water of a place, and how have the land and water affected the people of a place?

Uses of Geography: How does geography influence events of the past, present, and future?

Five Themes of Geography

You have just read about six essential elements. The five themes of geography are another way to divide the ideas of geography. These themes are location, place, region, movement, and human interaction. They help us think about the world around us. Look for these themes as you read the Map Skill questions throughout the book.

1. Location

The White House

In geography, location means an exact spot on the planet. A location often means a street name and number, such as 1600 Pennsylvania Avenue, the address of the White House. You write a location when you address a letter.

2. Place

Chicago, Illinois

What makes one place different from another? Every place has physical and human features such as mountains or lakes, that describe it. Place also includes human features such as where people live, how they work, and what languages they speak.

3. Region

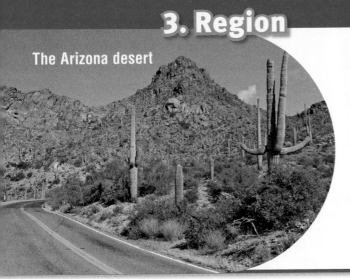

The Arizona desert

A region is a larger area than a place or location. A region is an area with common features that set it apart from other areas. One region may have many mountains or be mostly desert. People in a region may share customs and language.

4. Movement

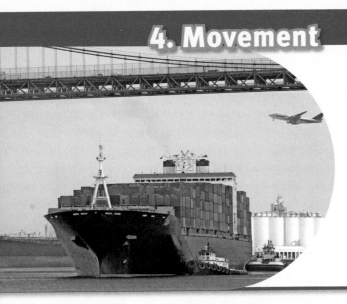

Throughout history people have moved things and themselves from one place to another. Geographers study why these movements happen. They also look at how people's movement changes an area.

5. Human Interaction

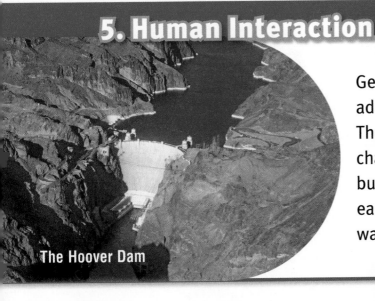

The Hoover Dam

Geographers study how people adapt to their environment. They also study how people change their environment. They build bridges to make travel easier, or build dams to store water and make electricity.

Dictionary of Geographic Terms

1. **BAY** Body of water partly surrounded by land

2. **BEACH** Land covered with sand or pebbles next to an ocean or lake

3. **CANAL** Waterway dug across the land to connect two bodies of water

4. **CANYON** Deep river valley with steep sides

5. **CLIFF** High steep face of rock

6. **COAST** Land next to an ocean

7. **DESERT** A dry environment with few plants and animals

8. **GULF** Body of water partly surrounded by land; larger than a bay

9. **HARBOR** Protected place by an ocean or river where ships can safely stay

10. **HILL** Rounded, raised landform; not as high as a mountain

11. **ISLAND** Land that is surrounded on all sides by water

12	**LAKE** Body of water completely surrounded by land	17	**PLAIN** Large area of flat land
13	**MESA** Landform that looks like a high, flat table	18	**PLATEAU** High flat area that rises steeply above the surrounding land
14	**MOUNTAIN** High landform with steep sides; higher than a hill	19	**PORT** Place where ships load and unload goods
15	**OCEAN** Large body of salt water	20	**RIVER** Long stream of water that empties into another body of water
16	**PENINSULA** Land that has water on all sides but one	21	**VALLEY** Area of low land between hills or mountains

Looking at Earth
Earth and the Globe

From outer space, Earth looks like a big blue ball with green and brown areas of land and white clouds. A globe is a model of Earth. It shows what the land and water look like on Earth.

You can see a line around the widest part of the globe. This is the equator. The equator is an imaginary line that separates the north from the south.

The farthest point north on the globe is called the North Pole. The farthest point south on the globe is called the South Pole.

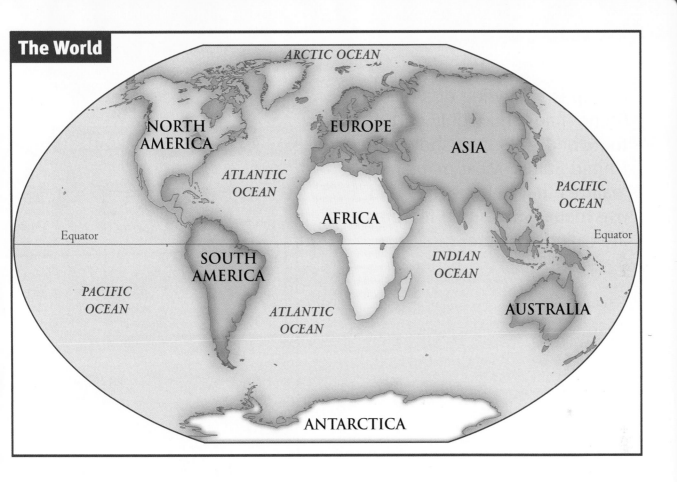

The World

ARCTIC OCEAN

NORTH AMERICA

EUROPE

ASIA

ATLANTIC OCEAN

PACIFIC OCEAN

AFRICA

Equator

SOUTH AMERICA

INDIAN OCEAN

PACIFIC OCEAN

ATLANTIC OCEAN

AUSTRALIA

Equator

ANTARCTICA

A Map of the World

A world map is a flat drawing of Earth. This map shows the continents and the oceans. Unlike a globe, a flat map can be used in a book.

The big areas of land on the Earth are called continents. The big bodies of water are called oceans.

There are seven continents on Earth. There are four major oceans. The equator divides the Earth into the northern half and the southern half.

What are the seven continents of the world?

What are the four oceans?

Reading a Map

A map is a drawing of a place. Some maps show only part of the world. This map shows the United States. Most maps have features that help us read and use maps. Some map features are called out here.

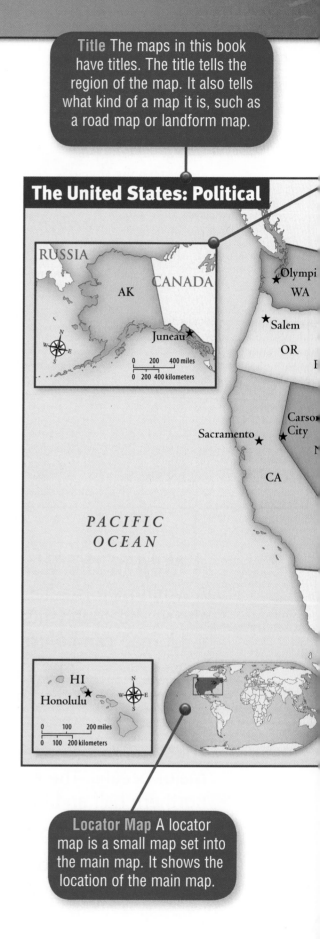

Title The maps in this book have titles. The title tells the region of the map. It also tells what kind of a map it is, such as a road map or landform map.

The United States: Political

RUSSIA
CANADA
AK
Juneau
0 200 400 miles
0 200 400 kilometers

Olympi
WA
Salem
OR

Carso
City
Sacramento
CA

PACIFIC
OCEAN

HI
Honolulu
0 100 200 miles
0 100 200 kilometers

Locator Map A locator map is a small map set into the main map. It shows the location of the main map.

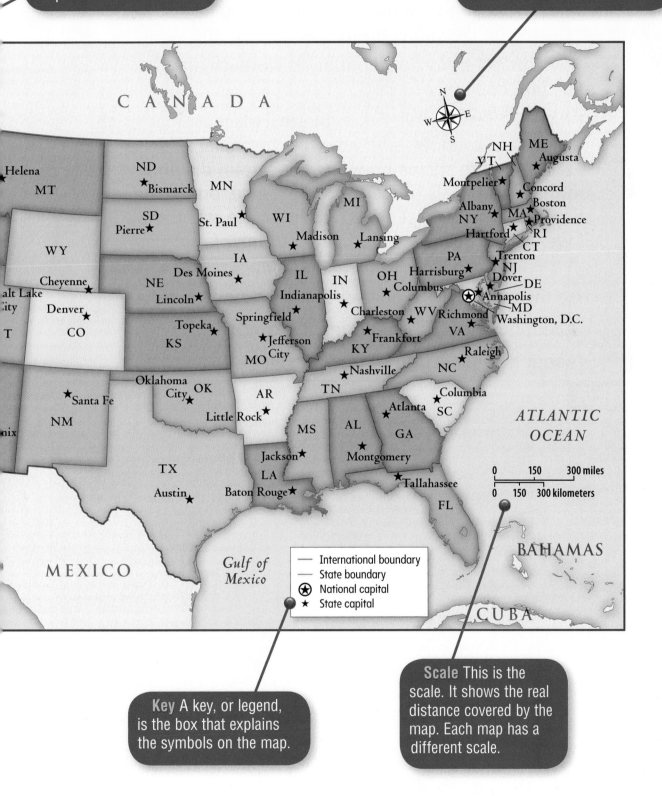

Inset Map An inset map is a small map. It shows an area that is too large, too small, or too far away to include on the main map.

Compass Rose A compass rose shows where north, south, east, and west are on the map.

Key A key, or legend, is the box that explains the symbols on the map.

Scale This is the scale. It shows the real distance covered by the map. Each map has a different scale.

CANADA

MEXICO

Gulf of Mexico

ATLANTIC OCEAN

BAHAMAS

CUBA

Helena
MT
ND ★Bismarck
MN
MI
NH ME ★Augusta
VT
Montpelier★ ★Concord
Albany ★Boston
NY MA ★Providence
Hartford★ RI
CT

SD
★Pierre
St. Paul★
WI
Madison
Lansing

WY
Cheyenne★
alt Lake City
IA
Des Moines★
NE ★Lincoln
IL
Indianapolis★
IN
OH
Columbus★
Harrisburg★
PA
Trenton★
NJ
Dover
★ ★DE
Annapolis
MD
Washington, D.C.

Denver★
CO
Topeka★
KS
Springfield★
★Jefferson City
MO
Charleston
WV
Richmond★
VA

T
Santa Fe★
NM
Oklahoma City
★OK
AR
Little Rock★
Nashville★
TN
Frankfort★
KY
Raleigh★
NC
Columbia★
SC

nix
TX
Austin★
Jackson★
LA
Baton Rouge★
MS
AL
Montgomery★
GA
Atlanta★
Tallahassee★
FL

——	International boundary
—	State boundary
✪	National capital
★	State capital

```
0        150      300 miles
|----|----|----|----|
0    150   300 kilometers
```

Finding Distance and Direction

To find direction on a map we use a compass rose. It shows the directions north, south, east, and west.

• If you travel from New London to Norwich, in what direction do you go?

A map is always smaller than the real place it represents. To understand how much smaller, we use a scale. A scale shows how much a certain distance on the map equals on Earth. For instance, on this map, one inch represents 20 miles on the real Earth. If we use the scale we can figure out how far places on the map really are from each other.

Use the map scale to answer the questions.

• About how far is it from Danbury to Waterbury?

• About how far is it from New Haven to Norwich?

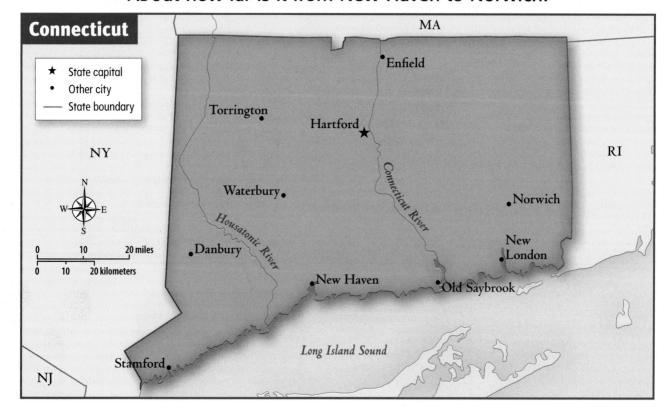

Special Maps

Maps can show many different kinds of information. Here are some kinds of special maps.

Landform Map

Landforms are different types of land on Earth. Mountains, hills, and deserts are all landforms. This map shows the landforms of Pennsylvania. You need to use the map key to understand what the the different colors on the map mean.

• Look at the map key. What does the color red show?

• What color is used for hills?

• On what kind of landform is Philadelphia located?

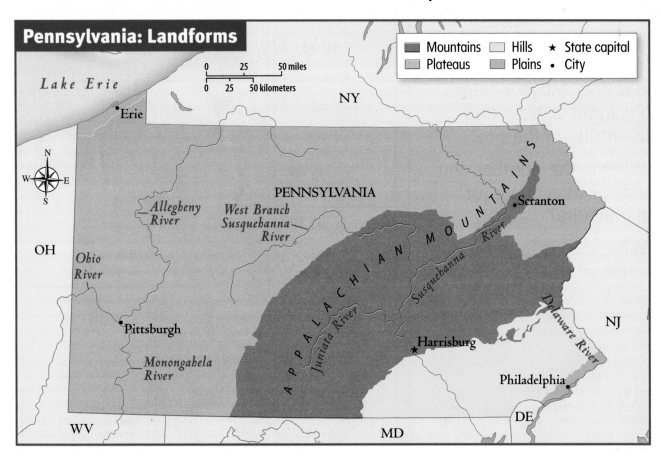

Pennsylvania: Landforms

Mountains   Hills   ★ State capital
Plateaus   Plains   • City

Lake Erie

Erie

NY

PENNSYLVANIA

N
W E
S

Allegheny River

West Branch Susquehanna River

Scranton

OH

Ohio River

Susquehanna River

Delaware River

NJ

Pittsburgh

Juniata River

Harrisburg

Monongahela River

Philadelphia

DE

WV

MD

APPALACHIAN MOUNTAINS

Road Map/Grid Map

A road map, sometimes called a route map, shows roads and highways. You would use a road map if you wanted to find know which road to take to go from one city to another, or from one state to another. This map shows the roads in New Jersey.

Grid maps help you locate exact areas. A grid map uses a pattern of lines that form boxes, or a grid. Each box is named using a letter and a number.

The map of New Jersey has a grid on it. Look at the key. The key helps you find things on the map. For instance, the key shows you that Union City is in box A2. To find Union City, put your finger on row A. Move it across to column 2. Now find Union City in the box.

• What is the number and letter of the square for Atlantic City?

• What lake is found in square A1?

New Jersey: Road Map/Grid Map

ATLANTIC OCEAN

Interstate highway
{206} U.S. highway
— Other state highway
★ State capital
• Other city

Index

Atlantic City................ D2
Cape May.................... DI
Cherry Hill................. CI
Jersey City................. A2
Lake Hopatcong.......... AI
New Brunswick........... B2
Newark...................... A2
Pine Barrens.............. C2
Trenton..................... BI
Union City................. A2
Wharton State Forest... C2

Historical Maps

A historical map shows how a place appeared at a certain time in the past. Use the key to understand symbols and colors on the map. The key gives details about the time in history. This map shows how our country looked when people from Europe first moved here. It shows the first thirteen colonies.

- What colonies were called the southern colonies?
- What city was a Pilgrim settlement?

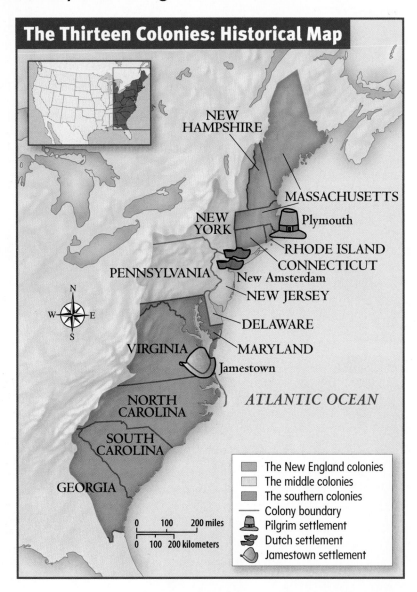

The Thirteen Colonies: Historical Map

NEW HAMPSHIRE

MASSACHUSETTS

NEW YORK

Plymouth

RHODE ISLAND
CONNECTICUT

PENNSYLVANIA

New Amsterdam

NEW JERSEY

DELAWARE

VIRGINIA

MARYLAND

Jamestown

ATLANTIC OCEAN

NORTH CAROLINA

SOUTH CAROLINA

GEORGIA

N
W E
S

0 100 200 miles
0 100 200 kilometers

- The New England colonies
- The middle colonies
- The southern colonies
— Colony boundary
- Pilgrim settlement
- Dutch settlement
- Jamestown settlement

United States: Political

ARCTIC OCEAN

RUSSIA

CANADA

Nome • Yukon River • Fairbanks

ALASKA

Anchorage •

Juneau •

N W E S

0   200   400 miles
0   200   400 kilometers

CANADA

Seattle •
Olympia ★
Spokane •
WASHINGTON

Great Falls •
Helena ★
MONTANA
Missouri R.
Billings •

Portland •
Salem ★
Eugene •
OREGON

IDAHO
Boise ★
Pocatello •

WYOMING
Casper •
Cheyenne

Eureka •
Redding •

Great Salt Lake
Ogden •
Salt Lake City ★
Provo •

Reno •
Carson City ★
Sacramento ★
NEVADA
UTAH

Denver •
COLORADO
Colorado Springs •
Pueblo •

San Francisco •
Oakland •
San Jose •
Fresno •

CALIFORNIA

Las Vegas •

Bakersfield •

Colorado River

Santa Fe ★
Albuquerque •

Los Angeles •
Long Beach •

ARIZONA
Phoenix ★

NEW MEXICO

San Diego •

Tucson •

El Paso •
Rio Grande

PACIFIC OCEAN

Gulf of California

MEXICO

Kauai   HAWAII
Niihau   Oahu
Honolulu ★   Molokai
PACIFIC   Lanai   Maui
OCEAN   Kahoolawe
Hilo •
Hawaii

N W E S

0   100   200 miles
0   100   200 kilometers

0   200   400 miles
0   200   400 kilometers

Legend:

— International boundary
— State boundary
⊛ National capital
★ State capital
• Other city

CANADA

Grand Forks
RTH KOTA
Fargo
Bismarck
UTH KOTA
re

MINNESOTA
Duluth
St. Paul
Minneapolis

Lake Superior

Marquette

MICHIGAN
Green Bay
WISCONSIN
Milwaukee
Madison

Lake Michigan

Grand Rapids
Lansing

Lake Huron

Detroit
Lake Erie

Lake Ontario

Buffalo

NEW HAMPSHIRE
VERMONT
Montpelier

MAINE
Augusta
Portland
Concord

MASSACHUSETTS

Albany
NEW YORK
Boston
Providence
Hartford
RHODE ISLAND
CONNECTICUT

Sioux Falls
BRASKA
Omaha
Lincoln

IOWA Cedar Rapids
Des Moines
ILLINOIS
Chicago
Davenport
Gary

Missouri River

INDIANA
Indianapolis
Springfield
Cincinnati

Toledo Cleveland
OHIO
Columbus

Ohio River

Pittsburgh

PENNSYLVANIA
Harrisburg

Newark New York
Trenton
Philadelphia
Dover

NEW JERSEY
DELAWARE

Baltimore
Washington, DC
Annapolis
MARYLAND

Topeka
KANSAS
Kansas City
Jefferson City
Wichita

Kansas City
St. Louis
MISSOURI
Evansville

Frankfort
Louisville
KENTUCKY

WEST VIRGINIA
Charleston

Richmond
Norfolk
VIRGINIA

Tulsa
lahoma City
OKLAHOMA

ARKANSAS
Fort Smith
Little Rock

Mississippi River

Nashville
TENNESSEE
Memphis

Tennessee River

Knoxville

NORTH CAROLINA
Raleigh
Charlotte

Columbia
SOUTH CAROLINA

ATLANTIC OCEAN

Dallas
Fort Worth
TEXAS
Austin
San Antonio

Shreveport
MISSISSIPPI
Jackson
LOUISIANA
Baton Rouge
New Orleans

Birmingham
ALABAMA
Montgomery
Mobile
Biloxi

Atlanta
GEORGIA
Columbus

Charleston
Savannah

Jacksonville

Tallahassee

Laredo
Corpus Christi

Houston

Gulf of Mexico

Orlando
FLORIDA
Tampa

Miami

BAHAMAS

N
W E
S

CUBA

GH15

United States: Physical

ARCTIC   OCEAN

RUSSIA

BROOKS RANGE
ALASKA
Mt. McKinley
20,320 ft.
(6,194 m)

Bering Strait

Arctic Circle

CANADA
Yukon River

ALASKA RANGE

Bering
Sea

Gulf of Alaska

N
W   E
S

Aleutian Islands

0   200   400 miles
0   200   400 kilometers

Puget
Sound

Mt. Rainier
14,410 ft. (4,392 m) ▲

Mt. St. Helens
8,363 ft. (2,549 m) ▲

Columbia R.

ROCKY

Missouri Ri

Mt. Hood
11,239 ft.
(3,426 m) ▲

CASCADE RANGE

COLUMBIA PLATEAU

Granite Peak
12,799 ft.
(3,901 m) ▲

Mt. Shasta
14,162 ft.
(4,317 m) ▲

Snake River

Cape
Mendocino

COAST   RANGES

Sacramento R.

SIERRA NEVADA

CENTRAL VALLEY

Great Salt
Lake

GREAT

BASIN

WASATCH RANGE

M
O
U
N
T
A
I
N
S

Lake
Tahoe

GREAT
SALT LAKE
DESERT

Kings Peak
13,528 ft.
(4,123 m) ▲

Mt. Elbert
14,433 ft.
(4,399 m) ▲

San Francisco
Bay

San Joaquin R.

Mt. Whitney
14,494 ft.
(4,418 m) ▲

Lake
Mead

COLORADO

PLATEAU

P
1
(4

PACIFIC

OCEAN

Death Valley
-282 ft.
(-86 m) ▼

Colorado River

Humphreys Peak
12,633 ft.
(3,851 m) ▲

CONTINENTAL DIVIDE

Wh
13,
(4,0

Pecos River

MOJAVE
DESERT

Channel
Islands

Salton
Sea

Gila River

SONORAN
DESERT

Gu
8,
(2,

Rio Grande

International
boundary
▲ Mountain peak
▲ Highest point
▼ Lowest point

HAWAII

Kauai

Oahu

N
W   E
S

Niihau

Molokai

PACIFIC
OCEAN

Lanai   Maui
Kahoolawe

Hawaii

0   100   200 miles
0   100   200 kilometers

Mauna Kea
13,796 ft.
(4,205 m) ▲

0   200   400 miles
0   200   400 kilometers

Gulf of California

MEXIC

CANADA

Lake of
the Woods

MESABI
RANGE

Lake Superior

GREAT LAKES

St. Lawrence River

Mt. Washington
6,288 ft.
(1,917 m)

GREEN MOUNTAINS

ADIRONDACK
MOUNTAINS

Lake
Huron

Lake
Ontario

Lake
Michigan

Mississippi River

Hudson River

Cape Cod

G R E A T

Lake Erie

ALLEGHENY
PLATEAU

Susquehanna
River

Long Island

CENTRAL PLAINS

River

ALLEGHENY
MOUNTAINS

APPALACHIAN MOUNTAINS

Delaware Bay

Platte
River

Missouri River

Ohio

River

Potomac
River

Chesapeake Bay

P L A I N S

Wabash

Arkansas

River

INTERIOR PLAINS

OZARK
PLATEAU

Tennessee River

PIEDMONT

▲ Mt. Mitchell
6,684 ft.
(2,037 m)

Cape Hatteras

ATLANTIC
OCEAN

Red River

OUACHITA
MOUNTAINS

Mississippi

River

Savannah River

ATLANTIC COASTAL PLAIN

Brazos River

Alabama

River

Chattahoochee River

Colorado River

OWARDS
LATEAU

GULF COASTAL PLAIN

Mobile
Bay

Mississippi
River Delta

Lake
Okeechobee

Galveston
Bay

Gulf of Mexico

BAHAMAS

Florida Keys

Straits of Florida

N

W   E

S

CUBA

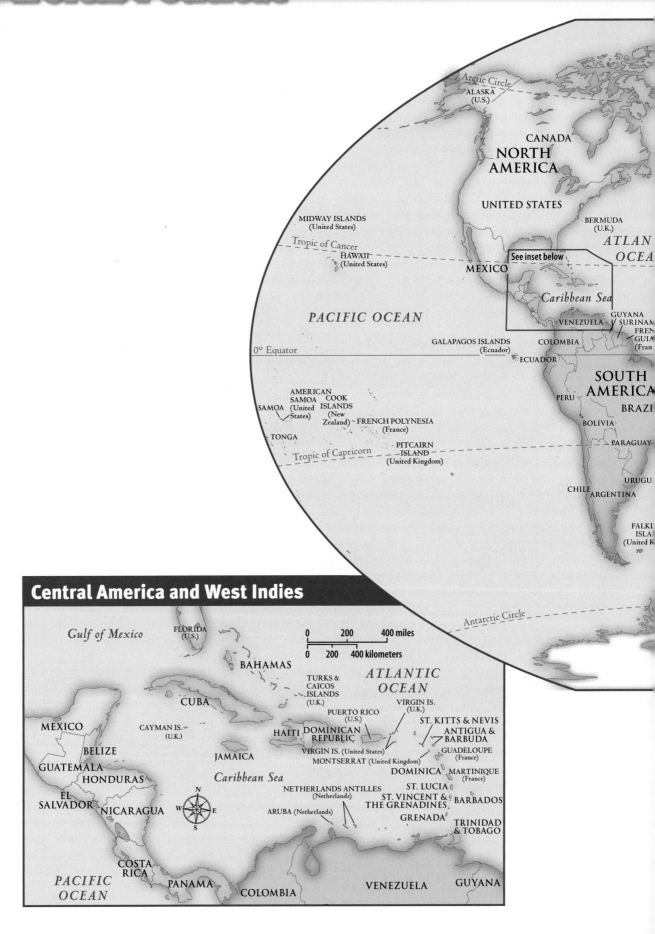

Central America and West Indies

ARCTIC OCEAN

NLAND
(mark)

SVALBARD
(Norway)

See inset below

RUSSIA

ICELAND

EUROPE

KAZAKHSTAN

MONGOLIA

ASIA

GEORGIA

UZBEKISTAN

KYRGYZSTAN

NORTH
KOREA

PACIFIC
OCEAN

ARMENIA
TURKEY

TURKMENISTAN

TAJIKISTAN

SOUTH
KOREA

JAPAN

TUNISIA

LEBANON

SYRIA

AZERBAIJAN

AFGHANISTAN

CHINA

MOROCCO

IRAQ

IRAN

PAKISTAN

BHUTAN
NEPAL

ALGERIA

LIBYA

ISRAEL
JORDAN

KUWAIT
BAHRAIN
QATAR

BANGLADESH

TAIWAN

WESTERN
SAHARA
(Morocco)

EGYPT

SAUDI
ARABIA

UNITED
ARAB
EMIRATES
OMAN

INDIA

MYANMAR
(BURMA)

LAOS

NORTHERN
MARIANA
ISLANDS
(United States)

WAKE
ISLAND
(United States)

MAURITANIA

MALI

NIGER

CHAD

SUDAN

ERITREA

YEMEN

THAILAND

VIETNAM

GUAM
(United States)

MARSHALL
ISLANDS

BURKINA
FASO

BENIN

AFRICA

NIGERIA

CENTRAL
AFRICAN
REPUBLIC

DJIBOUTI

ETHIOPIA

PHILIPPINES

GUINEA

SRI
LANKA

CAMBODIA

FEDERATED STATES
OF MICRONESIA

GHANA

IBERIA

D'IVOIRE

TOGO

CAMEROON

SOMALIA

MALDIVES

BRUNEI
MALAYSIA

PALAU

KIRIBATI

E AND PRINCIPE

UGANDA

KENYA

Equator

0°

EQUATORIAL GUINEA

GABON

RWANDA

NAURU

CONGO

DEM.
REPUBLIC
OF THE
CONGO

BURUNDI

TANZANIA

SEYCHELLES

INDIAN
OCEAN

INDONESIA

EAST
TIMOR

PAPUA
NEW
GUINEA

SOLOMON
ISLANDS

ANGOLA

COMOROS

ATLANTIC
OCEAN

ZAMBIA

MALAWI

TUVALU

NAMIBIA

ZIMBABWE

MADAGASCAR

MAURITIUS

BOTSWANA

N

REUNION
(France)

AUSTRALIA

VANUATU

FIJI
ISLANDS

W   E

MOZAMBIQUE

SWAZILAND

NEW
CALEDONIA
(France)

SOUTH
AFRICA

LESOTHO

S

FRENCH SOUTHERN &
ANTARCTIC LANDS
(France)

GEORGIA &
SANDWICH
DS (United Kingdom)

0   1,000   2,000 miles

0   1,000   2,000 kilometers

NEW
ZEALAND

ANTARCTICA

Europe

NORWAY

FINLAND

RUSSIA

SWEDEN

0   200   400 miles

ESTONIA

0   200   400 kilometers

North
Sea

DENMARK

Baltic Sea

LATVIA

N

IRELAND

UNITED
KINGDOM

LITHUANIA

RUSSIA

W   E

BELARUS

S

NETHERLANDS

ATLANTIC
OCEAN

BELGIUM

GERMANY

POLAND

LUXEMBOURG

CZECH
REPUBLIC

UKRAINE

LIECHTENSTEIN

FRANCE

AUSTRIA

SLOVAKIA

SWITZERLAND

HUNGARY

MOLDOVA

RUSSIA

SLOVENIA

ROMANIA

MONACO

SAN
MARINO

CROATIA

ANDORRA

BOSNIA &
HERZEGOVINA

SERBIA

BLACK Sea

GEORGIA

PORTUGAL

SPAIN

CORSICA
(France)

ITALY

MONT.
MACEDONIA

BULGARIA

BALEARIC IS.
(Spain)

SARDINIA
(Italy)

ALBANIA

TURKEY

GIBRALTAR (U.K.)

SICILY
(Italy)

GREECE

MOROCCO

ALGERIA

TUNISIA

MALTA

CRETE (Gr.)

CYPRUS

SYRIA

Mediterranean Sea

LEBANON

North America: Political

ASIA

ARCTIC OCEAN

EUROPE

North Pole +

Chukchi Sea

Bering Strait

Bering Sea

Beaufort Sea

GREENLAND (Denmark)

Baffin Bay

ALASKA (U.S.)

Fairbanks •

Anchorage •

Nuuk •

Davis Strait

Gulf of Alaska

Juneau •

Iqaluit •

Labrador Sea

Yellowknife •

Hudson Bay

CANADA

Newfoundland

Edmonton •

Vancouver •

Seattle •

Winnipeg •

Quebec •

Montreal •

Ottawa ⊛

Portland •

Boston •

Minneapolis •

Toronto •

New York •

ATLANTIC OCEAN

Salt Lake City •

Chicago •

Detroit •

Philadelphia •

Washington, DC ⊛

San Francisco •

Denver •

St. Louis •

UNITED STATES

BERMUDA (U.K.)

Los Angeles •

Phoenix •

Atlanta •

PACIFIC OCEAN

Dallas •

Ciudad Juarez •

Houston •

New Orleans •

BAHAMAS

Miami •

DOMINICAN REPUBLIC

ST. KITTS & NEVIS

Monterrey •

Gulf of Mexico

ANTIGUA & BARBUDA

PUERTO RICO (U.S.)

DOMINICA

MEXICO

CUBA

ST. LUCIA

Guadalajara •

HAITI

BARBADOS

JAMAICA

ST. VINCENT & THE GRENADINES

Mexico City ⊛

BELIZE

Caribbean Sea

GRENADA

TRINIDAD & TOBAGO

GUATEMALA

HONDURAS

EL SALVADOR

NICARAGUA

COSTA RICA

PANAMA

SOUTH AMERICA

— International boundary

⊛ National capital

• Other city

0   300   600 miles

0   300   600 kilometers

N
W   E
S

GH20

North America: Physical

ASIA

ARCTIC OCEAN

EUROPE

Lincoln Sea

Greenland Sea

Greenland

Baffin Bay

Point Barrow

Beaufort Sea

BROOKS RANGE

Bering Strait

Mt. McKinley
20,320 ft.
(6,194 m)

Yukon R.

ALASKA RANGE

YUKON PLATEAU

Mackenzie R.

Davis Strait

Cape Farewell

Mt. Logan
19,551 ft.
(5,959 m)

Peace R.

Churchill R.

CANADIAN SHIELD

Hudson Bay

Newfoundland

Gulf of St. Lawrence

Vancouver Island

Saskatchewan R.

Lake Winnipeg

COAST MOUNTAINS

ROCKY

Snake R.

Missouri River

Great Lakes

Gulf of Maine

Cape Cod

APPALACHIAN MOUNTAINS

Long Island

ATLANTIC OCEAN

PACIFIC OCEAN

COAST RANGES

GREAT BASIN

GREAT

Ohio R.

Chesapeake Bay

Bermuda (U.K.)

MOUNTAINS

PLAINS

Mt. Whitney
14,494 ft. (4,418 m)

Colorado R.

OZARK PLATEAU

Mississippi R.

Cape Hatteras

Death Valley
-282 ft. (-86 m)

SONORAN DESERT

Red R.

COASTAL PLAIN

BAJA CALIFORNIA

Rio Grande

SIERRA MADRE ORIENTAL

SIERRA MADRE OCCIDENTAL

Gulf of Mexico

WEST INDIES

Gulf of California

Orizaba
18,855 ft.
(5,747 m)

YUCATAN PENINSULA

Puerto Rico (U.S.)

Caribbean Sea

Lake Nicaragua

Isthmus of Panama

SOUTH AMERICA

CENTRAL AMERICA

— International boundary
⊛ National capital
▲ Mountain peak

| 0 | 300 | 600 miles |
| 0 | 300 | 600 kilometers |

N
W E
S

Ohio: Political

CANADA

Lake Erie

MI

IN

PA

WV

KY

Scale
0 — 15 — 30 miles
0 — 15 — 30 kilometers

Cities and places:

- Bryan
- Toledo ✈
- Maumee
- Bowling Green
- Defiance
- Fostoria
- Findlay
- Van Wert
- Lima
- Celina
- Wapakoneta
- Grand Lake St. Marys
- Indian Lake
- Bellefontaine
- Greenville
- Piqua
- Troy
- Marysville
- Dayton ✈
- Kettering
- Xenia
- Middletown
- Hamilton
- Wilmington
- Washington Court House
- Cincinnati ✈
- Batavia
- Point Pleasant
- Hillsboro
- Rocky Fork Lake
- Ripley
- Portsmouth
- Sandusky
- Fremont
- Tiffin
- Shelby
- Ashland
- Mansfield
- Marion
- Delaware Lake
- Mt. Vernon
- Delaware
- Columbus ✈ ★
- Chillicothe
- Circleville
- Lancaster
- Jackson
- Gallipolis
- Ironton
- Norwalk
- Elyria
- Lorain
- Cleveland ✈
- Parma
- Euclid
- Mentor
- Painesville
- Ashtabula
- Warren
- Youngstown
- Akron ✈
- Wooster
- Canton
- East Liverpool
- New Philadelphia
- Steubenville
- Coshocton
- Martins Ferry
- Newark
- Zanesville
- Dillon Lake
- Athens
- Marietta
- Belpre

Rivers:
- Maumee River
- Auglaize River
- Sandusky River
- Scioto River
- Mad River
- Little Miami River
- Miami River
- Mohican River
- Walhonding River
- Tuscarawas River
- Cuyahoga River
- Muskingum River
- Ohio River

Legend
— State boundary
✈ Airport
★ State capital
• Other city

GH22

Ohio: Physical

CANADA

Lake Erie

MI

Kelleys
Island

Maumee River

Auglaize River

Sandusky River

Cuyahoga Valley
National Park

Cuyahoga River

PA

I N T E R I O R   P L A I N S

Mobican River

Tuscarawas River

Scioto River

*Delaware
Lake*

Grand Lake
St. Marys

Indian Lake

*Walhonding
River*

A P P A L A C H I A N   P L A T E A U

IN

▲ Campbell Hill
1,550 ft. (472 m)

Mad River

Columbus ★

*Dillon
Lake*

Muskingum River

Ohio River

Dayton Aviation
Heritage National
Historical Park ■

Little Miami River

Wayne
National
Forest

WV

Great Miami River

Hopewell Culture
National Historical Park ■

Rocky Knob
1,280 ft.
(390 m) ▲

Wayne
National
Forest

*Rocky Fork
Lake*

William Howard Taft
National Historical Park ■

Washburn Hill
1,343 ft. (409 m) ▲

N
W ✦ E
S

Ohio River

Wayne
National
Forest

KY

0   15   30 miles
0   15   30 kilometers

▨	National Forest
■	National Park
—	State boundary
★	State capital
▲	Hill
▲	Highest point in Ohio

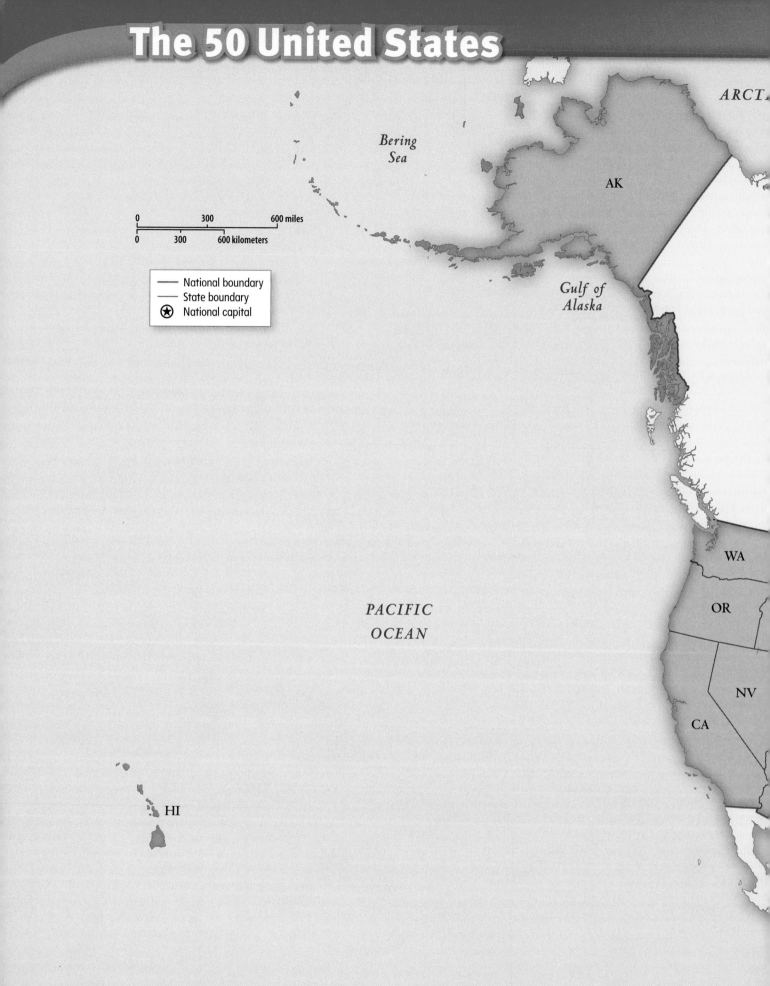

ARCT

Bering
Sea

AK

0   300   600 miles
0   300   600 kilometers

— National boundary
— State boundary
⊛ National capital

Gulf of
Alaska

PACIFIC

OCEAN

WA

OR

NV

CA

HI

GREENLAND
(Denmark)

Labrador
Sea

Hudson
Bay

CANADA

Lake
Superior

ME

Lake
Huron

Lake
Ontario

VT

NH

NY

MA

CT

RI

ND

MN

WI

MI

WY

SD

Lake
Michigan

Lake
Erie

PA

NJ

DE

MD

IA

IL

IN

OH

Washington, DC

NE

CO

KS

MO

KY

WV

VA

ATLANTIC
OCEAN

NM

OK

AR

TN

NC

SC

MS

AL

GA

TX

LA

FL

BAHAMAS

MEXICO

N

W   E

S

Gulf of
Mexico

CUBA

NT

GH25

Glossary

The Glossary will help you to pronounce and understand the meanings of the vocabulary terms in this book. The page number at the end of the definition tells where the term first appears.

Pronunciation Key									
a	at	ī	ice	u	up	th	thin		
ā	ape	î	pierce	ū	use	th	this		
ä	far	o	hot	ü	rule	zh	measure		
âr	care	ō	old	ů	pull	ə	about, taken,		
e	end	ô	fork	ûr	turn		pencil, lemon,		
ē	me	oi	oil	hw	white		circus		
i	it	ou	out	ng	song				

A

adapt (ə dapt′) To change the way you live. (p. 19)

ancestor (an′ ses tər) An early member of a family who came before you, such as a great-grandparent. (p. 133)

architecture (är′ ki tek′chər) The art or science of designing and making buildings. (p. 110)

artifact (är′ ti fakt) Something that was made or used by people in the past. (p. 53)

assembly line (ə sem′ blē līn) A line of workers performing a certain task. (p. 91)

B

bar graph (bär graf) A graph that uses bars to show information. (p. 84)

barter (bär′ tər) To trade things without using money. (p. 53)

bill (bil) A written idea for a law. (p. 231)

Bill of Rights (bil uv rīts) The first ten changes to the Constitution that protect the rights of citizens. (p. 223)

budget (buj′it) A plan for using money. (p. 157)

C

capital (kap′i təl) A city where a country or a state has its government. (p. 6)

capital resource (kap′i təl rē′ sôrs) The tools, machines, and factories people use to produce goods. (p. 165)

capitol (kap′ i təl) The building in which the state or national government meets. (p. 207)

cardinal directions (kär′də nal di rek′shəns) The directions north, east, south, and west. (p. 10)

century (sen′chərē) One hundred years. (p. 68)

citizen (sit′i zən) A person who is a member of a community, state, or country. (p. 197)

colony (kol′ ə nē) A place that is ruled by another country. (p. 61)

common good (kom′ən gu̇d) What is best for the most people. (p. 222)

community (kə mū′ ni tē) A place where people live, work, and play. (p. 5)

commute (kə mūt′) To travel a distance to and from work. (p. 16)

constitution (kän stə tü′ shən) A written plan of government. (p. 66)

consumer (kən sü′ mər) A person who buys a good or uses a service. (p. 150)

cooperate (kō äpə rāt) To work together. (p. 186)

council (sit′i koun′səl) The branch of local government that makes laws. (p. 216)

culture (kul′ chər) A way of life shared by a group of people. (p. 53)

custom (kus′təm) A way of doing something that is shared by many people. (p. 103)

D

dam (dam) A wall built across a stream or river that holds back and controls the water. (p. 37)

decade (dek′ ād) Ten years. (p. 68)

degree (di grē′) A unit of measuring distance on Earth's surface. (p. 138)

demand (di mand′) The number of people who want certain goods or sevices. (p. 168)

discrimination (di skrim′i nā′ shən) An unfair difference in the way people are treated. (p. 83)

diverse (di vûrs) Not all the same. (p. 109)

domestic trade (də mes′ tik trād) Trade that takes place within the borders of a country. (p. 184)

E

economy (i kon′ə mē) The way a place uses its money, goods, natural resources, and services. (p. 152)

ecosystem (ē′ kō sis′ təm) A community of living and nonliving things in a certain area. (p. 40)

elevator (el′ə vā tər) A machine that moves people and things up and down in a building. (p. 89)

employee (em ploi′ ē) Someone who gets paid to work for a person or a business. (p. 149)

environment (en vī′ rən mənt) The air, water, land, and other things that surround animals, people, and plants. (p. 32)

equator (i kwā′tər) An imaginary line around Earth halfway between the North Pole and the South Pole. (p. 76)

ethnic group (eth′ nik grüp) A group of people that shares the same language and culture. (p. 109)

executive branch (eg zek′ū tiv branch) The part of government that carries out laws. (p. 198)

expense (ek spens′) Something people spend money on to buy or to do. (p. 157)

explorer (ek splôr′ ər) A person who goes to a new place to find out about it. (p. 71)

export (ek spôrt′) To send goods out of a country to be sold. (p. 179)

F

factory (fak′tə rē) A place where things are manufactured. (p. 173)

festival (fes′tə vəl) A celebration. (p. 7)

flow chart (flō chärt) A chart that shows the different steps necessary to complete a process. (p. 204)

founder (found′ er) A person who starts something, such as a business or a town. (p. 125)

frontier (frun tîr) The far edge of a country where new people are just beginning to settle. (p. 71)

G

generation (jen′ə rā shn) A group of people born and living around the same time. (p. 103)

geography (jē og′rə fē) The study of Earth and the way people and animals live on it. (p. 5)

governor (guv′ər nər) The person elected to be in charge of the state government. (p. 207)

graph (graf) A drawing that shows information, such as the relationship between two things. (p. 84)

grid (grid) Lines that cross each other on a map. (p. 138)

H

hemisphere (hem′ is fîr) One half of Earth or another sphere. (p. 76)

heritage (her′i tij) Something handed down from the past. (p. 103)

hero (hîr ō) Someone you respect because of his or her achievements or personal qualities. (p. 117)

holiday (hol′ i dā) A day on which people or events are honored and celebrated. (p. 130)

human resource (hyü mən rē sôrs) A person who works for a business. (p. 165)

I

immigrant (im′i grənt) A person who comes from one country to live in another. (p. 80)

import (im pôrt′) To bring in goods made or grown in another country. (p. 178)

income (in′ kum) Money someone receives for working. (p. 157)

industry (in′ də strē) A special type of business that makes things or provides a service. (p. 79)

intermediate directions (in tər mēd′dē it di rek′shəns) A direction halfway between two cardinal directions. (p. 10)

international trade (in tər nash′ə nəl trād) Trade between different countries. (p. 182)

interstate highway (in tər stāt hī′wā′) A road that connects two or more states. (p. 212)

J

judicial branch (jü dish′ əl branch) The part of government that decides if laws are fair and follow the Constitution. (p. 199)

jury (jür′ē) A group of citizens chosen to hear the facts in a case that has been brought before a court of law, and to make a decision based on the facts and the law. (p. 222)

L

landform (land′ fôrm) The shapes of Earth's surface. (p. 19)

latitude (lat′ i tüd) A measure of distance north or south of the equator. (p. 138)

legislative branch (lej′is lā tiv branch) The part of government that writes and passes laws. (p. 199)

levee (le′ vē) A long wall made of dirt or concrete built next to a river or a lake to prevent flooding. (p. 39)

line graph (līn graf) A graph that shows information that changes over time. (p. 170)

local government (lō′kəl guv′ərn mənt) A group of people who run a town or city. (p. 215)

longitude (lon′ ji tüd) A measure of distance east or west of the prime meridian. (p. 138)

M

manufacture (man yə fak′ chər) To make a product using machines, often in large amounts. (p. 91)

map scale (map skāl) The measurement a map uses to show the real distance between places on Earth. (p. 26)

mayor (mā′ər) The head of a local government. (p. 215)

migration (mī grā′ shən) Movement from one part of the country to another. (p. 82)

mineral (min′ər əl) A natural resource that is not a plant or an animal. (p. 29)

N

natural resource (nach′ər əl rē′ sôrs) A material found in nature that people use. (p. 23)

nonprofit (non prof'it) Something that does not make money. (p. 230)

nonrenewable resource (non ri nü' ə bəl rē'sôrs) A natural resource that cannot be replaced. (p. 30)

━━━━━━━ O ━━━━━━━

opportunity cost (op' ər tü' ni tē kôst) The value of the next best choice when you choose one thing instead of another. (p. 161)

━━━━━━━ P ━━━━━━━

Patriot (pā'trē ət) A colonist who supported independence. (p. 65)

pioneer (pī' nîr') The first of a group of people to settle in an area. (p. 71)

plain (plān) An area of flat or almost flat land. (p. 20)

plateau (pla tō') An area of flat land higher than the land around it. (p. 21)

primary source (prī' mer ē sôrs) A firsthand account of events. (pp. 74, 105, 158, 202)

prime meridian (prīm mə rid' ē ən) An imaginary line that runs from the North Pole to the South Pole through Greenwich, England. (p. 76)

producer (pro dü' sər) Someone who makes, grows, or supplies goods or services. (p. 150)

profit (prof'it) The money a business makes after paying for tools, employees, and other costs. (p. 151)

━━━━━━━ R ━━━━━━━

recycle (rē sī' kəl) To reuse a product and turn it into something that can be used again. (p. 34)

region (rē jen) An area with common features that set it apart from other areas. (p. 20)

reservoir (rez'ər vwär) A place to store water. (p. 37)

revolution (rev' ə lü' shən) A fight that often leads to the end of one government and the beginning of a new one. (p. 65)

road map (rōd map) A map that shows roads. (p. 212)

rural (rüe'əl) Of or about an area that is far from a city and has farms or open country. (p. 15)

━━━━━━━ S ━━━━━━━

savings account (sā vingz ə kaunt) Money a person keeps in a bank that pays interest. (p. 162)

scarcity (skâr' si tē) A shortage of goods and services that are available. (p. 168)

settler (set' lər) A person who moves to find land. (p. 56)

skyscraper (skī'skrā pər) A very tall building. (p. 89)

slavery (slā' və rē) Forcing people to work without pay and without freedom. (p. 59)

sovereign (sov' ərin) Independent; not controlled by others. (p. 219)

specialize (spesh'ə līz) To make one thing very well. (p. 176)

sphere (sfîr) A round object like a ball. (p. 76)

state highway (stāt hī'wā') A road that begins and finishes inside a state. (p. 212)

suburb (sub'ûrb) A community near a large city. (p. 14)

supply (sə plī') The amount of goods or services that are available. (p. 168)

T

tax (taks) Money paid to a government for services. (p. 62)

territory (ter'i tôr'ē) An area of land owned by a country. (p. 72)

time line (tīm līn) A list that tells the order of important events. (p. 68)

tradition (trə dish' ən) A custom handed down from the past . (p. 133)

transcontinental (trans kon tə nen'təl) Crossing an entire continent. (p. 87)

transportation (trans pər tā'shən) A way of getting from one place to another. (p. 16)

U

urban (ûr'bən) Relating to a city and its surrounding communties. (p. 13)

V

value (val' yū) An idea that people in a culture care about and think is important. (p. 117)

volunteer (vol' ən tîr') A person who chooses to do something without getting paid. (p. 229)

Y

year (yîr) Any period of 12 months. (p. 68)

Index

This index lists many topics that appear in the book, along with the pages on which they are found. Page numbers after an *m* refer you to a map.

A

Adams, Samuel, 64
Adaptation, 19
Adelaide, Australia, 218, *m218*
Adelaide Festival of Arts, 218
Aesop, 119
Africa
 animals of, 41
 goods of, *m177*
 immigrants from, 58–59, 101, 106
 map, *m77*
 musical instruments of, 112
African Americans
 in American Revolution, 65
 and discrimination, 83
 and employment, 82, 83
 and equal rights, 130, 223, 234
 and Harlem Renaissance, 112
 and Juneteenth, 130
 and Martin Luther King, Jr. Day, 130
 migration of, 82, 110
 and music, 99, 112
 and slavery, 59, 130, 203
Africans in America, 58–59. *See also* Slavery
Agriculture. *See* Farmers and farming
Air, 29, 32, 40
Airplanes, 90
Akron, Ohio, 115
Alaska, 19, 128
Aldabran giant tortoise, 41

America, 56. *See also* Colonies and colonists
American Equal Rights Association, 234
American flag, 200, 202
American Indians. *See* Native Americans
American Revolution
 See also Colonies and colonists
 and Boston Tea Party, 64
 and British rules, 62–63, 64
 and Declaration of Independence, 65
 on time line, 69
Amish, 146
Ancestors, 133
Animals
 and ecosystems, 40
 and environment, 32, 40, 41, 42–43
 and 4-H clubs, 126
 of the Great Lakes, 42–43
 and Lewis and Clark, 73
 livestock, 15, 166, 167
 as natural resource, 29
 pets, 15, 126
 protecting, 41, 211
 in stories, 118, 119
Ansonia, Ohio, 17
Antarctica, *m77, m177*
Anthony, Susan B., 234
Appalachian Mountains,71
Apples, 166
Appleseed, Johnny, 120
Arbor Day, 126
Architecture, 110–11
 See also Buildings

Arctic Ocean, *m77*
Arizona
 and Children's Day, Book Day, 127
 Grand Canyon, 18, 120
 Hoover Dam, 36, 37
 Kartchner Caverns State Park, 211
 and Native Americans, *m225*
 plateaus of, 21
 taxes in, 208, 209
Arkansas, 232
Armed forces, 128
Armstrong, Louis, 112
Artifacts, 53, 58
Artists, 110–11, 112
Asia
 See also specific countries
 goods of, *m177*
 immigrants from, 80, 101
 map, *m77*
 and money, 155
 music from, 109
Assembly lines, 91, 147, 173
Athens, Ohio, 163
Atlantic Ocean, 61, *m77*
Austin, Texas, 130
Australia, *m77, m177*, 218, *m218*
Automobiles
 and assembly lines, 147, 173
 and cross-country travel, 90
 and licenses, 210
 and mountains, 21

and natural resources, 32
and steel, 174, 175
and trade, 182, 183, *m183*

B

Babe, the blue ox, 120
Bald eagles, 203
Banks, 162, 165
Barbourville, Kentucky, 125
Barges, 23
Bar graphs, 84–85, 102
Barnesville, Minnesota, 125
Bartering, 53, 154
Baseball, 13
Basketball, 113
Battle of St. Clair, 51
Beliefs, 117
Bellamy, Francis, 202
Benson, Arizona, 211
Big Darby Creek, 7
Bill of Rights, 223, 233
Bills, 205, 231. *See also* Laws
Blendon Woods State Park, 7
Blizzards, 24, 25
Blue Jacket, 51
Blues music, 112
Boats, 23
Bogor, Indonesia, 187
Books
 accordion book project, 188–89
 Children's Day, Book Day, 127
 textbook publication, 184–85

Boone, Daniel, 70, 71, 125
Boston, Massachusetts
    and taxes, 62
Boston Tea Party, 64
    and British rules, 63, 64, 65
Boston Harbor, 51, 63, 64
Branches of government
    in local government, 215, 216–17
    in national government, 198–99
    in state government, 207
Brazil, *m176*
Bread for the Day of the Dead, 133
Bridges, 19
British soldiers, 65, 200.
    See also Great Britain
Budgets
    about, 157
    of businesses, 158, 160–61
    and expenses, 157, 158, 159, 160–61
    of families, 159
    of governments, 158
    and income, 157, 159, 160–61
    and making choices, 160–61
    and opportunity costs, 161
    project, 192
Buildings
    changes in, 88, 89
    cultural influences on, 110–11
    and geography, 19
    green buildings, 33
    of Native Americans, 54
    points of view on, 115
    and trees, 35
Bunyan, Paul, 120–21
Buses, 16
Businesses, 148–55
    See also Goods
    and accordion book project, 188–89

and budgets, 158, 160–61
and the community, 152
and employees, 149, 151, 158
farming, 165 (*see also* farmers and farming)
and free enterprise, 169
and money, 154–55
and prices, 150–51, 168, 169, 174
producers and consumers, 150–51
specialization of, 176, *m176–77*, 184

Cahokia, 52, 53, 54
Cairo, Egypt, *m139*
Caledonian Club of San Francisco, California, 134
California
    and Earth Day celebrations, 38
    food from, 152, 166, *m166*
    highland dancing in, 134
    map of, *m139*
    and Yosemite National Park, 33
Campbell, Ben Nighthorse, 219
Canada
    goods of, *m176*, 178
    and Louisiana Purchase, 73
    map of, *m153*
    money of, 153
    and sports, 113
    and trade, 179, 182, 183, *m183*
Canoes, 55
Cans, 34
Canton, Ohio, 194
Capital resources, 165, 169
Capitals
    national capital, 198–99 (*see also* Washington, D.C.)

state capitals, 6, 207
Capitol Buildings
    in national government, 199
    in state government, 207
Cardinal directions, 10–11
Caribbean, 101, *m101*
Cars. *See* Automobiles
Caverns, 2
Celebrations, 124–31
    about, 125
    of heritage, 130–31
    of independence, 128–29
    reasons for, 126–27
Celtic Society of Southern Maryland, 134
Central America, 101, *m101*, 178
Central Pacific Railroad, 87
Centuries, 68
Chapman, John, 120
Chart and graph skills
    using bar graphs, 84–85, 102
    using flow charts, 204–5
    using line graphs, 170–71
    using pictographs, 96, 102
    using time lines, 68–69
Chicago, Illinois
    and African Americans, 82
    commuting to, 16
    sister cities, 186
    steel factories of, 174, 176
Children, 81, 127
China
    Chinese Moon Festival, 133
    Chinese New Year, 114, 135
    goods of, 176, *m177*, 178, 182
    immigrants from, 87
Cincinnati, Ohio, 1, 85, 99
Cinco de Mayo, 114, 131

Circleville Pumpkin Show, 168
Cities, 78–83
    See also specific cities
    about, 13
    and African Americans, 82–83
    and buildings, 89
    and ecosystems, 42
    and germs, 88
    growth of, 79
    and immigrants, 80–81
    migration to, 82
    of Native Americans, 53, 54
    sister cities, 186–87
    and suburban areas, 14
    and water, 37
    and weather, 39
Citizens and citizenship
    and being informed, 227
    and compromise, 67
    good citizens, 222, 229, 233
    and money management, 163
    and old buildings, 115
    participation in government, 197, 232
    rights of, 197
    and taxes, 208
    and trees, 35
    and volunteer work, 229, 230–31
    and voting, 233, 234–35
City councils, 216, 218
City seals, 236–37
Civilizations, 54
Clark, William, *m72*, 72–73
Class presidents, 204
Clay models, 45
Claysville, Pennsylvania, 227
Cleveland, Ohio, 3, 13, 115
Climate, 24–25, 79, 166, 178
Clothing
    clothing factories, 79
    and culture, 109

of immigrants, 106, 107
sold from carts, 80
and trade, 182
and weather, 24
Coal
mining of, 79
nonrenewable
resource, 30
and steel factories,
174, 176
uses for, 29, 31
Coins, 153
Colonies and colonists,
60–66
See also Boston,
Massachusetts
Jamestown
about, 61
and American
Revolution, 65, 69
and British rules, 63, 64
goods from, 58
map of, *m61*
and taxes, 62
Colorado, 21
Colorado River, 36, 37
Columbia, Missouri, 40
Columbus, Christopher,
56, 68
Columbus Jazz and Rib
Fest, 7
Columbus Museum of
Art, 147
Columbus, Ohio, 4, 5, 6, 7,
8-9, 17, 147, 163, 207
Common good, 222, 240
Communities, 4–9, 12–17,
52–59
about, 5
activities, 48
and businesses, 152
celebrations of, 126
changes in, 96, 144
fun in, 7
and geography, 5
helping in, 8–9, 230–31
history of, 92–93
of immigrants, 106
of Native Americans,

53–55 (*see also* Native
Americans)
and natural resources,
30–31, 32, 44
in nature (*see*
Ecosystems)
in rural areas, 15, 17
of settlers, 56–58
(*see also* Jamestown)
in suburban areas, 14, 16
on a time line, 68
and transportation,
16–17
in urban areas, 13
work in, 6
Commuting, 16
Compass roses on maps,
10, *m11*
Competition, 151
Composition project, 192
Congress
and executive
branch, 198
and laws, 199, 205
Constitution of the United
States,
about, 66, 197, 224
and balance of
power, 198
and Bill of Rights,
223, 233
and judicial branch, 199
and voting rights, 235
Consumers, 150, 151, 152
Continents, *m76*
Cooking, 9. *See* also Food
Cooperation, 180–87
about, 186
and compromise, 67
of countries, 181,
182–83
of sister cities, 186–87
of states, 184–85
Copper, 29, 30, 31
Corn, 52, 167
Costs, 151
Cotton, 166, 167
Councils, 216, 218

Countries, cooperation
between, 181, 182–83
County Fairs, 126
Courts and judges, 199,
222. *See also* Judicial
branch
Covered wagons, 74, 75
Cowries, 155
Cows, 167
Coyotes, 118
Creek Street, Ketchikan,
Alaska, 19
Crownsville, Maryland, 106
Culture, 108–14, 132–37
See also Stories
and architecture, 110–11
and dance, 114, 133,
134, 135
and ethnic groups, 109,
131, 140, 141
and festivals, 133, 186
and food, 109, 133
and immigrants, 80, 81,
106-7, 109
and music, 99, 109, 112
of Native Americans,
53, 54
and painting, 110–11
and puppet shows,
136–37
and sports, 113
and traditions, 133
of United States, 107,
110–11
and values, 117
Customs
of ethnic groups, 109
of immigrants, 103,
106–7
and storytelling, 118

D

Dams, 36, 37
Dance
about, 114
in China, 114, 135
in Ghana, 133
in Mexico, 114
in Scotland, 134

Daniel Boone Festival, 125
Datagraphics, 90, 102, 183
Day of the Dead, 133
Dayton, Ohio, 115
Decades, 68
Declaration of
Independence, 65,
69, 203
Deer, 73
Degrees on maps,
138, *m138*
Demand, 168, 169, 174
Democracy in Action,
67, 227
DeSoto, Texas, 185
Detroit, Michigan, 82,
91, 173
Directions, 10, *m11*,
m212–13
Discrimination, 83
Disease, 88, 89
Distances, 26–27
Diversity, 109
Doctors, 210
Doctors Without
Borders, 181
Domestic trade, 184–85
Dragon dance, 114, 135
Durban, South Africa, *m139*

E

Eagle Bluffs, Missouri, 40
Eagles, 203
Earth Day, 38
Earth Force, 34
East (direction), 10, *m11*,
m212–13
East (region), 87
Eastern Hemisphere,
m76, m77
Economy
about, 152
and automobile
manufacturing, 174
and businesses, 152
and free enterprise, 169
imports and exports,
178–79 (*see also* Trade)
and scarcity, 168, 169

Ecosystems
about, 40
of the Great Lakes,
42–43
of Mauritius, 41
Edison, Thomas, 89
Education, 208, 209, 210
Eisenhower, President
Dwight D., 186
El Día de los Muertos, 133
El Día de los Niños, El Día
de los Libros, 127
Elections and voting, 194,
222, 233, 234–35
Electricity
and dams, 36, 37
and green buildings, 33
and hybrid cars, 32
sources of, 31, 39
and wind, 39
Elevators, 89
Elizabeth II, 153
Elkhart County 4-H Fair, 126
Emergencies, 158, 159
Employees
about, 149
paying, 158
and profits, 151
Employment. *See* Work
England
See also Great Britain
and Boston Tea
Party, 64
colonists and settlers
from, 56
and goods from
America, 58
puppet shows of, 136
English (language), 104
Entertainment, 81
Environment, 36–43
See also Natural
Resources
and animals, 32, 40, 41,
42–43
changing, 37
importance of, 32
and National & Global
Youth Service Day, 229

and plants, 32, 40,
42–43
protecting, 32, 33,
38–39, 211
and recycling, 34
Equal rights, 130, 223, 234
Equator, *m76–77*, 138
Ethnic groups
and celebrations, 131
customs of, 109
and food, 140, 141
and holidays, 131
Europe
and American
colonies, 61
goods of, *m177*
immigrants from, 80, 101
map, *m77*
Executive Branch
in local government, 215
in national government,
198 (*see also* President
of the United States)
in state government, 207
Expenses
about, 157
of businesses, 158
and choices, 160–61
of families, 159
of governments, 158
Explorers, 71, 72–73
Exports, 179
Expository composition
project, 192

Fables, 119
Factories
about, 173
and assembly lines,
91, 173
clothing factories, 79
and environment, 42
steel factories, 174, 175
Fairs, 126
Families
and ancestors, 133
and budgets, 159
and heritage, 103

Fan dance, 114
Farmers and farming,
164–69, 170
about, 165
and bartering, 154
colonial farmers, 61
and consumers, 150,
151, 152
crops of, 166, *m166–67*
farmers' markets, 5
farms and farmland in
U.S., 170–71
and free enterprise, 169
and livestock, 166, 167
as producers, 150–51
resources of, 165
and rural
communities, 15
supply and demand,
168–69
and water, 23, 37
and weather, 39
Festival of Candles, 128
Festivals
about, 7
celebrating
independence, 128
and communities, 125
and culture, 133, 186
and food, 125, 133
and local
government, 218
and puppet shows,
136–37
Fifteenth Amendment, 234
Fire departments, 214,
215, 216
Flag, American, 200, 202
Flooding, 39
Florida, 25, 99, 167
Flow charts, 204–5
Food
of animals, 40
celebrating, 125
and consumers, 150–51
crops, 166, *m166–67*
(*see also* Farmers and
farming)
and culture, 109, 133

and ethnic groups,
140, 141
food sharing programs,
8–9
of immigrants, 106
imports of, 178
of Native Americans,
52, 55
and natural resources, 29
and settlers, 56, 57
sold from carts, 80
and trade, 152, *m152*
and traditions, 133
and water, 23
Ford, Henry, 91, 173
Ford Motor Company, 173
Forests, 118
Fort Boonesborough, 71
Fort Recovery, Ohio, 51
Fort Wayne, Indiana, 187
Founders, 125
Founder's Day, 126
4-H, 126
"The Fox and the
Grapes," 119
France
and Doctors Without
Borders, 181
and Louisiana
Purchase, 72
and marionettes, 137
and Mexico, 131
and sports, 113
Freedom in America
See also Rights
and African servants, 59
and American
Revolution, 65, 69, 200
and Bill of Rights,
223, 233
celebrations of, 128
in colonies, 61
and Constitution, 197
and flag, 202
and immigrants, 80, 101
and Liberty Bell, 203
and national anthem,
200–201

and Pledge of
Allegiance, 202
and settlers, 56
Free enterprise, 169
Frog jumping contests, 125
Frontier, 71. *See also* West
(frontier)

Gary, Indiana, 174, 176
Gasoline, 30, 31, 32
Generations, 103
Geographers, 138–39
Geography, 18–25
    and communities, 5
    and landforms, 19
    and population, 79
    regions, *m20–21*, 20–21
    and water, 19, 22–23
    and weather, 24–25
George III, 65
Ghana, 133
Giant tortoises, 41
Glass, 34, 58
Glenn, John and Annie, 195
Global Connections, 41,
    54, 129, 153, 218
Globes, *m76–77*
Goddesses and gods, 118
Gold, 30, 56, 75
Golden Spike, 87
Goods, 172–79
    See also Businesses
    and demand, 168
    imports and exports,
    178–79
    manufacturing of, 91,
    173, 174–75
    of Native Americans, 53
    prices of, 150–51, 168,
    169, 174
    producers of, 150–51
    and specialization, 176,
    m176–77, 184
    of states, 184
    and trade, 53, 178–79,
    182–85, *m183*
Goshen, Indiana, 126

Government
    See also Local
    government; National
    government; State
    government
    in Australia, 218
    branches of, 198–99,
    207, 215, 216–17
    and budget, 158
    capital, national,
    198–99 (*see also*
    Washington, D.C.)
    capitals, state, 6, 207
    capitol buildings,
    199, 207
    and elections, 222, 233
    employees of, 6, 210,
    215, 216
    expenses, 158
    and laws, 198–99, 205,
    222, 223, 224
    of Native Americans,
    219, 225, 226
    need for, 240
    participation in, 197, 232
    right to petition, 197
    and services, 208–11,
    216–18, 240
    and taxes, 208–9,
    216–17
Governors, 207
Grand Canyon, Arizona,
    18, 120
Graph skills. *See* Chart and
    graph skills
Great Britain, 62–63, 64,
    65. *See also* England
Great Lakes
    beaches of, 13
    ecosystems of, 42–43
    maps, *m11, m42–43*
    and Paul Bunyan, 121
Great Lakes Basin
    Ecosystem Team, 43
Great Migration, 82, 110
Greece, 176, m177
Greek architecture, 110, 111
Green buildings, 33

Greenville, Ohio, 17
Greenwich, England, m76
Gulf of Mexico, 30

Habitat for Humanity, 230
Hand puppets, 136
Hannibal, Missouri, 125
Harlem Renaissance, 112
Health
    health issues, 88, 89
    health programs, 210
Hearst Tower, 33
Helping people, 8–9
Hemispheres, m76–77
Henry, Joseph, 89
Heritage, 103, 130–31
Heroes, 117, 118
Highland games, 134
Highways
    and government, 217
    and road maps, 212,
    m213
    taxes for, 208
Hockey, 113
Holidays
    about, 130–31
    and American flag, 202
    and dance, 114
    and food, 133
    and heritage, 130–31
Holtz-Eakin, Douglas, 158
Holmes County, Ohio, 146
Homes, 230
Honesty, 123
Hong Kong, 182
Hoover Dam, 36, 37
Hoover Reservoir, 7
Hopi, 118, 225, *m225*, 226
Horses, 73, 88
House of Representatives,
    U.S., 199
Houses, 6, 24
"How Coyote Placed the
    Stars," 118
Human resources, 165, 169
Hurricanes
    danger of, 25

Hurricane Katrina,
    39, 230
Hybrid cars, 32

Idaho, 166
Illinois
    See also Chicago, Illinois
    food from, 166
    map of, *m11*
    and Native Americans, 53
    and steel, 174, 176
    volunteers in, 231
Immigrants, 100–107
    about, 101
    communities of, 80–81
    and culture, 80, 81,
    106–7, 109
    customs of, 103, 106–7
    new lives of, 104–5
    and population, 102
    reasons for
    immigration, 101
    and transcontinental
    railroad, 87
Imports, 178–79
Income, 157, 159, 160–61
Income tax, 208
Independence
    of India, 129
    of United States, 65,
    128 (*see also* American
    Revolution)
Independence, Missouri, 74
Independence Day (July
    4th), 65, 128
Independence Hall, 64
India, 129, *m129*
Indiana
    Fort Wayne, 187
    maps, *m11, m212–13*
    and steel, 174, 176
Indian Ocean, *m77*
Indonesia, 136, 187
Industries, 79
Interest, 162
Intermediate directions,
    10–11

International Space Station, 180, 181
International Trade, 182–83, 184
Interstate highways, 212, *m213*
Interviews, 92–93, 188
Inventions, 88, 89
Iowa, *m11*
Irish immigrants, 87
Iron, 30, 176
Italy, 137

J

Jacobs Field, Cleveland, Ohio, 13
Jamestown
  Africans in, 58–59
  arrival of settlers, 56, 68
  growth of, 58, 61
  trades of, 58
  winter in, 56–57
Japan
  goods of, 176, *m177*
  imports of, 179
  money of, 153
  sister cities in, 187
Jazz, 112
Jefferson, Thomas, 65, 72
Jersey City, New Jersey, 140
Jobs. *See* Work
John and Annie Glenn Historic Site and Exploration Center, 195
Judicial branch
  in local government, 216
  in national government, 199
  in state government, 207
July 4, 1776, 65, 128
Juneteenth, 130
Jury duty, 222

K

Kartchner Caverns State Park, 211

Kennecott Copper Mine in Utah, 29
Kentucky, 71, 125
Ketchikan, Alaska, 19
Key, Francis Scott, 200
King, Martin Luther, Jr., 130, 223
Kite flying, 129
Knives, 55
Kykotsmovi Village, 225

L

Lacrosse, 113
Lake Erie, *m11*, 13, *m43*
Lake Huron, *m11*, *m43*
Lake Mead, 37
Lake Michigan, *m11*, *m42*
Lake Ontario, *m11*
Lakes, *m20–21*, 22, 23. *See also* specific lakes
Lake Superior, *m11*, *m42*
Land and Landforms
  about, 19
  clay models of, 45
  and daily life, 20
  learning about, 44
  levees, 39
  as natural resource, 32
  open land, 15
  types of, 20–21
Language, 13, 104, 109
Latitude, *m138–39*, 138–39
Lawmakers. *See* Legislative branch
Lawrence, Jacob, 110, 111
Laws, 220–26
  about, 197, 221
  and bills, 205, 231
  and citizenship, 222
  and common good, 222
  and Constitution, 224
  and executive branch, 198
  flow chart about, 205
  and government, 205, 222, 223, 224
  and judicial branch, 199
  and legislative branch, 199, 207, 224

  and Native Americans, 225–26
Legends, 122–23
Legislative branch
  and laws, 199, 205, 207, 224
  in local government, 216
  in national government, 199
  role of, 232
  in state government, 207
Lessons in stories, 119
Levees, 39
Lewis, Meriwether, *m72*, 72–73
Liberty Bell, 203
Libraries, 216
Licenses, 210
"The Life of Washington" (Weems), 123
Light, 88, 89
Line graphs, 170–71
Lititz, Pennsylvania, 128
Littering, 222, 227
Livestock, 15, 166, 167
Local government, 214–19
  about, 215
  branches of, 215, 216–17
  and Native Americans, 219
  in other countries, 218
  and services, 216–17, 218, 240
  and taxes, 216–17
Longitude, *m138–39*, 138–39
Los Angeles, California, 38
Louisiana, 39
Louisiana Purchase, 72, *m72*, 73
Lumberjacks, 120
Lutz, Florida, 67

M

Manufacturing, 91, 173, 174–75
Map skills
  and direction, 10–11, *m11*

  and hemispheres, 76, *m76–77*
  and landforms, 44, *m45*
  and latitude and longitude, 138, *m138–39*
  and Lewis and Clark, 72, *m72–73*
  and map scale, 26–27, *m27*
  and road maps, 212–13, *m213*
Marietta, Ohio, 50
Marionettes, 137
Martin Luther King, Jr. Day, 130
Maryland, 106, 134
Mauritius, 41, *m41*
Mayors, 215, 218
McKinley, William, 194
Medicine, 89
Meeting in groups (freedom), 197
Memorial Day, 128
Mexico
  and Cinco de Mayo, 114, 131
  dances in, 114
  festivals in, 133
  goods of, *m176*
  immigrants from, 101
  maps, *m54*, *m101*
  money of, 153
  and Native Americans, 54
  and trade, 183, *m183*
Miami, Florida, 99
Michigan
  and Ford Motor Company, 91, 173
  maps, *m11*, *m115*
  migration to, 82
  points of view from, 115
Middle East, 182
Mid-Ohio FoodBank, 8-9
Midwest (region), 20–21, *m21*, 167
Migration, 82, 110
Military, 128
Minerals, 29
Minnesota, *m11*, 120

Mississippi River, 39, 72
Missouri
  levees of, 39
  map of, *m163*
  and National Tom
    Sawyer Days, 125
  prairie ecosystem of, 40
  sister city of, 187
Mitchell, Edgar, 22
Model T cars, 91
Money, 156–62
  See also Budgets
  and banks, 162, 165
  and bartering, 154
  borrowing, 165
  earning, 149, 150–51,
    160
  expenses, 157, 158,
    159, 160–61
  of families, 159
  of governments, 158
  history of, 155
  income, 157, 159,
    160–61
  kinds of, 153
  managing money, 157,
    161, 163
  saving, 162
Moon Festival of China, 133
Mora, Pat, 127
Morals in stories, 119
Morgan, Garrett, 3
Mott, Lucretia, 233, 234
Mound building of Native
  Americans, 53, 54
Mountains, 20, *m20–21*,
  21, 118
Muir, John, 33
Museums
  and immigrants, 81
  Columbus Museum of
    Art, 147
  National Museum of the
    American Indian, 131
  Rock and Roll Hall of
    Fame and Museum, 13
Music
  and culture, 99, 109, 112
  and dance, 114

of immigrants, 106
as tradition, 133
Myths, 118

National & Global Youth
  Service Day, 229
National anthem, 200–201
National government,
  196–203
  See also Symbols
  about, 197
  branches of, 198–99
  and taxes, 208
National Museum of the
  American Indian, 131
National Park Service, 33
National Tom Sawyer
  Days, 125
National Underground
  Railroad Freedom
  Center, 99
Native Americans
  celebrations of, 131
  cities, 53, 54
  and Daniel Boone, 71
  food of, 52, 55
  government of, 219,
    225, 226
  and Lewis and Clark, 73
  mound buildings, 53, 54
  and National Museum of
    the American
    Indian, 131
  and natural resources, 55
  and pioneers, 74
  and Pocahontas, 55, 57
  reservations, 225, *m225*
  and sports, 113
  and storytelling, 117, 118
Natural disasters, 158
Natural resources, 28–34
  See also specific natural
  resources, such as Water
  about, 23, 29
  activities, 48
  and communities,
    30–31, 32, 44
  and farming, 165

and manufacturing, 175
and Native Americans, 55
nonrenewable, 30, 31
protecting, 32–33, 211
and recycling, 34
regions for, *m31*
renewable, 39
and specialization, 176
and state
  government, 211
types of, 30–31
Navajo, 225
Needs and wants, 157, 192
Neighborhoods, 13, 80–81
Nelson, Gaylord, 38
Nevada, 37
New Concord, Ohio, 195
New Delhi, India, 129
New Hampshire, 231
New Mexico, 127
New Orleans, Louisiana
  and Hurricane Katrina, 39
  and Louisiana Purchase,
    72, 73
News, 88
Newspapers, 34
New Year in China, 114, 135
New York
  food from, 167
  landforms in, 20
  maps, *m11*, *m115*
  points of view from, 115
  and Seneca Falls
    Convention, 233, 234
New York City
  goods of, 152, *m152*
  green buildings of, 33
  and Harlem
    Renaissance, 112
  and immigrants, 81, 105
  and jobs, 82, 83
  population, 13, 79, 84
  and textbook
    publication, 184
  and travel, *m90*
Nigeria, 106, *m177*
Nineteenth Amendment,
  235
Nonprofit groups, 230

Nonrenewable resources,
  30, 31
North (direction), 10, *m11*,
  m212–13
North America, *m77*, 113,
  m176
North Carolina
  International Festival,
  186
Northeast (region), 20–21,
  m21
Northern Cheyenne Nation,
  219
Northern Hemisphere,
  m76, *m77*
North Pole, *m76*, *m77*

Oak Park, Illinois, 16
Oceans, 22
Ohio
  Akron, 115
  Ansonia, 17
  Athens, 163
  Canton, 194
  Capitol building, 207
  Caverns, 2
  Cincinnati, 1, 85, 99
  Circleville, 168
  Cleveland, 3, 13
    government in,
      215, 216
    maps, *m11*, *m115*
    points of view
      from, 115
    and textbook
      publication, 184
  Columbus, 4, 5, 6, 7,
    8-9, 17, 147, 163, 207
    about, 5
    capitol city role of, 6
    and festivals, 186
    fun in, 7
    helping one another
      in, 8, 9
    map of, *m5*
    and state fair, 7
    work in, 6
  Dayton, 115

Fort Recovery, 51
Holmes County, 146
Marietta, 50
New Concord, 195
Portsmouth, 115
Rendville, 13
Rossburg, 15, 17
State University, 98
Toledo, 26, 27, 35
Urbana, 35
West Liberty, 2
Wooster, 35
Youngstown, 163
Ohio Connections, 44-45,
    92-93, 140–41, 188-89,
    236-37
Ohio State University, 98
Oil, 30, 31, 32, 182
Omaha, Nebraska, 87
Opportunity costs, 161
Oranges, 167
Oregon Trail, 74–75, 96
Otis, Elisha, 89

Pacific Ocean, m77
Painting, 110–11
Pan de Muerto, 133
Paper, 29
Parades, 128
Parks, 208, 211, 217
Parthenon, 111
Patriots, 65, 69
Pennsylvania
    and American
    Revolution, 64, 66, 203
    community projects in,
    227
    Independence Day in,
    128
    and Liberty Bell, 203
    maps, m11
    migration to, 82
    and steel, 174
Performers, 81
Pesos, 153
Petitioning the government
    (freedom), 197

Pets, 15, 126
Philadelphia,
    Pennsylvania, 64, 66,
    203
Pictographs, 96, 102
Pierce, Elijah, 147
Pigeons, 41
Pilgrims, 130
Pink pigeons, 41
Pioneers, 71, 74–75, 120
Pittsburgh, Pennsylvania,
    82, 174, 176
Plains, 20, m20–21
Plains gray wolf, 73
Planes, 90
Plants
    and ecosystems, 40
    and environment, 32,
    40, 42–43
    and 4-H clubs, 126
    of the Great Lakes, 42
    and Lewis and Clark, 73
    as natural resource, 29
    protecting, 211
Plastics, 34
Plateaus, m20–21, 21
Pledge of Allegiance, 202
Plymouth,
    Massachusetts, 130
Pocahontas, 55, 57
Points of View
    on money
    management, 163
    on old buildings, 115
    on trees, 35
Police officers
    and local government,
    215, 216
    in Native American
    communities, 226
    and state
    governments, 210
Polio, 89
Ponds, 22, 23
Population, 79, 84–85, 102
Portsmouth, Ohio, 115
Poster projects, 93,
    192, 240

Potato Days Festival, 125
Potatoes, 125, 166
Powhatan, 55, 56, 57, 68
Powwows, 131
Prairie ecosystems, 40
President of the United
    States,
    first president, 65, 69
    and laws, 198, 205
President's Day, 65
Press, freedom of, 197, 223
Prices, 150–51, 168,
    169, 174
Primary sources, 74, 105,
    158, 202
Prime meridian, m76–77,
    138, m139
Producers, 150–51
Products, 176–77. See
    also Goods
Profits, 151
Project Backpack, 230
Promontory, Utah, 86
Property, 221
Public transportation, 16
Pumas, 40
Pumpkins, 168, 231
Punch and Judy puppet
    shows, 136
Puppets, 136–37
Putnam, Rufus, 50
Pyramids, 54

Ragtime, 112
Railroads and trains
    and mountains, 21
    and news, 88
    and public
    transportation, 16
    transcontinental
    railroad, 86, 87
Rain, 24, 25
Recycling, 34, 175
Red Cross, 230
Reel, 134
Regions of United States,
    m20–21, 20–21

Religion, 61, 197
Rendville, Ohio, 13
Reservations, 225, m225
Reservoirs, 37
Revolution, American.
    See American Revolution
Rights, 197. See also
    Freedom in America
Riverboats, 23
Rivers
    and levees, 39
    in myths, 118
    as natural resource,
    22, 23
    and Oregon Trail, 74
Roads
    and communities, 5
    and land, 19
    repair of, 215, 216, 217
    road maps, 212, m213
    taxes for, 208
Robinson, Aminah, 99
Rock and Roll Hall of Fame
    and Museum, 13
Rocky Mountains, 21
Rolfe, John, 57
Rossburg, Ohio, 15, 17
Rubles, 153
Rules, 221, 224. See
    also Laws
Rural communities, 15, 17
Russia, m139, 153, 181

Sacagawea, 73
Sacramento, California, 87
Safety, 221
Sales tax, 208
Salk, Jonas, 89
Salt, 29
San Francisco, California,
    m90, 134, m139
Saudi Arabia, 182
Savings accounts, 162
Scale of maps, 26–27
Scarcity, 168, 169
Schools
    and health issues, 88
    and immigrants, 105

Index

school government,
204, 232
and state
government, 210
taxes for, 208, 209
and volunteers, 229, 230
Scotland, 134
Scott, Abigail Jane, 74
Seals, 236–37
Seashells, 155
Seattle, Washington, 2, 38
Senate, 199
Seneca Falls Convention,
233, 234
Servants, 59
Services
government services,
208–11, 216–18, 240
producers of, 150
specialization of, 184
supply and demand for,
168
Settlers
See also Colonies and
colonists; Jamestown
about, 56
and Africans, 58–59
arrival of, 56, 68
and explorers, 72
and food, 56, 57
moving west, 74–75
Seward, Alaska, 128
Shadow puppets, 136
Shipping, 179
Shopping, 80
Sister cities, 186–87
Skyscrapers, 89
Slavery, 59, 130, 203
Slavic Village of Cleveland,
Ohio, 13
Smith, John, 57
Smith, Shirley, 232
Soccer, 113
Soil, 29
Song, national, 200–201
South (direction), 10, *m11*,
m212–13
South (region), 82, 167

South Africa, *m139*
South America, *m77*,
m176, 178
Southeast (region),
20–21, *m21*
Southern Hemisphere,
m76, m77
South Pole, *m76, m77*
Southwest (region),
m20–21, 20–21
Sovereign
governments, 219
Soybeans, 167
Space, view from, 22
Space station, 180, 181
Spain, 176
Spanish settlers, 68
Sparrows, 43
Specialized products, 176,
m176–77, 184
Speech, freedom of,
197, 223
Spheres, *m76–77*
Sports, 13, 113, 233
Stairs, 88
Stamp Act, 62
Stanton, Elizabeth Cady,
233, 234
Stars, 118
"The Star-Spangled
Banner," 200–201
State government, 206–11
branches of, 207
capitals, 6, 207
and services, 208–9,
210–11
and taxes, 208–9
State highways, 212, *m213*
States
See also specific states
Congressional
representatives of, 199
cooperation between,
184–85
domestic trade of, 184
parks in, 211
specialized goods of, 184
state symbols, 195, 231

Steel, 174, 175, 176
St. Louis, Missouri, 39, 187
Stone tools, 55
Stores, 152, 165, 169
Stories, 116–23
about, 117
fables, 119
legends, 122–23
myths, 118
tall tales, 120–21
and values, 117,
120, 123
Storms, 24–25
Stough, Craig, 215, 216,
217
St. Petersburg, Russia,
m139
Strawberries, 166
Streets. *See* Roads
Strickland, Ted, 206-07
Suburban areas, 14, 17
Sun ceremonies, 53
Sunlight, 30, 40
Supply, 168–69
Supreme Court, 199
Sweet Honey in the
Rock, 112
Switzerland, 176, *m177*
Sword dance, 134
Sylvania, Ohio, 215,
216–17
Symbols
American symbols,
200–201, 202, 203
community symbols,
236–37
state symbols, 195, 231

T

Takaoka, Japan, 187
Tall tales, 120–21
Tam, Vivienne, 182
Taxes
and American
Revolution, 62, 64
kinds of, 208–9
and services, 216–17
Taylor, Wayne, Jr., 226

Tea, taxes on, 62, 64
Telegraph, 88
Tenements, 81
Teotihuacan, Mexico, 54,
m54
Territories, 72
Texas, 127, 130, 185
Textbook production,
184–85
Thanksgiving Day, 130
Time lines, 68–69
Tobacco, 58
Toledo, Ohio, 26, 27, 35
Topographic maps, 44
Tornados, 25
Tortoises, 41
Tour Down Under bicycle
race, 218
Towns, 15
Trade, 53, 178–79,
182–85, *m183*. *See also*
Goods
Trading, 53. *See also* Goods
Traditions, 133
Traffic
traffic laws, 221
traffic lights, 3, 215
traffic tickets, 216, 221
Trains. *See* Railroads and
trains
Transcontinental railroad,
86, 87
Transportation and travel
See also Automobiles
changes in, *m90*, 90–91
by covered wagon, 74, 75
and mountains, 21
and news, 88
on Oregon Trail,
74–75, 96
and pictograph
activity, 96
by plane, 90
in rural areas, 17
in suburbs, 14
by train, 16, 21, 86,
87, 88
in urban areas, 16
and water, 23

Trash
    and citizenship, 227
    and littering, 222, 227
    and local government,
        215, 216
    and volunteer
        projects, 229
Trees
    and Arbor Day, 126
    and ecosystems, 41
    and environment, 32
    as natural resources,
        28, 29, 30
    protection of, 35
Tressel, Jim, 98
Tribal Councils, 226
Tsunamis, 187
Tunnels, 19, 21
Turkey, *m177*
Turn taking, 221
Twain, Mark, 125

Union Pacific Railroad, 87
United States, *m11, m101*
United States Supreme
    Court Building, 110, 111
Urbana, Ohio, 35
Urban areas, 13, 14, 82.
    See also Cities
Utah, 29

Vaccines, 89
Values, 117, 120, 123, 202
Veterans' Day, 128
Veto, 198
Vietnamese immigrants,
    104–5
Virginia, 55
Volunteers
    about, 229

and making a
    difference, 231
and nonprofit groups,
    230, 233
opportunities for, 229
and President
    Carter, 233
Voting and elections, 194,
    222, 233, 234–35

Wagon trains, 74, 75
Wants and needs, 157, 192
Wars, 65, 128
Washington
    and Earth Day
        celebrations, 38
    food from, 152, *m152,*
        166
Washington, D.C.
    as capital, 198–99
    map of, *m198–99*
    and National Museum of
        the American
        Indian, 131
Washington, George
    and American
        Revolution, 65
    honesty of, 122–23
    presidency of, 65, 69
    on U.S. money, 153
Water
    and dams, 37
    and ecosystems, 40
    and farming, 23, 37
    fresh water, 42 (*see also*
        Great Lakes)
    and geography, 19,
        22–23
    in green buildings, 33
    learning about, 44
    and levees, 39

as natural resource, 23,
    29, 30, 31, 32
and reservoirs, 37
and transportation, 23
types of, 22
water rights, 226
Weather, 24–25, 39
Weems, Mason L., 123
West (direction), 10, *m11,*
    m212–13
West (frontier), 70–75
    difficulty of travel,
        74–75, 87
    explorers and pioneers,
        71, 72–73, 74–75
    Louisiana Purchase, 72,
        m72, 73
    and Native Americans,
        71, 73
    and Oregon Trail,
        74–75, 96
    and railroad, 87
    why people traveled
        west, 75
West (region), *m20–21,*
    20–21
West Africa, 106, 133
Western Hemisphere, *m76,*
    m77
West Liberty, Ohio, 2
Wetlands, 40, 42
Wheat, 167
White House, 198
White-tailed deer, 73
Willard, Ohio, 184
Wind, 30, 39
Wisconsin, *m11,* 44
Wolves, 73
Women, rights of, 194
Wood, 28, 29, 58
Woods, Granville T., 88
Wooster, Ohio, 35

Work
    about, 149
    and African Americans,
        82, 83
    and Amish, 146
    and commuting, 16
    of government
        employees, 6, 210,
        215, 216
    and immigrants, 80, 81
    and income, 149
    and population
        growth, 79
    and skills, 6
    of volunteers, 229
Working together.
    See Cooperation
Writers, 112

Yahikans, 55
Yam festival in Ghana, 133
Yen, 153
Yosemite National Park, 33
Youngstown, Ohio, 163

Zinc, 31

Index

Maps: XNR.

Illustrations: 8-9: Bridget Starr Taylor. 14-15: Chris O'Leary. 23: Fiona Sansom. 42-43: John Megahan. 49: Chi Chung. 52-53: Bill Farnsworth. 62-63: Sonja Lamut. 74-75: Jeffrey Ebbeler. 80-81: Ellen Beier. 87: Rodica Prato. 88-89: John Kocon. 90: Jim Starr. 101: Ilene Richard. 103: Susan Tolonen. 105: Ilene Richard. 106: Nicole Tadgell. 118: Neecy Twinem. 119: Bridget Starr Taylor. 121: Ed Gazsi. 122-123: Elizabeth Dulemba. 125: Ilene Richard. 127: Michelle Dorenkamp. 150-151: Fiona Sansom. 152: Linda Howard Bittner. 154-155: Elizabeth Dulemba. 157: John Bendall-Brunello. 160-161: Tory & Norman Taber. 168: Fiona Sansom. 174-175: Chris Lyons/lindgrensmith.com. 178: Ed Gazsi. 182: Valeria Cis. 183: Jim Starr. 184-185: Laura Beingessner. 198-199: Tom Barrett. 200-201: Ellen Beier. 204: Ginger Nielson. 205: Ginger Nielson. 209: Jauna Martinez-Neal. 210: Chris Lyons/lindgrensmith.com. 216-217: Necdet Yilmaz. 222: Pamela Leavens. 226-227: Mary Teichman. 239: Ginger Nielson.

Photography Credits: Photography Credits: All Photographs are by Macmillan/McGraw-Hill (MMH) except as noted below.

v: Jeff Greenberg/PhotoEdit. vi-vii: ImageState/Alamy Images. viii: NASA/Photo Researchers, Inc.

1: Jon Arnold Images Ltd/Alamy Images. 2: (b) Ohio Caverns; (tl) Ohio Caverns, Inc.; (tr) Ohio Caverns, Inc. 3: (b) Bass Photo Co Collection, Indiana Historical Society; (tl) Western Reserve Historical Society; (tr) AP Photo/Mark Duncan. 4: (bc) David Young-Wolff/PhotoEdit; (bl) Jeff Greenberg/Alamy Images; (br) Bryan Regan Photography. 4-5: Randall Schieber; 5: (b) Jeff Greenberg/Alamy Images. 6: (t) David Young-Wolff/PhotoEdit. 6-7: (b)Terry Jordan, The Ohio State Exposition Center Shooter for Ohio Expo Center She does not own rights to their photos. 7: (t) Courtesy City of Raleigh Parks and Recreation Department. 8: (b) Bob Rowan; Progressive Image/CORBIS; (tl) Bryan Regan Photography; (tr) Bryan Regan Photography. 9: (b) Dale Tincher, Consultwebs, Inc.; (tl) Robert Campell Photography; (tr) Inter-Faith Food Shuttle. 10-11: (b) M Stock/Alamy Images. 12: (bc) Jerzyworks/Masterfile; (bl) Tim Hursley/SuperStock; (br) Miles Ertman/Masterfile. 12-13: Mark Duncan/AP Photos. 13: (c) Tim Hursley/SuperStock. 14: (bc) Jerzyworks/Masterfile; (tl) Michael Newman/PhotoEdit. 15: (t) Susan Findlay/Masterfile. 16: (b) Kevin O. Mooney/Odyssey Productions, Chicago. 17: (b) Michael Newman/PhotoEdit; (t) Miles Ertman/Masterfile. 18: (bcl) Tom Till Photography; (bcr) Annie Griffiths Belt/CORBIS; (bl) Wolfgang Kaehler Photography; (br) Aaron Horowitz/CORBIS. 18-19: Tom Bean/Getty Images. 19: (b) Wolfgang Kaehler Photography. 20: (b) Tom Till Photography; (c) Maxwell MacKenzie/Panoramic Images. 20-21: (bkgd) Maxwell MacKenzie/Panoramic Images; (cl) Linde Waidhofer/Getty Images. 21: (br) Wally Bauman/Alamy Images; (tcl) Momatiuk - Eastcott/CORBIS; (tcr) Craig Aurness/CORBIS; (tl) Linde Waidhofer/Getty Images; (tr) Max Alexander/Dorling Kindersley/Getty Images. 22: (b) Kevin Anthony Horgan/Getty Images; (br) Time Life Pictures/Getty Images; (cr) MMH. 23: (b) Visions of America, LLC/Alamy Images; (tr) Layne Kennedy/CORBIS. 24: (b) David Pollack/CORBIS; (t) SuperStock/Alamy Images. 25: (c) Tom Bean/Getty Images; (tl) Mike Theiss/Jim Reed Photography/CORBIS; (tr) Aaron Horowitz/CORBIS. 26-27: L. Clarke/CORBIS. 28: (bcl) Terry Vine/Getty Images; (bcr) Denis Felix/Getty Images; (bl) Time Life Pictures/Getty Images; (br) Jim Cummins/Getty Images. 28-29: Kaz Mori/Getty Images. 29: (b) Time Life Pictures/Getty Images. 30-31: (b) Terry Vine/Getty Images. 31: (tr) SuperStock. 32: (b) Colin Young-Wolff/PhotoEdit; (t) Denis Felix/Getty Images. 33: (b) © Chuck Choi Architectural Photography; (t) CORBIS. 34: (b) Jim Cummins/Getty Images; (c) Kaz Mori/Getty Images. 35: (b)Spencer Grant/PhotoEdit; (c) Bob Daemmrich/PhotoEdit; (t) David Olsen/Alamy Images. 36: (bcl) Robb Kendrick/Aurora Photos; (bcr) Francois Gohier/Ardea.com; (bl) Steve Bly/Alamy Images; (br) Allen Blake Sheldon/Animals Animals. 36-37: Aerial/Terrestrial Photography. 37: (b) Steve Bly/Alamy Images. 38: (b) Mark Hoffman/AP Images; (tl) Mary Kate Denny/PhotoEdit; (tr) Mary Kate Denny/PhotoEdit. 39: (b) Robb Kendrick/Aurora Photos; (cr) AFP/Getty Images; (t) Mark E. Gibson/Unicorn Stock Photos. 40: (b) David R. Frazier Photolibrary, Inc./Alamy Images; (cr) Photograph courtesy of Joseph M. Richards, U.S. Geological Survey; (t) Francois Gohier/Ardea.com. 41: (b) J Marshall - Tribaleye Images/Alamy Images; (c) Nick Garbutt/Nature Picture Library; (t) Martin Harvey/CORBIS. 43: (br) Mary Kate Denny/PhotoEdit; (tr) Allen Blake Sheldon/Animals Animals. 44: (br) Walter Bibikow/Index Stock Imagery; (br) Ken Karp for MMH. 45: (b) Ken Karp for MMH. 48: (t) Ken Karp for MMH. 50: (b) CORBIS; (tl)Getty Images; (tr)Andre Jenny/Alamy Images; Photography.

51: (b) CORBIS; (tl) Lorence Bjorklund; (tr) Ohio Historical Society. 52: (bcl) Marilyn "Angel" Wynn/Nativestock Pictures; (bcr) Richard T. Nowitz/CORBIS; (bl) Nativestock Pictures; (br) Richard T. Nowitz/CORBIS. 53: (b) Nativestock Pictures; (t) Nativestock Pictures. 54: (b) Cahokia Mounds State Historic Site, painting by Michael Hampshire; (t) Neil Beer/Getty Images. 55: (b) Marilyn "Angel" Wynn/Nativestock Pictures; (t) Marilyn "Angel" Wynn/Nativestock Pictures. 56: (t) Steve Helber/AP Images. 56-57: (b) Richard T. Nowitz/CORBIS. 57: (c) Newberry Library/SuperStock; (t) The Granger Collection, New York. 58: (bkgd) Arthur S. Aubry/Photodisc; (tr) National Park Service, Colonial National Historical Park; (tr) Pat & Chuck Blackley. 59: (bkgd) Wetzel & Company; (br) Marilyn "Angel" Wynn/Nativestock Pictures; (br) Richard T. Nowitz/CORBIS. 60: (bcr) North Wind Picture Archives/Alamy Images; (bl) North Wind Picture Archives/Alamy Images; (br) SuperStock. 60-61: Nancy Martin/Martin Photography. 61: (b) Burke/Triolo Productions/FoodPix/Jupiterimages; (t) North Wind Picture Archives/Alamy Images. 62: (t) The Colonial Williamsburg Foundation. 64: (b) The Granger Collection, New York; (t) North Wind Picture Archives. 65: (b) The Granger Collection, New York; (t) North Wind Picture Archives/Alamy Images. 66: (t) SuperStock. 67: (b) ImageDJ/Alamy Images. 68: (bl) North Wind Picture Archives; (br) Steve Helber/AP Images; (t) Marilyn "Angel" Wynn/Nativestock Pictures. 69: (bl) The Granger Collection, New York; (cr) Museum of the City of New York/CORBIS; (t) North Wind Picture Archives/Alamy Images. 70: (bc) Painting: "Lewis and Clark: The Departure from the Wood River Encampment, May 14, 1804" by Gary R. Lucy. Courtesy of the Gary R. Lucy Gallery, Inc., Washington, MO; (bl) Bettmann/CORBIS; (br) MPI/Hulton Archive/Getty Images. 70-71: Bettmann/CORBIS. 71: (b) James P. Rowan Photography. 72: (tr) Painting: "Lewis and Clark: The Departure from the Wood River Encampment, May 14, 1804" by Gary R. Lucy. Courtesy of the Gary R. Lucy Gallery, Inc., Washington, MO. 73: (b) The Granger Collection, New York; (tl) Detail of "Lewis and Clark at Three Forks" by E.S. Paxson, Oil on Canvas, 1912, Courtesy of the Montana Historical Society. Don Beatty photographer 10/1999; (tr) Dorling Kindersley/Getty Images. 74: (c) Jerome Wilson/Alamy Images; (c) MMH. 75: (b) Detail of "Lewis and Clark at Three Forks" by E.S. Paxson, Oil on Canvas, 1912, Courtesy of the Montana Historical Society. Don Beatty photographer 10/1999; (t) MPI/Hulton Archive/Getty Images. 76: (b) NASA/Photo Researchers, Inc. 78: (bl) Schenectady Museum; Hall of Electrical History Foundation/CORBIS; (br) Library of Congress, Prints & Photographs Division, FSA-OWI Collection, [reproduction number,: LC-USF34-040820-D DLC]. 78-79: Bettmann/CORBIS. 79: (br) Schenectady Museum; Hall of Electrical History Foundation/CORBIS. 81: (br) Brown Brothers. 82: (b) Library of Congress, Prints & Photographs Division, FSA-OWI Collection, [reproduction number, LC-USF34-040820-D DLC]. 83: (b) Bettmann/CORBIS; (c) CORBIS. 84: (tl) Lake County Museum/CORBIS. 85: (tl) www.cincinnativiews:net; (tr) Jon Arnold Images Ltd/Alamy Images. 86: (bc) CORBIS; (br) National Motor Museum / HIP/The Image Works, Inc. 86-87: The Granger Collection, New York. 87: (b) The Granger Collection, New York. 88: (b) The Granger Collection, New York; (c) The Granger Collection, New York; (tl) Phil Schermeister/CORBIS. 89: (b) Richard Cummins/CORBIS; (c) © Smithsonian Institution, National Museum of American History; (t) CORBIS. 91: (b) Richard Cummins/CORBIS; (tl) National Motor Museum / HIP/The Image Works, Inc.; (tr) Mary Evans Picture Library/The Image Works, Inc. 92: (b) MMH; (t) Jeff Greenberg/PhotoEdit. 93: (bl) MMH. 95: (cl) The Granger Collection, New York; (cr) Museum of the City of New York/CORBIS; (tl) The Granger Collection, New York; (tr) North Wind Picture Archives/Alamy Images. 96: (tr) Ken Karp for MMH.

97: Paul Barton/CORBIS. 98: (b) Getty Images; (tl) Aminah Brenda Lynn Robinson American born 1940 Artist in her Studio Courtesy of the Columbus Museum of Art, Ohio; (t) AFP/Getty Images. 99: (b) Elsa/Getty Images; (tl) Jed Jacobsohn/Getty Images; (tr) ASSOCIATED PRESS Kiichiro Sato. 100: (bcl) Jose Luis Pelaez, Inc./CORBIS; (br) Nanine Hartzenbusch/The Baltimore Sun. 100-101: Kevin Dodge/CORBIS. 103: (br) Jose Luis Pelaez, Inc./CORBIS. 104: (b) Bob Krist/CORBIS. 105: (b) Stuart Pearce/age fotostock; (t) Lam Family Photo, Courtesy of Chau Lam; (tr) MMH. 106: (bl) Nanine Hartzenbusch/The Baltimore Sun; (br) Nanine Hartzenbusch/The Baltimore Sun. 107: (b) Kevin Dodge/CORBIS; (t) Jane Sweeney/Lonely Planet Images. 108: (bcl) Joe Sohm/Visions of America, LLC/Alamy Images; (bcr) Eliot Elisofon/Time Life Pictures/Getty Images; (bl) Photo Resource Hawaii/Danita Delimont Stock Photography; (br) David Young-Wolff/PhotoEdit. 108-109: Photo Resource Hawaii/Danita Delimont Stock Photography. 109: (bc) C Squared Studios/Photodisc/Getty Images; (br) C Squared Studios/Photodisc/Getty Images. 110: (b) Joe Sohm/Visions of America, LLC/Alamy Images; (t) Lawrence, Jacob (1917-2000) "The migrants arrived in great numbers." Panel 40 from The Migration ; Series. (1940-41; text and title revised by the artist, 1993).

Tempera on gesso on composition board, 12 x 18". ; Gift of Mrs. David M. Levy. (28.1942.20). Digital Image © The Museum of Modern Art/Licensed by SCALA ; © ARS, NY/Art Resource, NY. 111: (b) Dynamic Graphics /JupiterImages; (t) Lindsay Hebberd/CORBIS. 112: (b) Marko Communications; (t) Eliot Elisofon/Time Life Pictures/Getty Images. 113: (b) James Nesterwitz/Alamy Images; (t) The Granger Collection, New York. 114: (bl) David Young-Wolff/PhotoEdit; (br) Dynamic Graphics/JupiterImages; (tr) David M. Grossman/The Image Works, Inc. 115: (t) Emilio Ereza/Alamy Images; (c) Camille Tokerud/Getty Images; (b)JUPITERIMAGES/BananaStock/Alamy Images. 116: (bcr) Andre Jenny/Alamy Images; (bl) Marilyn "Angel" Wynn/Nativestock Pictures. 116-117: Brand X Pictures/PunchStock. 117: (b) Marilyn "Angel" Wynn/Nativestock Pictures. 120: (b) The Granger Collection, New York. 123: (b) Andre Jenny/Alamy Images. 124: (bcl) Kristine Ambrosen; (bcr) Dinodia Photo Library; (bl) Amanda Stratford/The Hannibal Courier-Post; (br) Deborah Davis/PhotoEdit. 124-125: Randall Hyman. 125: (b) Amanda Stratford/The Hannibal Courier-Post. 126: (b) Getty Images; (t) Kristine Ambrosen. 127: (b) Cheron Bayna/Image Courtesy of Pat Mora. 128: (b) Blend Images/Alamy Images; (t) Jeff Hunter/Getty Images. 129: (b) Dinodia Photo Library; (t) Xinhua/Landov. 130: (bl) Bob Daemmrich/Bob Daemmrich Photography; (br) Bob Daemmrich/Bob Daemmrich Photography; (t) Larry Kolvoor/Austin Am-Statesman/WPN. 131: (b) Jeff Hunter/Getty Images; (t) Deborah Davis/PhotoEdit. 132: (bc) ImageState/Alamy Images; (bl) Anders Ryman/CORBIS; (br) David Muscroft/Alamy Images. 132-133: Craig Pershouse/Lonely Planet Images. 133: (b) Anders Ryman/CORBIS. 134: (b) Jon Arnold/Danita Delimont Stock Photography; (t) Marcus Brooke/Getty Images. 134-135: (b) ImageState/Alamy Images. 135: (t) Rodolfo Arpia/Alamy Images. 136: (b) Adams Picture Library/Alamy Images; (br) David Muscroft/Alamy Images; (tl) SCPhotos/Alamy Images. 137: (b) Marcus Brooke/Getty Images; (t) Arco Images/Alamy Images. 139: (b) Sergio Pitamitz/Danita Delimont Stock Photography. 140: (b) Ken Karp for MMH; (t) Peter Byron/PhotoEdit. 144: (t) MMH.

145: James Lauritz/Digital Vision/Getty Images. 146: (b) James L. Amos/Getty Images; (tl) Clay Perry/CORBIS; (tr) Galen Rowell/CORBIS. 147: (b) Elijah Pierce; (tl) Columbus Museum of Art, Ohio Museum Purchase, Alfred L. Willson Fund of the Colubus Foundation 1989.008; (tr) Andre Jenny/Alamy Images. 148: (bcr) Comstock Images/PunchStock; (bl) Jose Luis Pelaez, Inc./CORBIS. 148-149: Gibson Stock Photography. 149: (br) Jose Luis Pelaez, Inc./CORBIS. 152: (br) Ambient Images Inc./Alamy Images; (tl) Comstock Images/PunchStock. 153: (bc) Chris Hammond/Alamy Images; (bl) Kitt Cooper-Smith/Alamy Images; (br) © Smithsonian Institution, National Numismatic Collection; (cr) MMH; (tr) Zedcor Wholly Owned/Jupiterimages. 155: (bl) Ken Karp for MMH; (br) Ambient Images Inc./Alamy Images. 156: (bcl) Marc Romanelli/Jupiterimages; (bl) Cindy Charles/PhotoEdit. 156-157: James Darell/Photodisc/Getty Images. 157: (br) Cindy Charles/PhotoEdit. 158: (b) AP Photos; (bl) MMH; (t) Michael Geissinger/The Image Works, Inc. 159: (t) Marc Romanelli/Jupiterimages. 161: (bl) Gabe Palmer/Alamy Images; (br) Tomi/PhotoLink/Photodisc/Getty Images; (tr) Stockdisc/PunchStock. 162: (b) James Darell/Photodisc/Getty Images. 163: (bl) Jose Luis Pelaez Inc./Getty Images; (br) Ed-Imaging; (t) Plain Picture/Jupiter Images; 164: (bc) David Frazier/CORBIS; (bl) Joeseph Sohm-Visions of America/Getty Images; (br) James Schwabel/Panoramic Images. 164 (bc) David Frazier/CORBIS 165: (br) Joeseph Sohm-Visions of America/Getty Images. 166: (c) isifa Image Service s.r.o./Alamy Images; (tl) Syracuse Newspapers / David Lassman/The Image Works, Inc.; (tr) Harald Theissen/Alamy Images. 167: (br) George Contorakes/Masterfile; (cl) David Frazier/CORBIS; (cr) Bill Barksdale/AgStockUSA; (tc) Lynn Stone/AgStockUSA. 168: (br) Paul Sakuma/AP Images. 168-169: (b) James Schwabel/Panoramic Images. 169: (b) isifa Image Service s.r.o./Alamy Images; (tr) Feldman & Associates. 170-171: (bkgd) Richard Price/Getty Images. 172: (bcl) CORBIS; (bcr) Ancient Art & Architecture/Danita Delimont Stock Photography; (bl) AFP/Getty Images; (br) William Caram/CORBIS. 172-173: David R. Frazier Photolibrary, Inc/Alamy Images. 173: (b) AFP/Getty Images.

174: (tl) The Granger Collection, New York; (tr) CORBIS. 175: (tl) Bruce Dale/National Geographic/Getty Images; (tr) © 2006 Stratus Imaging. 176: (b) David Buffington/Photodisc/Getty Images; (cb) Dave G. Houser/CORBIS; (ct) Erik Simonsen/Transtock Inc./Alamy Images; (t) Stockbyte/Getty Images. 177: (bl) J Marshall - Tribaleye Images/Alamy Images; (br) Siede Preis/Photodisc/Getty Images; (c) Ancient Art & Architecture/Danita Delimont Stock Photography; (tcl) Brand X Pictures/Alamy Images; (tcr) Matthew Ward/Dorling Kindersley/Getty Images; (tl) Hugh Threlfall/Alamy Images; (tr) Nikreates/Alamy Images. 178: (b) MMH; (tl) Nature Picture Library/Alamy Images. 179: (b) J Marshall - Tribaleye Images/Alamy Images; (t) William Caram/CORBIS. 180: (bcr) MMH; (bl) Tina Manley/Alamy Images; (br) Elyse Lewin/Getty Images. 180-181: NASA Human Space Flight Gallery. 181: (b) Tina Manley/Alamy Images. 182: (br) Getty Images. 184: (bl) MMH; (br) Amanda J. Freeman/RR Donnelly/MMH. 185: (b) MMH; (t) Jeff Cadge/Getty Images. 186: (b) Steve Barsky; (tc) AP Photos; (tl) Elyse Lewin/Getty Images; (tr) Art Kowalsky/Alamy Images. 187: (tcl) BennettPhoto/Alamy Images; (tcr) Kristi J. Black/CORBIS; (tl) Andrew Ward/Life File/Getty Images; (tr) Dallas and John Heaton/Free Agents Limited/CORBIS. 188: (b) Ken Karp for MMH; (t) David R. Frazier Photolibrary, Inc./Alamy Images. 189: (b) MMH. 192: (t) Ken Karp for MMH.

193: Wally McNamee/CORBIS; (t) Photodisc/Getty Images. 194: (tl) Bettman/CORBIS; (tr) Andre Jenny/Alamy Images; (b)CORBIS. 195: (b) CORBIS/SYGMA; (tl) Bettmann/CORBIS; (tr) John Glenn Archives. 196: (bcl) Dean Fox/SuperStock; (bl) Evan Vucci/AP Photos; (br) Pete Saloutos/CORBIS. 196-197: Bill Brooks/Alamy Images. 197: (b) Evan Vucci/AP Photos. 198: (t) Dennis O'Clair/Getty Images. 199: (tl) Dean Fox/SuperStock; (tr) Hisham F. Ibrahim/Photodisc/Getty Images. 202: (bl) Steve Allen/Brand X/CORBIS; (br) Comstock/Jupiterimages; (cl) MMH. 203: (b) Dennis O'Clair/Getty Images; (tl) age fotos-tock/SuperStock; (tr) Pete Saloutos/CORBIS. 206: (bc) Ryan McVay/Getty Images; (bl) Lee Snider/Photo Images/CORBIS; (br) John Miller/AP Photos. 206-207: (b) Kiichiro Sato/AP Images; 207: (b)Lee Snider/Photo Images/CORBIS. 208: (b) Digital Vision/PunchStock; (t) Ryan McVay/Getty Images. 210: (bc) Courtesy of the Arizona Department of Public Safety; (t) David Schmidt/Masterfile. 211: (b) Bob Daemmrich/CORBIS; (t) John Miller/AP Photos. 213: (br) Peter Horree/Alamy Images. 214: (bl) Peter Steiner/Alamy Images; (br) Paul J. Richards/AFP/Getty Images. 214-215: Philip Rostron/Masterfile. 215: (b) Peter Steiner/Alamy Images. 218: (b) Peter Mundy/Alamy Images; (cr) Doug Pearson/Jon Arnold Images/Alamy Images. 219: (t) Paul J. Richards/AFP/Getty Images. 220: (bcr) Jonathan Ernst/Reuters/CORBIS; (bl) Jeff Cadge/Getty Images; (br) Jerry Jacka, 2006. 220-221: George Shelley/Masterfile. 221: (b) Jeff Cadge/Getty Images. 222: (tc) Tony Freeman/PhotoEdit. 223: (b) Flip Schulke/CORBIS; (t) Jason Reed/Reuters/Landov. 224: (b) Jonathan Ernst/Reuters/CORBIS. 225: (t) Rick Scuteri/AP Photos. 226: (b) Jason Reed/Reuters/Landov; (t) Jerry Jacka, 2006. 227: (b) Bonnie Kamin/PhotoEdit. 228: (bcl) Billy Hustace/Getty Images; (bcr) David Ashley/CORBIS; (bl) Youth Service America 2007; (br) Bob Daemmrich/PhotoEdit. 228-229: Jeffry Myers/Index Stock Imagery. 229: (b) Youth Service America 2007. 230: (b) Erik S. Lesser/Getty Images; (bl) Billy Hustace/Getty Images; (t) Jennifer Hearn. 231: (c) Siede Preis/Photodisc; (tr) Bob Lapree/Union Leader Corporation. 232: (b) David Ashley/CORBIS; (t) Anthony Gray Photography. 233: (b) Bettmann/CORBIS; (br) Bettmann/CORBIS; (t) Tom & Dee Ann McCarthy/CORBIS. 234: (tl) The Granger Collection, New York; (tr) The Granger Collection, New York. 235: (b) Erik S. Lesser/Getty Images; (tl) The Granger Collection, New York; (tr) Bob Daemmrich/PhotoEdit. 236: (b) MMH; (t) David R. Frazier Photolibrary, Inc./Alamy Images; 240: (t) MMH.

R3: (b) Chuck Savage/CORBIS. R7: (b) Amanda Stratford/The Hannibal Courier-Post. R8: (c) Stockdisc/PunchStock. R9: (b) Cindy Charles/PhotoEdit. R11: (c) Pete Saloutos/CORBIS. GH4: (b) Ed Boettcher/CORBIS; (t) Dennis O'Clair/Getty Images. GH5: (b) Aerial/Terrestrial Photography; (c) Steve Allen/Getty Images; (t) F. Schussler/PhotoLink/Getty Images. GH8: (l) Bryan Allen/CORBIS; (r) MMH.

ACKNOWLEDGMENTS
Grateful acknowledgment is given to the following authors and publishers. Every effort has been made to trace the ownership of all copyrighted material and to secure the necessary permissions to reprint these selections. In the case of some selections for which acknowledgment is not given, extensive research has failed to locate the copyright holders.

"… there emerges…" Institute of Noetic Sciences brochure, 1973. Reprinted by permission of the Institute of Noetic Sciences.

"Paul Bunyan, the Mightiest Logger of Them All" from American Tall Tales by Mary Pope Osborn, copyright © 1991 by Mary Pope Osborn. Alfred A. Knopf

from "House supports making the pumpkin the state fruit" by Anne Saunders. Copyright March 8, 2006, Associated Press.